The National Register of

HISTORIC PLACES
IN MINNESOTA

A GUIDE

The National Register of
HISTORIC
PLACES IN
MINNESOTA

A GUIDE

Compiled by Mary Ann Nord
Foreword by Larry Millett

Minnesota Historical Society Press

This book has been financed in part with Federal funds from the National Park Service, U.S. Department of the Interior. However, the contents and opinions do not necessarily reflect the views or policies of the Department of the Interior, nor does the mention of trade names or commercial products constitute endorsement or recommendations by the Department of the Interior.

This program receives Federal financial assistance for identification and protection of historic properties. Under Title VI of the Civil Rights Act of 1964 and Section 504 of the Rehabilitation Act of 1973, the U.S. Department of the Interior prohibits discrimination on the basis of race, color, national origin, or handicap in its federally assisted programs. If you believe you have been discriminated against in any program, activity, or facility as described above, or if you desire further information, please write to: Office of Equal Opportunity, U.S. Department of the Interior, National Park Service, 1849 C Street, N.W., Washington, D.C. 20240.

www.mnhs.org/mhspress

The Minnesota Historical Society Press is a member of the Association of American University Presses.

Manufactured in Canada

10 9 8 7 6 5 4 3 2 1

♾ The paper used in this publication meets the minimum requirements of the American National Standard for Information Sciences—Permanence for Printed Library materials, ANSI Z39.48-1984.

Title pages: Paul Bunyan, Bemidji, Beltrami County, ca. 1938; water tower with observation deck, Lake Bronson State Park, Kittson County

International Standard Book Number 0-87351-448-3

Library of Congress Cataloging-in-Publication Data
The national register of historic places in Minnesota : a guide / compiled by Mary Ann Nord ; foreword by Larry Millett.
     p. cm.
Includes index.
ISBN 0-87351-448-3 (pbk. : alk. paper)
    1. Historic sites—Minnesota—Directories.
    2. Historic buildings—Minnesota—Directories.
    3. Minnesota—Directories.
    4. Minnesota—History, Local.
    I. Nord, Mary Ann.
F607.N38 2003
977.6—dc21   2003000004

The National Register of

HISTORIC PLACES IN MINNESOTA

A GUIDE

NATIONAL REGISTER PROPERTIES

FOREWORD

This guide to Minnesota's historic buildings and places is, among many other things, an invitation to memory. No matter if you're from the heart of the city or the most rural corner of the state, you'll find within these pages some old and treasured architectural friends that have earned a listing on the National Register of Historic Places.

I grew up on the North Side of Minneapolis in the 1950s, before clean-sweep urban renewal had undone far too much of the city's past, and I still carry in my mind a map of the city as it was then. Churches, schools, libraries, industrial buildings, stores, and, of course, houses were all part of my young life. A good many of the buildings I remember are gone—St. Joseph's Church, where I was baptized; the old downtown library on Hennepin Avenue, a brownstone haven from the din of the city that featured a mysterious mummy among its collections; the marvelous Loeb Arcade and its curving row of shops; the incomparable Metropolitan Building, the loss of which still haunts Minneapolis.

Fortunately, much also remains. As I ran down the list of National Register properties for Hennepin County, I was pleased to find many buildings that had inter-sected with my life at one time or another. In each case old memories instantly stepped forward, like eager schoolchildren with raised hands, begging to be called on. Old buildings have that power—to remind us of who we are and where we have been. They collect memories the way cisterns collect water, and when we lose them we lose part of ourselves.

One of the buildings in this guide that holds special memories for me is the Basilica of St. Mary, a thundering Classical/Baroque monument that was the scene, long ago, of my high-school graduation ceremonies. The church seemed a wonder to me then and still does today, especially now that its huge dome has received a gleaming new coat of copper. I remember, too, night-time cab rides past the basilica and through the infamous "bottleneck," where Lyndale and Hennepin Avenues came together at a dizzyingly acute angle. The old white-knuckle intersection is gone now, replaced by another sort of bottleneck (the Lowry Hill tunnel on Interstate 94), but the basilica continues to reign, as powerful as ever, over this subterranean tide of traffic.

Another building I recall well is the Butler Brothers Company (now Butler Square), a muscular warehouse from 1906–08 that always struck me as particularly grand. Riding the Number 5 bus in from North Minneapolis, I'd see the building almost every day as I went downtown. Stern and rock-solid, it loomed over the sooty old warehouse district like a huge Gothic fortress. Now, like so many of its kin, it has been adapted for new uses and seems ready to go on for centuries to come if we'll allow it to.

I also have vivid memories of the Chicago Milwaukee St. Paul and Pacific Depot (or simply the Milwaukee Depot, as everyone called it). I took many trains to Chicago from the depot, which always seemed to be a sort of poor cousin of the much grander Great Northern Station a few blocks away. Cities, however, work in mysterious ways, and the biggest and best buildings are not always the ones that survive. The mighty Great Northern Station was gone by 1978, but the Milwaukee hung on— through many travails and false hopes—and has now been turned into a swank hotel.

Other buildings on my personal memory list include the Church of St. Stephen, where my parents were married in the 1940s; the old Farmers and Mechanics Savings Bank, a fine little Beaux Arts/Classical temple that I knew as Schiek's restaurant and that has now evolved

(if that is the right word) into a "gentlemen's club"; the
Foshay Tower, long the summit of Minneapolis, and best
known for its tiny open-air observatory that was always
a thrilling place to visit as a child; the Fredrika Bremer
School, a fine old Romanesque pile from the 1880s
located just a few blocks from where I grew up; and the
Minneapolis Armory, a big streamlined Moderne barn
where I watched Catholic high-school basketball tour-
naments and many other events.

But the building I seem to remember best of all is
the old North Branch of the Minneapolis Public Library.
Vaguely medieval in style, the library was a warm and
inviting place, a home away from home for a hopelessly
curious youngster like myself. It's no longer used as a
library—a bigger, more modern, and far less lovely
structure has long since supplanted it—but I suspect it
remains engraved in the memories of many old North
Siders like myself.

If you grew up in St. Paul or the suburbs or some-
where out in what we city kids used to call the country,
you'll also find familiar buildings and places in this
guide. Some are still being used for their original purposes. Others have been rehabilitated to serve some new
use. And still others are empty and shuttered, waiting
for a second chance at life. Any of them will reward a
visit. In fact, the pleasures of memory and recognition
offered in this guide make it a handy roadside companion. Take it along the next time you travel through
Minnesota. It will lead you to wonders and surprises.
It will help you see familiar places with fresh eyes. And
it will give you a new appreciation for the state's rich
architectural legacy.

That legacy is extremely fragile. Many people assume that the National Register is a shield, capable of
deflecting all the forces—urban renewal, institutional
abandonment, dilapidation, changing uses—that can
bring about the destruction of historic buildings. But the
register in and of itself offers no magic armor. It is, after
all, simply a list, a kind of honor roll of buildings and
places that possess significant architectural, historic,

and cultural value. Ultimately, it is people who make buildings, and it is only people who can save them. As much as anything else, this guide is a testament to the thousands of men and women who, in ways large and small, have helped to preserve Minnesota's built history.

Winston Churchill once famously remarked that we shape our buildings only to have them shape us. There is much truth to this observation. Most of the buildings listed in this guide are neither famous nor monumental, but they have shaped us all and, one hopes, will continue to do so for many years to come.

Larry Millett

ACKNOWLEDGMENTS

With this guide, the Minnesota Historical Society's State Historic Preservation Office furthers its mission to protect the state's historic properties by fostering an understanding and appreciation of these irreplaceable resources. Many people had a hand in ushering the project to completion. Thanks go to:

Britta Bloomberg, Deputy State Historic Preservation Officer and head of the Society's Historic Preservation, Field Services, and Grants Department, whose vision and persistence helped to make the book a reality.

Susan Roth, National Register Historian, for her tireless pursuit of the salient fact and perfect picture that would capture the essence of each county. Her nearly thirty-year involvement with Minnesota's National Register program makes her a walking compendium of knowledge about the state's historic properties.

Charles Nelson, Historical Architect, and Scott Anfinson, National Register Archaeologist, for invaluable guidance in their respective areas of expertise, bred from years of yeoman service to preserving Minnesota's built environment and archaeological past.

Michael Koop, Historic Preservation Program Specialist, who traveled many miles photographing historic properties for this publication.

Michele Decker, Administrative Secretary for the Historic Preservation, Field Services, and Grants Department, who greatly aided the work flow.

David Grabitske, Grants and Field Programs Assistant, for sharing his research on Sarah Jane Sibley.

Greg Britton, Director, and Ann Regan, Managing

Editor, Minnesota Historical Society Press, for committing the resources to bring the guide to fruition.

Deborah Swanson, Associate Editor, whose meticulous attention to detail was essential to a book that's all about the details.

Finally, special thanks to all Minnesotans who are stewards of the state's historic properties, for their dedication to preserving these treasured pieces of our past.

INTRODUCTION

As far back as 1849, Minnesotans recognized the importance of preserving their history. That year, well before Minnesota became a state, the first territorial legislature created the Minnesota Historical Society as an institution charged expressly with collecting, preserving, and interpreting evidence of the past.

It was a similar desire to protect evidence of America's beginnings that brought historic preservation to Minnesota in the statehood year of 1858. The first to assume a leadership role was Sarah Jane Sibley, wife of Governor Henry H. Sibley. The daughter of a Revolutionary War veteran, Sarah Sibley headed state fundraising for a nationwide effort by the Mount Vernon Ladies' Association of the Union to preserve George Washington's Virginia estate. Although an economic crisis, the reluctance of some people to give money for the home of a slave owner, and ill health limited her success, Sarah and her work would provide an example for others to follow in saving historic places closer to home.

One of them was Sarah Sibley's own house. A two-story, yellow limestone dwelling built by Henry in the late 1830s, the residence stood in the heart of Mendota, a fur-trading center at the confluence of the Mississippi and Minnesota Rivers. As Henry Sibley's influence spread and his social position changed—from trader to constitutional convention delegate to Minnesota's first state governor—his home became the business, social, and political center of the fast-growing region. But after the Sibleys moved down the Mississippi River to St. Paul in 1862, the house served a succession of other uses—Catholic girls' boarding school, summer art colony, produce warehouse—until, in ruins, it was abandoned.

It took another group of civic-minded women to rescue the crumbling house. In 1909, fifty years after Sarah Sibley trumpeted the cause of preservation in the name of patriotism, the Sibley house was acquired by the Minnesota Society of the Daughters of the American Revolution. Sustained by their vision of creating a midwestern Mount Vernon, the MSDAR repaired the house and operated it as a public museum until 1996, when the property was transferred to the Minnesota Historical Society.

MSDAR members gathered about 1917 at the Henry H. Sibley House in Dakota County.

Minnesota abounded with other early preservation efforts. Fort Snelling, established in 1819, was described as a historic site as early as 1863. In 1873 Minnesotans first began marking sites associated with the Dakota War of 1862. And by 1895, two St. Paul men had completed a survey of many of the state's archaeological sites. A sizeable number of Minnesota's state parks were established to help protect historic sites within their borders. And across the state, private organizations began acquiring locally significant landmarks. These efforts helped save some of Minnesota's best-known and most-beloved historic places.

After World War II—eager to look ahead, not back—Minnesota joined the rest of the nation in an ambitious effort to renew blighted urban areas and build a system of interstate highways. By the late 1950s, it became clear that these projects were rapidly changing the American landscape. Irreplaceable pieces of the past disappeared at an alarming rate. It was against this backdrop that preservationists began seeking a way to protect the country's cultural resources.

On October 15, 1966, the National Historic Preservation Act was signed into law, creating a comprehensive, nationwide historic preservation program. Its most important product was the National Register of Historic Places, which established a formal way to recognize properties that make up the essential fabric of the nation's history. The legislation also provided a framework for the preservation program built on partnerships among federal, state, tribal, and local governments. A key component was the network of State Historic Preservation Offices that would spearhead state preservation initiatives and help carry out the national program.

In 1969 the Minnesota Legislature designated the director of the Minnesota Historical Society as the State Historic Preservation Officer, and Minnesota's historic preservation program took shape. Since then the State Historic Preservation Office of the Minnesota Historical Society has engaged in an ongoing effort to identify significant sites throughout the state. Numerous individuals from federal, state, and local agencies, county and local historical societies, and research organizations, as well as private property owners, contributed to the effort. With their help, the Minnesota Historical Society has surveyed historic resources in all 87 counties, resulting in an inventory of more than 63,000 historic and archaeological resources.

The process of identifying, evaluating, and listing historic properties continues. By the end of 2002, the National Register of Historic Places contained 1,515 Minnesota listings representing more than 6,000 individual properties. This book is a guide to those properties.

ABOUT THE NATIONAL REGISTER OF
HISTORIC PLACES

The National Register of Historic Places is the nation's official list of properties deemed worthy of preservation. Operated by the National Park Service of the U.S. Department of the Interior, the National Register program is administered in each state by its State Historic Preservation Office. To learn more about the National Register, go to http://www.cr.nps.gov/nr. Some helpful facts about the Register to keep in mind:

■ **Eligibility:** The National Register recognizes properties that have local, state, or national significance. Properties may be listed on the National Register because of their association with significant persons and events, because of their architectural or engineering significance, or because they contain important information about our history or prehistory (see National Register Criteria, page 302–3, for a more complete definition of historical significance). Properties that have transcendent value to the nation as a whole may be designated as National Historic Landmarks.

■ **Property types:** Properties on the National Register fall into five broad types. *Buildings* are properties created principally to shelter human activity. *Sites* mark the location of a significant event or activity where the location itself possesses historic or archaeological value. The term *structure* is used for functional constructions other than buildings—a bridge or water tower, for example. *Objects* are constructions other than buildings and structures that are primarily artistic in nature. *Districts* possess a significant concentration of resources.

■ **Process:** Each National Register nomination begins with research to establish the property's significance. The case for significance is recorded on a nomination form and then presented to the Minnesota Historical Society State Review Board, a volunteer group of citizens and professionals with expertise in history, architecture, and archaeology. If the nominated property is found to meet National Register criteria, it is sent to the State Historic Preservation Officer for signature and then to the Keeper of the Register in Washington, D.C., for final review. Once the nomination is approved, the property is placed on the National Register.

■ **What listing means:** Listing on the National Register constitutes official recognition that a property is worthy of preservation. National Register listing often changes the way communities perceive their historic properties, giving impetus to efforts to preserve them. Preservation of such properties is further encouraged through certain federal tax benefits and state and federal grant funds. While listing does not guarantee that historic properties will be preserved, they receive a measure of protection from an environmental review process that monitors compliance with federal and state laws intended to safeguard them. Listing does not interfere with the right of private property owners to alter, manage, or dispose of their property.

USING THE GUIDE

This guide identifies all Minnesota properties listed on the National Register of Historic Places as of December 31, 2002. Grouped by county, they are described in alphabetical order under each county heading. Peruse the entries for the county that you are interested in to learn about its historic properties or check the index to find a particular property. A few things to remember:

■ **Property names:** Properties are identified by the name in use during the period of significance.

■ **Addresses:** Street addresses given are generally those used at the time of the property's listing. Locations for archaeological properties are purposely nonspecific to protect them from harm.

- **Historic districts:** The many historic districts on the National Register encompass thousands of properties not listed individually in this guide. Information about those properties may be found in the files of the State Historic Preservation Office or in the online database described below.

- **Ownership:** Most of Minnesota's National Register properties are privately owned and not open to the public. Many continue to serve their communities as homes and businesses. Access to properties that serve public purposes, such as schools, city halls, courthouses, or libraries, may be restricted. Only a small percentage of properties in this guide are open to the public as museums.

- **Removals:** Properties may be removed from the National Register if the qualities for which they were listed have been lost due to destruction by fire or storm, demolition, removal from original site, or severe alteration. On pages 289–301, the guide lists 95 Minnesota properties that have been officially removed from the National Register. This list is a compelling reminder of the many ways in which our historic resources are at risk. Additional properties in the guide—such as the Territorial/ State Prison in Washington County, destroyed by arson in September 2002—may have lost their eligibility for listing but have not yet gone through the formal process for removal from the Register.

For more information about Minnesota's National Register properties, go to the Minnesota Historical Society's web site at http://nrhp.mnhs.org. A searchable database enables you to find information about individual properties within historic districts, for example, and to conduct searches based on such factors as architectural style, property type, or construction date. Be sure to check in periodically. New properties are added to the database as they are listed on the National Register, and other information is updated on an ongoing basis.

National Register files for all of Minnesota's historic properties are housed in the State Historic Preservation Office at the Minnesota History Center operated by the Minnesota Historical Society in St. Paul. These files are open to the public by appointment; to schedule your visit or to learn more about other historic preservation activities in Minnesota, contact:

State Historic Preservation Office
Minnesota Historical Society
Minnesota History Center
345 Kellogg Blvd. W.
St. Paul, MN 55102-1906
Telephone: 651-296-5434
TTY: 800-627-3529
Fax: 651-282-2374
E-mail: mnshpo@mnhs.org

The National Register of

HISTORIC PLACES
IN MINNESOTA

A GUIDE

ABBREVIATIONS AND TERMS

The date that a property was placed on the National Register is shown in this manner: **(4/16/82)** *means* April 16, 1982

ca. *circa;* about this time

Carnegie library A public-library building constructed with funds granted to a community during 1886–1919 by industrialist and philanthropist Andrew Carnegie (1835–1919) or his Carnegie Corporation of New York, a philanthropic and educational organization created in 1911. Grants were made for 1,679 libraries in the United States, including 65 libraries in 58 Minnesota communities; 33 Carnegie libraries in Minnesota are on the National Register.

CCC Civilian Conservation Corps, a program of the federal government that employed young men on conservation and construction projects during the Great Depression of the 1930s

Contact Period 1650–1837; the period of time following the first substantial contact between Indians and Europeans in present-day Minnesota up to the signing in 1837 by the Dakota and the Ojibwe of the first major treaties in which the Indians began to cede large portions of their lands in Minnesota to the United States

CWA Civil Works Administration, a federal program that provided temporary employment in public-works projects during the Great Depression

fur trade era 1650–1850; the period of time during which Indians in present-day Minnesota traded furs and hides to Europeans and European Americans in exchange for manufactured goods

IOOF   Independent Order of Odd Fellows, a fraternal organization

NYA   National Youth Administration, a federal program that provided assistance, including employment, to young persons during the Great Depression

Old-Stock Americans   Members of European families whose ancestors were primarily British and had mostly resided in North America for at least two generations before arriving in Minnesota

Postcontact Period   1837–present; the period of time following the signing of the treaties of 1837 to the present day in Minnesota

Precontact Period   10,000 B.C.–A.D. 1650; the period of time before the first substantial contact between Indians and Europeans in present-day Minnesota

PWA   Public Works Administration, a federal program that provided jobs in public-construction projects during the Great Depression

SERA   State Emergency Relief Administration, a state program that provided employment in work projects during the Great Depression

WPA   Works Progress Administration or Work Projects Administration, federal programs that provided employment in a wide variety of construction and cultural projects during the Great Depression

Some properties in this guide may have lost their eligibility for listing but have not yet gone through the formal process for removal from the National Register.

Please note that most National Register properties are privately owned and are not open to the public.

NATIONAL REGISTER PROPERTIES

AITKIN COUNTY

AITKIN CARNEGIE LIBRARY (4/16/82)
121 2nd St. N.W., Aitkin
Classical Revival brick community library built in 1911.

AITKIN COUNTY COURTHOUSE AND JAIL (4/16/82)
209 and 217 2nd St. N.W., Aitkin
Beaux Arts, brick-and-stone, second-generation courthouse constructed in 1929, with adjacent 1915 jail.

ARTHYDE STONE HOUSE (4/16/82)
Co. Rd. 27, unorganized territory (Arthyde)
Fieldstone structure representing speculative attempts
to settle northern Minnesota's logged-over land after
World War I.

BETHLEHEM LUTHERAN CHURCH (4/16/82)
off Co. Hwy. 12, Nordland Twp.
Swedish Evangelical Lutheran frame church built in 1897
to serve county's large Swedish immigrant population.

PATRICK CASEY HOUSE (4/16/82)
4th St. S.E. and 2nd Ave. S.E., Aitkin
Queen Anne/Classical Revival frame residence built in
1901 by one of Aitkin's leading merchants.

MALMO MOUNDS AND VILLAGE SITE (4/3/75)
Malmo Twp.
Group of mounds dating from Precontact Period
(ca. 200 B.C.–A.D. 400).

NATIONAL WOODENWARE COMPANY
SUPERINTENDENT'S RESIDENCE (4/16/82)
Elm St. and Ione Ave., Hill City
Residence (1910) of chief administrator for city's principal industry, a mill complex that manufactured barrels and tubs for Armour & Co.

NORTHERN PACIFIC DEPOT (4/16/82)
20 Pacific St. S.W., Aitkin
Brick passenger depot built in 1916, symbolizing importance of railroad in Aitkin's growth and development.

POTTER-CASEY COMPANY BUILDING (4/16/82)
Minnesota Ave., Aitkin
One of Aitkin's largest brick commercial buildings, constructed in 1902 to house county's leading mercantile business.

SAVANNA PORTAGE (4/23/73)
Balsam Twp.
Transportation route between Upper Mississippi Valley and Great Lakes used by Indians, fur traders, missionaries, and travelers.

Northern Pacific Depot

ANOKA COUNTY

ANOKA-CHAMPLIN MISSISSIPPI RIVER BRIDGE (12/31/79)
U.S. Hwy. 52 over Mississippi River, Anoka (also in Hennepin County)
Continuous-arch, steel-reinforced concrete bridge designed by C. M. Babcock and built in 1929 by Minneapolis Bridge Company.

ANOKA POST OFFICE (12/31/79)
300 E. Main St., Anoka
Georgian Revival brick post office built in 1916.

Banfill Tavern

BANFILL TAVERN (12/12/76)
6666 E. River Rd., Fridley
One of Minnesota's early wayside inns, built in 1847 near major transportation routes and operated by John Banfill.

CARLOS AVERY GAME FARM (8/9/91)
off Co. Hwys. 17 and 18, Columbus Twp.
Picturesque Colonial Revival frame buildings (1936–41)

constituting one of first large-scale efforts at wildlife management in Minnesota.

COLONIAL HALL AND MASONIC LODGE NO. 30 (12/31/79)
1900 3rd Ave. S., Anoka
Georgian Revival frame house and medical office built in 1904 for Drs. Alanson and Flora Aldrich; brick Masonic hall added in 1922.

CRESCENT GRANGE HALL NO. 512 (12/26/79)
Type Lake Rd., Linwood Twp.
Meeting hall (1881–82) affiliated with Minnesota State Grange, established to benefit farmers and promote education in agriculture.

DISTRICT NO. 28 SCHOOL (12/27/79)
14100 St. Francis Blvd. N.W., Ramsey
One-room brick schoolhouse erected in 1892 to serve county's growing rural population.

JACKSON HOTEL (12/8/78)
214 Jackson St., Anoka
Anoka's leading hotel when built in 1884, serving a clientele of businessmen, entertainers, and tourists.

PORTER KELSEY HOUSE (12/26/79)
14853 7th Ave. N., Andover
Italianate brick residence built in 1887 by owner of Kelsey Brick Company.

KLINE SANITARIUM (12/26/79)
1500 S. Ferry Pkwy., Anoka
Anoka's first hospital, built in 1902 and operated by local physician Dr. James Franklin Kline.

HENRY G. LEATHERS HOUSE (12/26/79)
22957 Rum River Blvd., St. Francis
Victorian frame residence built in 1883 for prominent druggist and local postmaster.

RICHARDSON BARN (12/26/79)
22814 Sunrise Rd. N.E., Linwood Twp.
Log barn with rubblestone foundation erected ca. 1870, used principally for storing hay.

RIVERSIDE HOTEL (12/26/79)
3631 Bridge St., St. Francis
Frame residence built ca. 1860 for Woodbury family of millers, expanded into hotel to house seasonal sawmill workers.

SHAW-HAMMONS HOUSE (12/26/79)
302 Fremont St., Anoka
Greek Revival house (1854) occupied by a succession of Anoka land speculators, lumbermen, business leaders, and politicians.

SPARRE BARN (1/10/80)
20071 Nowthen Blvd., Burns Twp.
Round dairy barn designed by architect Ernest Marsh and constructed in 1924.

SWEDISH EVANGELICAL LUTHERAN CHURCH (12/26/79)
2200 Swedish Dr. N.E., Ham Lake
Frame church with bell tower built in 1872 by Ham Lake's Swedish settlers, with furnishings made by local Swedish craftsmen.

HEMAN L. TICKNOR HOUSE (12/27/79)
1625 3rd Ave. S., Anoka
Residence built in 1867 for early Anoka business leader, landowner, and county commissioner.

WINDEGO PARK AUDITORIUM/OPEN AIR THEATER (1/8/80)
between S. Ferry St. and Rum River, Anoka
Semicircular open-air theater built in 1914 for community plays and pageants.

WOODBURY HOUSE (12/26/79)
1632 S. Ferry Pkwy., Anoka
Federal/Greek Revival–style home built in 1850s by Dr. Samuel Shaw, later occupied by Woodbury family of business and civic leaders.

BECKER COUNTY

DETROIT LAKES CARNEGIE LIBRARY (3/16/76)
1000 Washington Ave., Detroit Lakes
Prairie School library built in 1911, based on design by Wisconsin architects Claude and Starck.

EDGEWATER BEACH COTTAGES (3/15/89)
321 Park Lake Blvd., Detroit Lakes
Tourist resort built in 1937–39 featuring rare stovewood construction.

GRAYSTONE HOTEL (7/1/99)
119 Pioneer St., Detroit Lakes
Hybrid of city hotel and rural resort, built in 1916–17 to stimulate region's tourism industry.

HOLMES BLOCK (7/19/2001)
710-718 Washington Ave., Detroit Lakes
Brick commercial building built in 1892 by entrepreneur Elon Galusha Holmes as town's business, cultural, and mercantile center.

Graystone Hotel, ca. 1920

ITASCA STATE PARK (5/7/73)
Co. Hwy. 113, Savanna Twp. (also in Clearwater and Hubbard Counties)
Minnesota's oldest state park (est. 1891), site of Mississippi headwaters, with rustic-style log and stone buildings/structures built in 1905–42.

NORTHERN PACIFIC PASSENGER DEPOT (12/22/88)
off U.S. Hwy. 10, Detroit Lakes
Brick depot built in 1908 to serve region's growing tourism industry.

HOMER E. AND REBECCA SARGENT HOUSE (12/22/88)
1036 Lake Ave., Detroit Lakes
Queen Anne summer house built in 1885 by a Chicago railroad executive and his wife.

BELTRAMI COUNTY

BELTRAMI COUNTY COURTHOUSE (5/26/88)
619 Beltrami Ave. N.W., Bemidji
Beaux Arts-inspired, brick-and-stone courthouse with domed tower, designed by Kinney and Detweiler and built in 1902.

David and Wanda Park House

BEMIDJI CARNEGIE LIBRARY (11/25/80)
426 Bemidji Ave., Bemidji
Classical Revival brick library with limestone trim, designed by Fargo architect W. D. Gillespie and built in 1909.

BUENA VISTA ARCHAEOLOGICAL HISTORIC DISTRICT (11/7/96)
Turtle Lake Twp.
Site of late-19th-century logging town, remains of William Maher Sawmill, and standing 1898 schoolhouse.

DISTRICT NO. 132 SCHOOL (10/27/88)
Co. Rd. 500, Roosevelt Twp.
Classical Revival frame school designed by local contractors and built ca. 1915.

GREAT NORTHERN DEPOT (5/26/88)
off Minnesota Ave., Bemidji
Classical Revival, brick-and-stone depot built in 1913 for passenger and freight service to booming logging town.

LAKE BEMIDJI STATE PARK CCC/NYA/RUSTIC STYLE HISTORIC RESOURCES (10/25/89)
off Co. Hwy. 20 (Lake Bemidji State Park), Northern Twp.
Log recreational facilities constructed in 1937–39 by NYA workers.

NYMORE BRIDGE (11/6/89)
1st St. over Mississippi River, Bemidji
Large barrel-vault, reinforced concrete bridge built in 1917 using patented reinforcing system.

DAVID AND WANDA PARK HOUSE (5/16/88)
1501 Birchmont Dr., Bemidji
Moderne-style residence designed by Edward K. Mahlum and built in 1936.

PAUL BUNYAN AND BABE THE BLUE OX (3/10/88)
3rd St. and Bemidji Ave., Bemidji
Colossal roadside statues of mythical giant lumberjack
and companion, erected in 1937–38 to stimulate tourism.

RABIDEAU CCC CAMP (6/16/76)
off Co. Hwy. 39 (Chippewa National Forest), Taylor Twp.
One of two surviving CCC camps in Minnesota, constructed in 1935–41.

SAUM SCHOOLS (3/27/80)
Co. Hwy. 23, Woodrow Twp.
One-room log school (1903) and two-story frame
schoolhouse (1912) built as one of Minnesota's first
consolidated schools.

BENTON COUNTY

CHURCH OF SS. PETER AND PAUL (CATHOLIC) (4/6/82)
State St., Gilman
Beaux Arts brick church built on basilica plan in 1930
for Polish Catholic parish.

COTA ROUND BARNS (4/6/82)
Co. Hwy. 48, St. George Twp.
Reinforced concrete barns built in 1920–23 by local
veterinarian-turned-contractor Al Cota.

ESSELMAN BROTHERS GENERAL STORE (4/6/82)
Co. Hwys. 1 and 13, Mayhew Lake Twp.
Multipurpose store built in 1897 that served as center
of crossroads community.

POSCH SITE (10/23/73)
Langola Twp.
Habitation site on sandy ridge overlooking Platte River
valley, yielding stone tools from Precontact Period
(5000–1000 B.C.).

Cota Round Barns

LEONARD ROBINSON HOUSE (4/6/82)
202 2nd Ave. S., Sauk Rapids
House of locally quarried granite built in 1873 by leading
pioneer of area's granite quarrying industry.

RONNEBY CHARCOAL KILN (4/6/82)
off Minn. Hwy. 23, Ronneby
Rare Minnesota example of early 20th-century industrial kiln, used to manufacture coal from hardwood
slabs.

BIG STONE COUNTY

BIG STONE COUNTY COURTHOUSE (8/15/85)
20 S.E. 2nd St., Ortonville
Monumental 1902 Victorian brick courthouse with
ornate central rotunda, designed by Fremont D. Orff.

CHICAGO MILWAUKEE ST. PAUL AND
PACIFIC DEPOT (7/31/86)
Main and Center Sts., Clinton
Small, standardized frame combination depot for
passenger and freight traffic, built ca. 1885.

COLUMBIAN HOTEL (8/15/85)
305 N.W. 2nd St., Ortonville
Large Victorian brick hotel built in 1892 as focal point
of downtown Ortonville.

DISTRICT NO. 13 SCHOOL (8/15/85)
Co. Rd. 25, Artichoke Twp.
Octagonal school building constructed in 1898 by
Ortonville contractor John Carlson and Company.

ODESSA JAIL (7/24/86)
Main and 2nd Sts., Odessa
Small, freestanding brick jail
(1913) of type constructed in
rural communities at turn of
20th century.

**ORTONVILLE COMMERCIAL
HISTORIC DISTRICT** (8/15/85)
*vicinity of 2nd St. and Madison
and Monroe Aves., Ortonville*
District No. 13 School
Central business district with
uniform collection of small Victorian brick commercial
buildings trimmed in locally quarried purple granite.

ORTONVILLE FREE LIBRARY (8/15/85)
412 N.W. 2nd St., Ortonville
Carnegie-funded, Mission Revival–style library designed
in 1915 by F. H. Ellerbe.

BLUE EARTH COUNTY

BLUE EARTH COUNTY COURTHOUSE (7/28/80)
204 S. 5th St., Mankato
Prominently sited courthouse of Mankato stone, designed
by Healy and Allen in French and Italian Renaissance
styles, built in 1886–89.

JEANS R. BRANDRUP HOUSE (7/28/80)
704 Byron, Mankato (also in Lincoln Park Historic District)

Classical Revival frame residence built in 1904 for founder of Mankato Commercial College for vocational training.

CHARLES CHAPMAN HOUSE (7/28/80)
418 McCauley, South Bend Twp. (LeHillier)

Blue Earth County Courthouse

Residence of Mankato stone built in 1858 for city engineer and town-lot surveyor.

LORIN CRAY HOUSE (7/28/80)
603 S. 2nd St., Mankato

Queen Anne brick residence designed in late 1890s by Frank Thayer for civic leader, judge, and philanthropist.

ADOLPH O. EBERHART HOUSE (7/28/80)
228 Pleasant St., Mankato (also in Lincoln Park Historic District)

Georgian Revival frame home of Minnesota's 17th governor, built ca. 1903.

FEDERAL COURTHOUSE AND POST OFFICE (6/17/80)
401 S. 2nd St., Mankato

Massive Richardsonian Romanesque government building of Mankato stone, built in 1896.

FIRST BAPTIST CHURCH (7/28/80)
U.S. Hwy. 169, Garden City Twp.

Solid-concrete-block building constructed in 1868 in pre-railroad settlement.

FIRST NATIONAL BANK OF MANKATO (7/30/74)
229 S. Front St., Mankato
Prairie School brick building with stone and terra cotta trim and stained glass windows, designed by Ellerbe and Round and built in 1913.

FIRST PRESBYTERIAN CHURCH (7/28/80)
S. Broad and Hickory Sts., Mankato
Richardsonian Romanesque church of Mankato stone designed by Warren H. Hayes and built in 1896.

JAMES P. GAIL FARMHOUSE (7/28/80)
off U.S. Hwy. 169, Garden City Twp.
Octagonal house built in late 1850s by owner using brick manufactured onsite; rare rural Minnesota example of 19th-century building fad.

RENSSELAER D. HUBBARD HOUSE (6/7/76)
606 S. Broad St., Mankato
French Second Empire residence of brick with Mankato stone trim, built in 1871 for owner of Hubbard Milling Company.

WILLIAM IRVING HOUSE (7/28/80)
320 Park Lane, Mankato
French Second Empire brick residence built in 1873.

JONES-ROBERTS FARMSTEAD (7/28/80)
Minn. Hwy. 68, Judson Twp.
Early farmstead with farmhouse, barn, outbuildings, and grove (1860–1900) that served as focus of Blue Earth County's Welsh community.

KENNEDY BRIDGE (11/6/89)
Twp. Rd. 167 over Le Sueur River, Mankato Twp.
One of Minnesota's few surviving wrought-iron through truss bridges, erected in 1883 as part of first countywide bridge-building program.

KERN BRIDGE (7/28/80)

Twp. Rd. 190 over Le Sueur River, Mankato and South Bend Twps.

Rare Minnesota example of bowstring-arch through truss, constructed in 1873.

Lincoln Park Residential Historic District

LINCOLN PARK RESIDENTIAL HISTORIC DISTRICT (6/20/95)

vicinity of Byron, 2nd, and Parson Sts. between Shaubut St. W. and Liberty St. E., Mankato

Collection of late-19th- and early-20th-century residences built for Mankato's merchant and professional classes.

MAIN STREET COMMERCIAL BUILDINGS (7/28/80)

north side of Main St. between 2nd and 3rd Sts., Mapleton

Uniform group of two-story brick commercial buildings constructed in 1890s by local contractor J. B. Nelsen and Company.

MANKATO HOLSTEIN FARM BARN (7/28/80)

Co. Hwy. 5, Lime Twp.

Clay-tile barn with rainbow-arch roof, built in 1917 for renowned dairy-cattle-breeding operation.

MANKATO PUBLIC LIBRARY AND READING ROOM (7/28/80)
120 S. Broad St., Mankato
Renaissance Revival, Carnegie-funded library of brick
and Mankato stone, designed by New York firm of
Jardine, Kent, and Jardine and built in 1902–03.

MANKATO UNION DEPOT (7/28/80)
112 Pike St., Mankato
County's sole
surviving depot,
constructed at city's
center jointly by
two competing rail
lines.

MARSH CONCRETE RAINBOW ARCH BRIDGE (7/28/80)
*Co. Rd. 101 over
Little Cottonwood
River, Cambria Twp.*

Seppman Mill

Early one-lane example of bridge type patented in 1911
by Marsh Engineering Company of Des Moines.

MINNEOPA STATE PARK WPA/RUSTIC STYLE HISTORIC RESOURCES (10/25/89)
off U.S. Hwy. 169 (Minneopa State Park), South Bend Twp.
Buildings and structures, many of native limestone,
developed in 1940 by WPA workers in park type
intended to serve nearby small communities.

NORTH FRONT STREET COMMERCIAL HISTORIC DISTRICT (7/28/80)
301-415 N. Riverfront Dr. (odd numbers only), Mankato
Grouping of late-19th- and early-20th-century, brick-
and-stone commercial buildings on northern edge of
central business district.

OLD MAIN, MANKATO STATE TEACHERS COLLEGE (6/2/83)
5th St. S. at Jackson St., Mankato
College's administrative, academic, and social center
(1908), a Jacobean Revival, brick-and-limestone building by State Architect Clarence H. Johnston Sr.

SEPPMAN MILL (8/26/71)
Minn. Hwy. 68 (Minneopa State Park), South Bend Twp.
Wind-powered mill built of local stone in 1863 to grind
flour and feed.

STERLING CONGREGATIONAL CHURCH (7/28/80)
Co. Rd. 151, Sterling Twp.
Frame church built in 1867 by members of the largely
Scottish-descent Minnesota Settlement Association.

LUCAS TROENDLE HOUSE (7/28/80)
2nd and Silver Sts., Mapleton
Queen Anne brick-and-stone residence designed in
1896 by Pass and Schippel of Mankato for railroad
townsite developer.

Lucas Troendle House, ca. 1910

ZIEGLERS FORD BRIDGE (11/6/89)
Twp. Rd. 96 over Big Cobb River, Decoria Twp.
Single-span steel through truss built in 1904 by Mayer
Brothers of Mankato.

BROWN COUNTY

AUGUST SCHELL BREWING COMPANY (12/27/74)
20th St. S., New Ulm
Residence (1880), garden, brew house (1880s), barrel
house and cellars of New Ulm's sole remaining early
brewery, founded in 1860.

BENDIXON-SCHMIDT HOUSE (12/31/79)
123 N. Marshall Ave., Springfield
Queen Anne frame residence built in 1894, owned successively by town's early business leaders.

BJORNEBERG GARAGE (12/31/79)
Broadway, Hanska
Brick automobile service garage with cast-concrete
bas-relief panels, built ca. 1919.

BOESCH-HUMMEL-MALTZAHN BLOCK (12/31/79)
6-12 Minnesota St. N., New Ulm
Brick commercial building constructed in 1890 in
central business district, featuring elaborately detailed
front façade.

CHICAGO NORTH WESTERN DEPOT (12/31/79)
Valley St. S., New Ulm
Second-generation stone depot, built ca. 1895 for
passenger and freight traffic.

CHICAGO NORTH WESTERN DEPOT (6/25/92)
Oak St. N.W., Sleepy Eye
Tudor Revival brick passenger depot designed by
Chicago architects Frost and Granger and built in 1902.

BERNARD FESENMAIER HOUSE (12/31/79)

426 State St. N., New Ulm

L-shaped, gable-roofed house with polychrome brick detailing built in late 1880s.

Superintendent's Residence, Flandrau State Park

FLANDRAU STATE PARK CCC/WPA/RUSTIC STYLE HISTORIC RESOURCES (10/25/89)

off Co. Hwy. 13 (Flandrau State Park), Cottonwood Twp.

Collection of buildings and structures featuring native quartzite, designed by Edward W. Barber to reflect area's German heritage, built in 1942.

WANDA GÁG CHILDHOOD HOME (12/31/79)

226 Washington St. N., New Ulm

Home of artist Anton Gág and family, including daughter Wanda (resident 1890s–1913), artist/author of *Millions of Cats* and other children's books.

GRAND HOTEL (6/21/90)

210 Minnesota St. N., New Ulm

Italianate brick hotel constructed in central business district in 1876.

Hermann Monument

HERMANN MONUMENT (10/2/73)
Hermann Heights Park, New Ulm
Colossal figure designed by Julius Berndt, commissioned in 1880s by Sons of Hermann, a German-American fraternal organization.

FREDERICK W. KIESLING HOUSE (2/23/72)
220 Minnesota St. N., New Ulm
Frame dwelling associated with the Dakota War of 1862.

KREITINGER GARAGE (12/31/79)
1 N. Cass Ave., Springfield
Two-story commercial building with ornamental brick-work built ca. 1911 as auto dealership.

LAMPERT LUMBER COMPANY LINE YARD (12/31/79)
Center St., Milford Twp.
Retail/office/storage building of Sleepy Eye–based company, one of several lumberyards built along rail line in early 20th century.

LIBERAL UNION HALL (12/31/79)
Broadway and Main St., Hanska
Community center built in 1910 with brick manufactured onsite by group affiliated with Nora Unitarian Church.

JOHN LIND HOUSE (12/31/74)
622 Center St., New Ulm
Queen Anne brick-and-stone home of Minnesota's 14th governor, built in 1887.

MELGES BAKERY (6/28/74)
213 Minnesota St. S., New Ulm
One-story commercial building with false front, built of local brick in 1865.

NEW ULM ARMORY (12/31/79)
205 Broadway N., New Ulm
Gothic Revival–style, brick-and-concrete armory built in 1914 for one of Minnesota's oldest National Guard companies.

NEW ULM OIL COMPANY SERVICE STATION (12/31/79)
Broadway and 5th St. N., New Ulm
One of several stations with fanciful features designed by Saffert Construction Company of New Ulm, built in 1926.

NEW ULM POST OFFICE (4/28/70)
Center St. and Broadway, New Ulm
Unique adaptation of German Renaissance style, built in 1909 of brick and locally manufactured concrete Artstone, with stepped gables and dormers.

NORA FREE CHRISTIAN CHURCH (8/4/88)
Minn. Hwy. 257, Linden Twp.
Church (1884) and parsonage (1906) of liberal Unitarian congregation established by Norwegian intellectual Kristofer Janson.

ADOLPH C. OCHS HOUSE (12/31/79)
303 N. Marshall, Springfield
Colonial Revival brick house built in 1911 for owner of
A. C. Ochs Brick and Tile Company.

OLD MAIN (12/31/79)
Dr. Martin Luther College, College Heights, New Ulm
Victorian Gothic brick-and-stone building constructed
in 1884 as first building on campus of Lutheran teacher
training college.

ST. MICHAEL'S SCHOOL AND CONVENT (12/31/79)
500 State St. N., New Ulm
Italianate example of early institutional architecture in
Minnesota, built in 1872 with later additions.

OTTO SCHELL HOUSE (12/31/79)
Point Lookout, New Ulm
Queen Anne frame residence (ca. 1895) of brewer Otto
Schell, son of Schell brewing company founder August
Schell.

SHADY LANE STOCK FARM (12/31/79)
U.S. Hwy. 14, Burnstown Twp.
Farmstead (ca. 1898–1913) of progressive livestock
breeder L. E. Potter, featuring prototype of clay block
silo developed at A. C. Ochs Brick and Tile Company.

SLEEPY EYE MILLING COMPANY (2/8/91)
4th and Oak Sts. N.E., Sleepy Eye
Most complete milling complex in southern Minnesota, built in 1901–20 to process grain for flour, feed,
and cereals.

W. W. SMITH HOUSE (12/31/79)
524 1st Ave. S., Sleepy Eye
Queen Anne frame residence with classical details, built
ca. 1901 for head of First National Bank of Sleepy Eye.

SOUTH BROADWAY HISTORIC DISTRICT (12/31/79)
200-308 Broadway S. (even numbers only), New Ulm
Eight brick residences of varying scales and styles, built at turn of 20th century with locally manufactured brick.

SOUTH GERMAN STREET HISTORIC DISTRICT (12/31/79)
110-312 German St. S. (even numbers only), New Ulm
Larger-scale homes built in late 19th century in Italianate and Queen Anne variations for leaders of New Ulm's commerce and industry.

SYNSTEBY SITE (5/12/75)
Lake Hanska Twp.
Precontact Period habitation site and mound groups, and site of 1863 Fort Hanska.

THORMODSON BARN (12/31/79)
off Minn. Hwy. 257, Linden Twp.
Sixteen-sided barn with central interior silo designed and built in 1912 by George Lee for a cattle-breeding operation.

Otto Schell House, 1979

TURNER HALL (12/31/79)
State St. and 1st St. S., New Ulm
Symbol of New Ulm's German cultural identity, built in 1873 for Turnverein, an immigrant organization promoting physical exercise.

WINONA AND ST. PETER FREIGHT DEPOT (12/31/79)
Oak St. N.E., Sleepy Eye
Early frame depot (ca. 1887) built for one of the first rail lines to reach western Minnesota.

CARLTON COUNTY

CARLTON COUNTY COURTHOUSE (8/29/85)
301 Walnut Ave., Carlton
Renaissance Revival brick-and-stone courthouse designed
in 1920s by Clyde Kelly.

CHURCH OF SS. JOSEPH AND MARY (CATHOLIC) (3/29/84)
Mission Rd., Perch Lake Twp.
Log church built in 1884 by Ojibwe parishioners.

Church of SS. Joseph and Mary

CLOQUET CITY HALL (9/11/85)
Ave. B and Arch St., Cloquet
City government center, built of brick in Georgian and Renaissance Revival styles in 1920 after city was destroyed by fire of 1918.

CLOQUET-NORTHERN OFFICE BUILDING (8/29/85)
Ave. C and Arch St., Cloquet
Brick-and-stone commercial building built after fire of
1918 to house city's main businesses.

GRAND PORTAGE OF THE ST. LOUIS RIVER (5/24/73)
off Minn. Hwy. 210 (Jay Cooke State Park), Silver Brook Twp.
Seven-mile portage on trade route between Upper
Mississippi Valley and Great Lakes used by Indians
and fur traders.

JAY COOKE STATE PARK CCC/WPA/RUSTIC STYLE HISTORIC DISTRICT (6/11/92)
off Minn. Hwy. 210 (Jay Cooke State Park), Thomson Twp.
Native stone inn (1940–42) and suspension bridge (1934) constructed by CCC workers.

JAY COOKE STATE PARK CCC/WPA/RUSTIC STYLE PICNIC GROUNDS (6/11/92)
off Minn. Hwy. 210 (Jay Cooke State Park), Thomson Twp.
Native stone shelter and stone-and-log water tower/latrine at Oldenburg Point picnic grounds developed by CCC workers in 1934–36.

JAY COOKE STATE PARK CCC/WPA/RUSTIC STYLE SERVICE YARD (6/11/92)
off Minn. Hwy. 210 (Jay Cooke State Park), Thomson Twp.
Native stone pump house and log custodian's cabin built in 1934–35 by CCC workers in part of park devoted to maintenance and administrative functions.

KALEVALA FINNISH EVANGELICAL NATIONAL LUTHERAN CHURCH (10/1/98)
off Minn. Hwy. 73, Kalevala Twp.
Finnish-language Lutheran church built in 1915, one of few frame buildings to survive 1918 fire.

LINDHOLM OIL COMPANY SERVICE STATION (9/11/85)
202 Cloquet Ave., Cloquet
Designed by Frank Lloyd Wright and completed in 1958, the only station built from his prototype drawings.

MINNEAPOLIS ST. PAUL AND SAULT STE. MARIE DEPOT (3/17/94)
840 Folz Blvd., Moose Lake
Standard first-class frame depot for the Soo Line, built in 1907; one of few buildings to survive 1918 fire, it offered shelter to the homeless.

NORTHEASTERN HOTEL (11/8/84)
115 St. Louis Ave., Cloquet
Brick hotel (1904) that survived 1918 fire and served as hospital, temporary shelter, and Red Cross headquarters for fire relief efforts.

Rudolph Weyerhaeuser House, 1 Park Place, Park Place Historic District

PARK PLACE HISTORIC DISTRICT (8/29/85)
1, 512, 520, and 528 Park Place, Cloquet
Four large frame houses constructed in 1919 during post-fire rebuilding boom; erected by Weyerhaeuser lumber companies as employee residences.

SHAW MEMORIAL LIBRARY (8/29/85)
406 Cloquet Ave., Cloquet
Renaissance Revival brick library (1920) designed by Kelly and Shefchik, one of several public buildings erected after fire of 1918; named for prominent lumberman George S. Shaw.

CARVER COUNTY

EMILE AMBLARD GUEST HOUSE (1/4/80)
32-36 N. Vine St., Waconia
Frame house on "mainland" designed and built ca. 1900 by developer of Coney Island resort area.

BRINKHAUS SALOON LIVERY BARN (1/4/80)
112 W. 4th St., Chaska
Building of Chaska brick constructed ca. 1875 to house livery business that provided transportation and mail service to surrounding communities.

CARVER HISTORIC DISTRICT (1/4/80)
vicinity of Lime, 1st, Walnut, and 6th Sts., Carver
Collection of 100 commercial, religious, residential, and social buildings in 19th-century Minnesota River town.

CHURCH OF ST. HUBERTUS (CATHOLIC) (3/19/82)
Great Plains Blvd. and W. 78th St., Chanhassen
Gothic-style church of red brick with cream-colored Chaska brick trim, built in 1887 for German Catholic community of Chanhassen.

CONEY ISLAND OF THE WEST (8/11/76)
Lake Waconia, Waconia Twp.
Summer resort/recreation area in Lake Waconia developed during late-19th and early-20th centuries.

FREDERICK E. DU TOIT HOUSE (1/4/80)
121 Hickory St., Chaska
House of cream-colored Chaska brick built ca. 1870 for state legislator and longtime publisher of *Chaska Herald* newspaper.

EDER-BAER HOUSE (1/4/80)
105 Elm St., Chaska
Queen Anne residence (ca. 1900) of cream-colored Chaska brick, a widely used, locally manufactured building material.

FREDERICK GREINER HOUSE (1/4/80)
319 E. 3rd St., Chaska
House of cream-colored Chaska brick built ca. 1870 for early political figure and proprietor of Chaska House, community's first hotel.

Wendelin Grimm Farmstead

WENDELIN GRIMM FARMSTEAD (12/30/74)
off Co. Hwy. 11 (Carver Park Reserve), Laketown Twp.
Farmhouse of cream-colored Chaska brick built in 1876 for developer of Grimm alfalfa, first U.S. strain of winter-hardy alfalfa.

PHILIP GUETTLER HOUSE (1/4/80)
Adams and Mill Sts., Cologne
House of cream-colored Chaska brick built in 1902 for owner of city's major industry, Cologne Milling.

HEBEISEN HARDWARE STORE (1/4/80)
Railroad and Maria Sts., Hamburg
Brick commercial building (1907), site of early cooperative association that provided goods and services to agricultural community.

JACOB HEBEISEN HOUSE (1/4/80)
off Co. Hwy. 50, Hamburg
Residence built in 1884 for one of Hamburg's leading merchants.

ALBERTINE AND FRED HECK HOUSE (12/27/2000)
8941 Audubon Rd., Chanhassen
Farmhouse (ca. 1895) of cream-colored Chaska brick, a widely used, locally manufactured building material.

HERALD BLOCK (1/4/80)
123 W. 2nd St., Chaska
Commercial building of cream-colored Chaska brick, home of *Chaska Herald* newspaper since 1871.

KING OSCAR'S SETTLEMENT (1/4/80)
Co. Hwy. 40, Dahlgren Twp.
Complex of church and parish buildings associated with early Swedish Lutheran settlement, established in 1853.

JOHN KNOTZ HOUSE (1/4/80)
Paul and Mill Sts., Cologne
Residence (1905) of Dr. John Knotz, medical doctor for railroad lines, and Rosa Partoll Knotz, women's rights advocate and Cologne mayor.

LAKETOWN MORAVIAN BRETHREN'S CHURCH (1/4/80)
Co. Hwy. 11, Victoria
Church of Chaska brick built in 1878 for one of two outposts of Chaska Moravian congregation.

E. H. LEWIS HOUSE (1/4/80)
321 W. 2nd St., Chaska
Ca. 1870 residence of Chaska brick, owned successively by Faber family of hoteliers and merchants and physician Lewis.

CHARLES MAISER HOUSE (1/4/80)
16 W. Main St., Waconia
Italianate frame house built ca. 1875 for Maiser family of grain millers.

MOCK CIGAR FACTORY AND HOUSE (1/4/80)
48 W. Main St., Waconia
False-front factory and attached Italianate house (ca. 1875) owned by E. H. Mock, proprietor of early Waconia industry.

PAUL MOHRBACHER HOUSE (1/4/80)
Paul and Market Sts., Cologne
Ca. 1880 brick home of Cologne founder and civic leader.

NORWOOD METHODIST EPISCOPAL CHURCH (1/4/80)
Hill and Union Sts., Norwood
Frame church with bell tower designed and built in 1876 by Norwood civic leader James Slocum Jr.

ANDREW PETERSON FARMSTEAD (10/11/79)
Minn. Hwy. 5, Laketown Twp.
Farmstead (ca. 1867–98) of Swedish immigrant farmer and horticulturist whose 43-year diary recorded life in 19th-century Minnesota.

JOHANN SCHIMMELPFENNIG FARMSTEAD (1/4/80)
off U.S. Hwy. 212, Benton Twp.
Log and frame farm buildings (1856–1909) documenting evolution of Minnesota farmsteads.

SIMONS BUILDING AND LIVERY BARN (1/4/80)
123 W. 3rd St., Chaska
Commercial/residential buildings of Chaska brick (1888–1890s) that housed a saloon, second-story hotel, and livery stable for patron use.

WACONIA CITY HALL (5/9/83)
9 W. 1st St., Waconia
Red brick civic building designed in 1909 by Charles S. Sedgwick to accommodate city offices, fire station, and public hall.

WALNUT STREET HISTORIC DISTRICT (1/4/80)
vicinity of Walnut, 2nd, Chestnut, and 6th Sts., Chaska
Buildings, structures, and burial mounds representing area's prehistory through its period of commercial, industrial, religious, and residential development.

WEST MAIN STREET HOUSES (1/4/80)

417, 429, and 453 W. Main St., Waconia
One Chaska brick residence (1886) and two frame "carpenter's catalogue" houses (1898, 1903) showing individual interpretation by local craftsmen.

WEST UNION (1/4/80)

Co. Hwy. 50, Hancock Twp.
Church (1868) and parish hall (1905) forming religious and social center of early Swedish Lutheran settlement.

WINTER SALOON (1/4/80)

Elm and Hazel Sts., Norwood
Saloon/meeting hall with second-floor proprietor's residence, built ca. 1890 for Winter brothers, holders of Norwood's first liquor license.

YOUNG AMERICA CITY HALL (1/4/80)

102 2nd Ave. S., Young America
Red brick building with corner tower built in 1909 as headquarters for municipal government.

ZOAR MORAVIAN CHURCH (1/4/80)

Co. Hwy. 10, Laketown Twp.
Greek Revival frame church built in 1863 for one of two outposts of Chaska Moravian congregation.

Zoar Moravian Church

CASS COUNTY

BATTLE POINT (8/17/90)
Leech Lake Reservation
Precontact Period Indian village and mounds, two Post-contact cemeteries, and site of one of last battles (1898) between Indians and U.S. military.

CHASE HOTEL (6/4/80)
329 Cleveland Ave., Walker
First-class resort hotel built by L. W. Chase in 1922 to cater to tourists in new age of automobile transportation.

CHIPPEWA AGENCY HISTORIC DISTRICT (5/22/73)
Sylvan Twp.
Mounds, Precontact Period village site (ca. A.D. 500–1300), oxcart trails, and 1850s building remnants from Chippewa Indian Agency.

GREAT NORTHERN RAILWAY COMPANY BRIDGE (10/14/80)
off Minn. Hwy. 371, Wilkinson Twp.
Through girder, swing span built ca. 1915 to accommodate tugboat traffic on Steamboat River between logging areas and sawmills.

Administration Building, Minnesota State Sanatorium for Consumptives, ca. 1925

GULL LAKE MOUNDS SITE (5/7/73)

East Gull Lake Twp.

Mound group and habitation site dating from Precontact Period (800 B.C.–A.D. 900).

HOLE-IN-THE-DAY II HOUSE SITE (6/19/73)

Sylvan Twp.

Site of log farmhouse built in 1850s by the U.S. government for influential Ojibwe leader.

MINNESOTA STATE SANATORIUM FOR CONSUMPTIVES (AH-GWAH-CHING) (7/25/2001)

7232 Ah-Gwah-Ching Rd. N.W., Shingobee Twp. (Ah-Gwah-Ching)

First state-operated facility for treatment of tuberculosis, opened in 1907; earliest buildings designed by State Architect Clarence H. Johnston Sr.

JULIUS NEILS HOUSE (6/20/80)

3rd St., Cass Lake

Large frame residence built in 1900 for prominent lumber entrepreneur and founder of Neils Lumber Company.

OLD BACKUS (12/24/74)

Powers and Pine River Twps.

Site of Backus and Brooks Lumber Company camp and first Backus townsite, 1885–1902.

RICE LAKE HUT RINGS (8/14/73)

Fairview Twp.

Depressions thought to be made by earth lodges dating from late Precontact Period or later.

SHERWOOD FOREST LODGE COMPLEX (6/16/80)

Co. Hwy. 77, Lake Shore

Hunting-and-fishing resort complex of rustic log lodge and cabins (ca. 1929, 1935) built during first major wave of Minnesota resort construction.

SOO LINE DEPOT (5/23/80)
off Main St., Remer
Frame depot built ca. 1910 in the Soo Line's standard second-class pattern, with living quarters for agent's family.

SUPERVISOR'S OFFICE HEADQUARTERS (1/31/76)
Ash Ave. N.W and 2nd St. N.W. (Chippewa National Forest), Pike Bay Twp.
Large example of chinkless log construction, built of native red pine by Finnish craftsmen and CCC and WPA workers in 1936.

WINNIBIGOSHISH LAKE DAM (5/11/82)
Itasca Co. Hwy. 9 at Mississippi River,
unorganized territory (also in Itasca County)
Reinforced concrete dam built in 1900 by the U.S. Army Corps of Engineers as part of reservoir system to stabilize Mississippi River flow.

WINNIBIGOSHISH RESORT (5/23/80)
U.S. Hwy. 2, Bena
Motor court and lake resort (1933) with central store/filling station, pagoda-roofed gas pumps, and guest cottages.

CHIPPEWA COUNTY

CHARLES H. BUDD HOUSE (9/19/77)
219 N. 3rd St., Montevideo
Shingled residence built in 1909 for early Montevideo resident, civic leader, and local government official.

CHICAGO MILWAUKEE AND ST. PAUL DEPOT (10/27/88)
S. 1st St. at Park Ave., Montevideo
Frame passenger depot constructed in 1901; only building remaining of a major Milwaukee Road division headquarters complex.

CHIPPEWA COUNTY BANK (9/19/77)

1st St. and Lincoln Ave., Montevideo
Commercial Queen Anne brick building with tower,
built in 1900.

HENRY GIPPE FARMSTEAD (9/25/85)

U.S. Hwy. 59, Tunsberg Twp.
Farmstead with 1887 farmhouse of brick made by
owner; home of educators Hilda and Louise Gippe.

LAC QUI PARLE MISSION HISTORIC DISTRICT (3/14/73)

Co. Hwy. 13, Kragero Twp. (also in Lac qui Parle County)
Sites of Fort Renville fur trading post, mission church,
missionary residences, and Dakota Indian village.

MONTEVIDEO CARNEGIE LIBRARY (8/26/82)

125 N. 3rd St., Montevideo
Brick library with limestone trim (1906), designed
by Martin Granum in local adaptation of Classical
Revival style.

OLOF SWENSSON FARMSTEAD (12/30/74)

Co. Hwys. 15 and 6, Granite Falls Twp.
Brick home (1901–03) and timber-frame barn (1880s)
on cut-granite foundations, designed by Swensson, a
farmer, preacher, and political activist.

Olof Swensson Farmstead

JULIAN A. WEAVER HOUSE (6/20/86)
837 Minnesota Ave., Granite Falls
Greek Revival/Italianate frame residence built ca. 1878
for town's first depot agent.

CHISAGO COUNTY

GUSTAF ANDERSON HOUSE (7/21/80)
13045 Lake Blvd., Lindstrom
Italianate brick residence built in 1879 for prominent
farmer and speculator.

ANGEL'S HILL HISTORIC DISTRICT (4/11/72)
*vicinity of W. Plateau
and Government Sts.
and Military Rd.,
Taylors Falls*
Homogenous group
of mid-19th-century
Greek Revival frame
residences, public
buildings, and church
in hills above busi-
ness district.

William H. C. Folsom House, Angel's Hill
Historic District, ca. 1975

**ARCHAEOLOGICAL
SITE 21CH23** (1/16/89)
Amador Twp.
Precontact Period riverside campsite probably used by
Indians harvesting mussels.

J. C. CARLSON HOUSE (7/21/80)
Bremer and 6th St., Rush City
Queen Anne frame residence designed in 1899 by
Augustus F. Gauger for bank president and civic leader.

CENTER CITY HISTORIC DISTRICT (7/21/80)
Summit Ave., Center City

Concentration of late-19th- and early-20th-century frame houses built largely by a local carpenter and lumberyard owner for prosperous residents.

JOHN DAUBNEY HOUSE (7/21/80)
Oak and River Sts., Taylors Falls
Italianate frame house (ca. 1870) acquired as retirement residence by early settler and farmer.

GEORGE FLANDERS HOUSE (7/21/80)
Co. Hwys. 30 and 9,
Harris
Italianate frame dwelling built in 1870s by local promoter as a residence and a stop for rail travelers.

FRANCONIA HISTORIC DISTRICT (6/17/80)
vicinity of Cornelian, Summer, and Henry Sts.,
Franconia Twp. (Franconia)
Frame residences of early settlers in St. Croix River milling town.

GRANT HOUSE (7/21/80)
4th St. and Bremer, Rush City
Brick hotel built in 1896 to serve railroad community.

INTERSTATE STATE PARK CCC/WPA/RUSTIC STYLE CAMPGROUND (6/11/92)
off U.S. Hwy. 8 (Interstate State Park), Shafer Twp.
Buildings and objects constructed in 1938 and 1941 by WPA workers with basalt stone quarried in park.

INTERSTATE STATE PARK CCC/WPA/RUSTIC STYLE HISTORIC DISTRICT (6/11/92)
off U.S. Hwy. 8 (Interstate State Park), Shafer Twp.
Buildings and structures of local basalt stone, including 1920s examples of rustic-style construction that later influenced WPA workers.

FRANK A. LARSON HOUSE (FRIDHEM) (7/21/80)
Newell Ave., Lindstrom
Lakeside, polychrome frame summer house (ca. 1898) used by Chicago publisher of Swedish-language newspaper.

Frank A. Larson House (Fridhem)

MOODY BARN (7/21/80)
Co. Hwy. 24, Chisago Lake Twp.
Round dairy barn with central silo built in 1915 for small owner-operated farm.

PAUL MUNCH HOUSE (5/4/76)
Summer St., Franconia Twp. (also in Franconia Historic District)
Greek Revival frame house built ca. 1855; residence of Civil War veteran and miller.

MUNCH-ROOS HOUSE (11/20/70)
360 Bench St., Taylors Falls
Greek Revival frame dwelling built in 1853 by Munch brothers as residence/carpenter shop, later occupied by Swedish banker/politician.

**POINT DOUGLAS TO SUPERIOR
MILITARY ROAD: DEER CREEK SECTION** (2/7/91)
*off Co. Hwy. 16 (St. Croix Wild River State Park),
Amador Twp.*
Fragment of road developed by U.S. government in
1850s between St. Croix and St. Louis Rivers.

TAYLORS FALLS PUBLIC LIBRARY (10/15/70)
473 Bench St., Taylors Falls
Frame residence and tailor shop built in 1854; later
acquired for use as town library.

CHARLES A. VICTOR HOUSE (7/21/80)
30495 Park St., Lindstrom
Large frame house built ca. 1905 by prominent merchant, civic leader, and Swedish-language newspaper
publisher.

CLAY COUNTY

BARNESVILLE CITY HALL (5/7/80)
Front and Main Sts., Barnesville
Small-town municipal services complex of 1899 city
hall with fire hall and opera house, and ca. 1910 jail,
all of local brick.

JOHN BERGQUIST HOUSE (5/7/80)
719 10th Ave. N., Moorhead
Log house built ca. 1870 by early homesteader.

BERNHARD BERNHARDSON HOUSE (5/7/80)
Co. Hwy. 59, Holy Cross Twp.
Log house built in 1870 by early homesteader.

**BUFFALO RIVER STATE PARK WPA/RUSTIC STYLE
HISTORIC RESOURCES** (10/25/89)
off U.S. Hwy. 10 (Buffalo River State Park), Riverton Twp.

Group of buildings and structures built by WPA workers in 1937, largely of local split stone.

BURNHAM BUILDING (5/7/80) *420 Main Ave., Moorhead*
False-front frame commercial/residential building typifying 1880s downtown Moorhead.

SOLOMON G. COMSTOCK HOUSE (12/30/74)
5th Ave. and S. 8th St., Moorhead
Late Victorian frame home designed by Kees and Fisk and built in 1883 for business leader and politician.

COMSTOCK SCHOOL (5/7/80)
Main St., Comstock
Brick school building begun in 1909 for Clay County's first consolidated school district.

FAIRMONT CREAMERY COMPANY (2/10/83)
801 2nd Ave. N., Moorhead
Brick industrial plant built in 1923 by company promoting agricultural diversification in Red River Valley.

FEDERAL COURTHOUSE AND POST OFFICE (5/7/80)
521 Main Ave., Moorhead
Classical Revival brick building designed by federal government architect Oscar Wenderoth and built in 1915.

LEW A. HUNTOON HOUSE (5/7/80)
709 8th St. S., Moorhead
English cottage–style residence designed by Bertrand and Chamberlain and built in 1910 for director of Moorhead State Normal School.

WULF C. KRABBENHOFT FARMSTEAD (5/7/80)
Co. Hwy. 69, Elmwood Twp.
Red River Valley farm with Queen Anne–inspired frame farmhouse and outbuildings (1890–1910), homesteaded by German immigrant family.

MAIN BUILDING, CONCORDIA COLLEGE (5/7/80)
S. 8th St., Moorhead
Classical Revival, brick-and-stone building constructed in 1906 as center of campus activity.

JOHN OLNESS HOUSE (5/7/80)
U.S. Hwy. 75, Kragnes Twp.
Frame house with Queen Anne details built in 1902 by community's leading merchant and land speculator.

PARK ELEMENTARY SCHOOL (12/22/88)
121 6th Ave. S., Moorhead
Classical Revival, yellow-brick neighborhood school built in 1900.

ROBERT PATTERSON HOUSE (5/7/80)
1st Ave. W. at Elm, Barnesville
Queen Anne fieldstone-and-frame residence built in 1898–1900.

RANDOLPH M. PROBSTFIELD HOUSE (5/7/80)
Co. Hwy. 96, Oakport Twp.
County's oldest known residence, built in 1869 by early settler and agricultural entrepreneur.

Lew A. Huntoon House

ST. JOHN THE DIVINE EPISCOPAL CHURCH (5/7/80)
120 S. 8th St., Moorhead
Shingled frame church with octagonal tower, designed
by Cass Gilbert and built in 1898–99.

HANNA C. AND PETER E. THOMPSON HOUSE (2/23/96)
361 2nd St. N.E., Barnesville
Classical Revival residence attributed to Hancock Brothers of Fargo and built in 1902–03 for community leaders
and mercantile business owner.

CLEARWATER COUNTY

GRAN EVANGELICAL LUTHERAN CHURCH (5/19/88)
Co. Hwys. 92 and 20, Popple Twp.
County's first church, built in 1897 with logs, land, and
labor donated by Norwegian congregation.

ITASCA BISON SITE (ITASCA STATE PARK) (12/29/70)
*unorganized territory
(Itasca State Park)*
Precontact Period
bison kill site
(7500–5500 B.C.) with
bison bone and arti-
facts embedded in
peat deposit.

ITASCA STATE PARK
(5/7/73)
*off Co. Hwy. 38, Itasca
Twp. and unorganized
territory (also in Becker
and Hubbard Counties)*

Old Timer's Cabin, Itasca State Park

Minnesota's oldest state park (est. 1891), site of Mississippi headwaters, with Rustic-style log and stone build-
ings/structures built in 1905–42.

LOWER RICE LAKE SITE (12/18/78)
LaPrairie Twp.
Precontact Period site (ca. A.D. 1000–1600) used by
Indians gathering and processing wild rice.

UPPER RICE LAKE SITE (12/19/78)
Minerva Twp.
Precontact Period site (ca. A.D. 1000–1600) used by
Indians gathering and processing wild rice.

COOK COUNTY

AMBOY AND *GEORGE SPENCER* SHIPWRECKS (4/14/94)
vicinity of Schroeder, Lake Superior
Wood-hulled schooner-barge (1874) and freight-carrying
steamship (1884) used to transport iron ore; both sunk
during 1905 *Mataafa* storm.

BALLY BLACKSMITH SHOP (8/13/86)
Broadway and 1st St., Grand Marais
False-front commercial building constructed in 1911 as
town's only general-purpose blacksmith shop.

CHURCH OF ST. FRANCIS XAVIER (CATHOLIC) (7/31/86)
U.S. Hwy. 61, unorganized territory
Small mission church built by local carpenter in 1895;
sole remaining structure from Chippewa City, late-19th-
and early-20th-century Ojibwe settlement.

CLEARWATER LODGE (12/2/85)
Co. Hwy. 66, unorganized territory
Log resort built in 1925–26 along Gunflint Trail by
homesteaders to capitalize on emerging tourist trade.

COOK COUNTY COURTHOUSE (5/9/83)
411 2nd St., Grand Marais
Classical Revival, county-government building designed
by Kelly and Lignell and constructed in 1911–12.

FOWL LAKE SITE (12/30/74)
unorganized territory (Superior National Forest)
Island habitation site from Precontact Period
(3000–1000 B.C.).

GRAND PORTAGE NATIONAL MONUMENT (10/15/66)
off U.S. Hwy. 61, Grand Portage Indian Reservation
Late-18th-century North West Company fur-trade depots
at Grand Portage and Fort Charlotte, connected by nine-
mile portage trail.

HEIGHT OF LAND (10/18/74)
unorganized territory (Superior National Forest)
Portage on Laurentian Divide, used by voyageurs and
Indians during fur trade era.

NANIBOUJOU LODGE (10/21/82)
U.S. Hwy. 61, unorganized territory
Private recreational club with massive rock fireplace
and Indian-motif décor, designed by Holstead and
Sullivan and built in 1928–29.

NORTH SUPERIOR LIFEBOAT STATION
LIGHTKEEPER'S HOUSE (11/28/78)
12 S. Broadway, Grand Marais
Frame house built in 1896 for keeper of lighthouse
marking Grand Marais harbor.

SCHROEDER LUMBER COMPANY BUNKHOUSE (7/31/86)
off U.S. Hwy. 61, Schroeder Twp.
Log building with open interior plan, remnant of one of
North Shore's most extensive logging operations ca. 1900.

JIM SCOTT FISH HOUSE (10/23/86)
U.S. Hwy. 61 and 5th Ave., Grand Marais
Waterfront frame building constructed in 1907 by commercial fisherman to process fish and repair and store
fishing equipment.

Grand Portage depot, Grand Portage National Monument

COTTONWOOD COUNTY

ISAAC BARGEN HOUSE (6/13/86)
1215 Mountain Lake Rd., Mountain Lake
Queen Anne–inspired pattern-book farmhouse built in
1888 for leading educator and newspaper publisher in
German Mennonite community.

CHICAGO ST. PAUL MINNEAPOLIS
AND OMAHA DEPOT (6/13/86)
4th St. and 1st Ave., Westbrook
Frame passenger/freight depot built ca. 1900 on branch
line that spurred town development and region's agricultural economy.

COTTONWOOD COUNTY COURTHOUSE (4/18/77)
900 3rd Ave., Windom
Classical Revival/Renaissance Revival brick courthouse
with domed atrium, designed by Omeyer and Thori
and built in 1904, with murals by Odin J. Oyen of
La Crosse, Wis.

Glyphs (filled with chalk for visibility) of shaman and turtle, Jeffers Petroglyphs Site

JEFFERS PETROGLYPHS SITE (10/15/70)
Delton Twp.
Largest known concentration of rock art from Precontact and Contact Periods in Minnesota; animal and human figures carved by Indians in outcropping of Sioux quartzite.

MOUNTAIN LAKE SITE (6/4/73)
Mountain Lake Twp.
Village site from Precontact Period (3000 B.C.–A.D. 1200) on island in dry lake bed.

CROW WING COUNTY

BRAINERD PUBLIC LIBRARY (5/23/80)
206 N. 7th St., Brainerd
Classical Revival brick community library built in 1904 with Carnegie grant.

BRAINERD WATER TOWER (7/17/74)
Washington and 6th Sts., Brainerd
Innovative concrete structure for municipal water storage built in 1918–21 according to design by engineer L. P. Wolff.

BRIDGE NO. 5265 (6/29/98)
U.S. Hwy. 169 near Mille Lacs Lake, Garrison
Masonry-decorated, multi-plate arch bridge built by the
National Park Service in 1938 as part of CCC-developed
wayside project.

H. H. BROACH HOUSE (SHAWANO) (5/23/80)
Pequot Blvd., Pequot Lakes
Log house with intricate round-stone masonry on foundation, fence, and other structures, built in 1920s as
summer residence.

CROW WING COUNTY COURTHOUSE AND JAIL (5/23/80)
326 Laurel St., Brainerd
Stone courthouse (1920) and adjacent brick sheriff's
residence/cell block (1916), both by Alden and Harris.

CROW WING STATE PARK (7/28/70)
Ft. Ripley Twp.
Habitation site at junction of land and water transportation routes spanning Precontact, fur trade, and 19th-
century lumbering eras.

**CUYUNA IRON RANGE MUNICIPALLY OWNED
ELEVATED METAL WATER TANKS:**
Crosby Tank (10/22/80) *1st Ave., Crosby*
Cuyuna Tank (10/22/80) *North St., Cuyuna*
Deerwood Tank (10/22/80) *211 Maple St., Deerwood*
Ironton Tank (10/22/80) *7th St., Ironton*
Trommald Tank (10/22/80) *Trommald*
Cylindrical tanks on latticework towers, built in 1912–18
during period of widespread public improvements in
mining towns.

DEERWOOD AUDITORIUM (11/29/95)
27 E. Forest Rd., Deerwood
Moderne-style, concrete-and-stone, multipurpose municipal building designed by Carl Buetow and built in
1935–37 under the SERA and the WPA.

WILFORD H. FAWCETT HOUSE (5/23/80)
off Co. Hwy. 4, Breezy Point
Rustic log residence designed by Magney and Tusler for publisher and resort developer, built in 1922–28.

FORT FLATMOUTH MOUNDS (8/14/73)
Mission Twp.
Mound group named for a 19th-century Ojibwe leader.

GORDON-SCHAUST SITE (12/23/74)
Cross Lake
Undated, linear mound groups now embedded in residential developments.

GRAND VIEW LODGE
(5/23/80)
off Co. Hwy. 77, Nisswa
Resort lodge built in 1918, one of most elaborate and well-articulated examples of rustic log architecture in northern Minnesota.

Grand View Lodge

WERNER HEMSTEAD HOUSE (5/23/80)
303 N. 4th St., Brainerd
Classical Revival frame residence (1903) of former Brainerd mayor, state legislator, and business leader.

IRONTON SINTERING PLANT COMPLEX (9/11/80)
off Co. Hwy. 30, Crosby
Processing plant built in 1924 by Hanna Mining Company to turn low-grade ore into a higher-grade, marketable product.

MINNESOTA AND INTERNATIONAL RAILROAD FREIGHT HOUSE AND SHELTER SHED (5/27/80)
Co. Hwy. 13, Lake Edward Twp. (Lake Hubert)

Open-sided station platform and enclosed freight house built ca. 1918 to serve summer resort–bound passengers.

MINNEWAWA LODGE (8/11/80)
Co. Hwy. 13, Nisswa
Lakeside resort developed in early 20th century by New York City journalist/actor Benjamin Heald as an actors' retreat.

NORTHERN PACIFIC RAILROAD SHOPS HISTORIC DISTRICT (1/3/89)
vicinity of Burlington Northern Railroad tracks, Laurel and 13th Sts., Brainerd
Large-scale repair-and-service operations for railroad headquarters, with complex of buildings and structures built in 1882–1925.

PARKER BUILDING (5/23/80)
623 Laurel St., Brainerd
Brick commercial block constructed in 1909 to house a bank and other businesses.

RED RIVER TRAIL: CROW WING SECTION (2/6/91)
Co. Hwy. 27 (Crow Wing State Park), Ft. Ripley Twp.
Section of Mississippi River crossing leading to Crow Wing village site, part of extensive system of 19th-century fur-trade routes.

ST. COLUMBA MISSION SITE (12/18/73)
Nisswa
Site of Episcopal mission church, school, and store, established in 1852 and burned during the Dakota War of 1862.

SEBRE LAKE SITE (11/16/84)
Ft. Ripley Twp.
Precontact Period habitation site with burial features (ca. 3000 B.C.–A.D. 900).

SOO LINE DEPOT (11/25/80)
1st St. N. and 1st Ave. E., Crosby
Brick depot built in 1910 as western terminus of railroad operations for Cuyuna Range iron ore transport.

SPINA HOTEL (5/23/80)
Curtis Ave. and 4th St., Ironton
Brick hotel with street-level shops, built in 1913 during boom years of Cuyuna Range.

UPPER HAY LAKE ARCHAEOLOGICAL DISTRICT (1/21/74)
Jenkins Twp.
Precontact Period village site and group of linear mounds (A.D. 900–1650).

DAKOTA COUNTY

DANIEL F. AKIN HOUSE (12/31/79)
19185 Akin Rd., Farmington
Farmhouse of locally quarried limestone built by civil engineer; site of continuous meteorological observation since 1885.

Church of St. Mary

CHURCH OF ST. MARY (CATHOLIC) (12/31/79)
8433 239th St. E., New Trier
Beaux Arts masonry church designed in 1909 by
George Ries for community of German immigrants.

CHURCH OF THE ADVENT (EPISCOPAL) (12/31/79)
412 Oak St., Farmington
Small Gothic Revival board-and-batten church built in
1872 with plans adapted from Upjohn's *Rural Architecture* plan book.

DAKOTA COUNTY COURTHOUSE (7/21/78)
Vermillion and Fourth Sts., Hastings
Italian Villa–style brick-and-stone courthouse built in
1869–71 from designs by A. M. Radcliff; Renaissance
dome added after 1900.

DISTRICT NO. 72 SCHOOL (12/31/79)
321st St. W. and Cornell Ave., Waterford Twp. (Waterford)
Frame rural school constructed in 1882.

EAST SECOND STREET COMMERCIAL HISTORIC DISTRICT (7/31/78)
E. 2nd St., Hastings
Downtown business district of 19th-century river town,
encompassing 35 largely Italianate brick buildings with
stone trim.

IGNATIUS ECKERT HOUSE (7/21/78)
724 Ashland St., Hastings
Cupolated Italian Villa–style frame residence, moved
from abandoned townsite of Nininger in 1857.

EXCHANGE BANK (12/31/79)
344 3rd St., Farmington
Italianate, two-story brick, multipurpose commercial
building constructed in 1880 to replace wood-frame
stores destroycd by fire.

Fasbender Clinic

FASBENDER CLINIC (12/31/79)
801 Pine St., Hastings
Example of Frank Lloyd Wright's later work: a brick
medical clinic with dramatic metal roof, completed in
1959 for Dr. Herman Fasbender.

FIRST PRESBYTERIAN CHURCH (7/7/95)
602 Vermillion St., Hastings
Romanesque Revival church built in 1875–81 from
designs by Charles N. Daniels; rebuilt after 1907 fire
from plans by Harry Wild Jones.

FORT SNELLING HISTORIC DISTRICT (10/15/66)
(National Historic Landmark, 12/19/60)
Minn. Hwys. 55 and 5 (Ft. Snelling State Park),
Mendota Heights (also in Hennepin County)
Minnesota's first military post, established in 1819 at the
confluence of the Mississippi and Minnesota Rivers to
protect U.S. interests.

FORT SNELLING–MENDOTA BRIDGE (10/15/66)
Minn. Hwy. 55 over Minnesota River, Mendota Heights
(also in Hennepin County)
Steel-reinforced, continuous-arch concrete bridge built
in 1925–26 according to plans by Walter Wheeler and
C. A. P. Turner.

REUBEN FREEMAN HOUSE (12/31/79)
9091 Inver Grove Trail, Inver Grove Heights
Imaginative vernacular house of coursed fieldstone
with eight-gabled roof built ca. 1875.

GOOD TEMPLARS HALL (12/31/79)
9965 124th St. E., Nininger Twp. (Nininger)
Greek Revival building (1858), one of few structures
remaining from townsite of Nininger, platted by specu-
lator/author/politician Ignatius Donnelly.

HASTINGS FOUNDRY–STAR IRON WORKS (12/31/79)
707 E. 1st St., Hastings
Industrial building erected in 1859; played pivotal role
in development of transportation and engineering
technology.

HASTINGS METHODIST EPISCOPAL CHURCH (6/7/78)
8th and Vermillion Sts., Hastings
Frame church, built in 1861 in mix of Greek Revival,
Gothic Revival, and Italianate styles.

BYRON HOWES HOUSE (6/15/78)
718 Vermillion St., Hastings
Italian Villa–style residence with tower, built in 1868–70
for banker and civic leader.

RUDOLPH LATTO HOUSE (5/23/78)
620 Ramsey St., Hastings
Brick residence in transitional Italianate/Eastlake style,
built in 1880–81 for local banker.

WILLIAM G. LE DUC HOUSE (6/22/70)
1629 Vermillion St., Hastings
Limestone mansion in Gothic Villa style, built in
1862–65 for noted merchant, writer, historian, promoter, and Civil War veteran.

MACDONALD-TODD HOUSE (12/31/79)
309 W. 7th St., Hastings
Greek Revival residence (1857) originally located in townsite of Nininger, owned successively by two prominent journalists, A. W. MacDonald and Irving Todd.

MENDOTA HISTORIC DISTRICT (6/22/70)
vicinity of Willow St. and Minn. Hwy. 13,
Mendota and Mendota Heights
American Fur Company trading center and region's first permanent white settlement, including trader and agent residences and church (1830s–1850s).

MINNEAPOLIS ST. PAUL ROCHESTER AND DUBUQUE ELECTRIC TRACTION COMPANY DEPOT (ORCHARD GARDENS) (12/31/79)
Co. Hwy. 5 at 155th St., Burnsville
Small, trackside flag-stop shelter built in 1910 to serve resident market farmers of new subdivision.

EMIL J. OBERHOFFER HOUSE (12/31/79)
17020 Judicial Rd. W., Lakeville
Prairie Style residence (1918) designed by Paul Haugen for first conductor of Minneapolis Symphony Orchestra.

RAMSEY MILL AND OLD MILL PARK (7/15/98)
junction of 18th St. and Vermillion River, Hastings
Ruins of 1856 flour mill and surrounding park (est. 1925) that grew into tourist site.

SERBIAN HOME (3/26/92)
404 3rd Ave. S., South St. Paul
Fraternal society hall built of brick in 1923 for community of Serbian immigrants working in city's meat-packing houses.

HENRY H. SIBLEY HOUSE (1/20/72)
Willow St., Mendota (also in Mendota Historic District)
Locally quarried limestone house built as a residence

and office ca. 1836 by Sibley, the district manager of the American Fur Company and later the first state governor and a general during the Dakota War of 1862; also the home of his wife, Sarah Jane Sibley.

Stockyards Exchange, 1898

STOCKYARDS EXCHANGE (3/7/79)
200 N. Concord St., South St. Paul
Victorian brick commercial building constructed in 1887 as base of operations for Minnesota's large meat-packing industry.

THOMPSON-FASBENDER HOUSE (5/22/78)
649 W. 3rd St., Hastings
French Second Empire brick residence built in 1880 for sawmill proprietor William Thompson; later owned by Dr. Herman Fasbender.

VAN DYKE-LIBBY HOUSE (10/2/78)
Vermillion St., Hastings
French Second Empire brick residence built in 1867 for lumberman William J. Van Dyke; later owned by Roland C. Libby.

GEORGE W. WENTWORTH HOUSE (12/31/79)
1575 Oakdale Ave., West St. Paul
Queen Anne brick residence built in 1887 by livestock raiser, landowner, and civic leader.

WEST SECOND STREET RESIDENTIAL
HISTORIC DISTRICT (7/31/78)
W. 2nd St., Hastings
Group of residences exhibiting major architectural styles in vogue in Minnesota between 1850 and 1890.

DODGE COUNTY

OLE CARLSON HOUSE (4/16/82)
Co. Hwy. 15, Canisteo Twp.
Large brick farmhouse built for Carlson in 1880 by a neighboring Norwegian immigrant farmer.

EUREKA HOTEL (4/16/82)
101 3rd Ave. S.W., Kasson
Brick hotel built in 1894 alongside railroad tracks.

KASSON MUNICIPAL BUILDING
(4/16/82)
12 W. Main, Kasson
Multipurpose municipal building in Prairie School style designed in 1917 by Purcell and Elmslie.

KASSON WATER TOWER (6/3/76)
4th Ave. N.W. and
2nd St. N.W., Kasson
Steel tank atop ornamental limestone tower, built in 1895 by local contractor.

Kasson Water Tower

JACOB LEUTHOLD JR. HOUSE (4/16/82)
108 2nd Ave. N.W., Kasson

Frame residence designed in 1905 by Kees and Colburn for founder of early clothing-store chain.

MANTORVILLE AND RED WING STAGE ROAD: MANTORVILLE SECTION (8/30/91)
off 5th St., Mantorville
Road built in 1855 to facilitate trade and mail service between towns settled after 1853 treaty ratification.

MANTORVILLE HISTORIC DISTRICT (6/28/74)
vicinity of Main and 5th Sts., Mantorville
Town center with group of residential, commercial, and government buildings dating 1856–1918, including 1871 limestone county courthouse.

PERRY NELSON HOUSE (4/16/82)
Co. Hwy. 22, Concord Twp.
Large Italianate stone farmhouse built in early 1870s for one of Concord's many Old-Stock American immigrants.

WASIOJA HISTORIC DISTRICT (3/13/75)
Co. Hwy. 16, Wasioja Twp.
1850s village with limestone quarry and kiln and numerous stone buildings built by resident stonemasons; includes a Civil War recruiting station.

DOUGLAS COUNTY

ALEXANDRIA POST OFFICE (4/16/79)
625 Broadway, Alexandria
Renaissance Revival brick-and-stone building completed in 1910.

ALEXANDRIA PUBLIC LIBRARY (8/23/85)
7th Ave. W. and Fillmore St., Alexandria
Large Beaux Arts brick-and-stone, Carnegie-funded library designed in 1903 by Wisconsin architect Henry A. Foeller.

ALEXANDRIA RESIDENTIAL HISTORIC DISTRICT (1/11/91)
vicinity of Cedar and Douglas Sts. and
Lincoln and 12th Aves., Alexandria
Group of 59 houses built in 1868–1930 in varied residential architectural styles for city's business and professional classes.

BASSWOOD SHORES SITE (4/8/94)
La Grand Twp.
Habitation site with evidence of early Dakota ceramics from Precontact Period (ca. A.D. 900–1650).

BRANDON AUDITORIUM AND FIRE HALL (8/29/85)
Holmes Ave., Brandon
Concrete municipal building with fieldstone facing and artist-designed interiors, constructed under the WPA in 1936 by local workers.

THOMAS F. COWING HOUSE (8/23/85)
316 Jefferson St., Alexandria
Pattern-book Gothic Revival cottage built ca. 1875 for business and political leader.

DOUGLAS COUNTY COURTHOUSE (8/23/85)
305 8th Ave. W., Alexandria
Victorian Romanesque courthouse (1895) of local brick with Kasota stone trim, designed by Buechner and Jacobson.

GREAT NORTHERN PASSENGER DEPOT (8/15/85)
N. Broadway and Agnes Blvd., Alexandria
Custom-designed depot, one of largest and most ornate on Great Northern line, completed in 1907 to serve growing resort industry.

JOHN B. JOHNSON HOUSE (12/9/77)
U.S. Hwy. 52, Osakis
Frame house with hexagonal plan and plunging roof-

lines, designed ca. 1886 by owner who theorized it would withstand wind storms.

LAKE CARLOS STATE PARK WPA/RUSTIC STYLE GROUP CAMP (7/2/92)
off Minn. Hwy. 29 (Lake Carlos State Park), Carlos Twp.
Rough-sided mess hall and recreation building for public use, constructed in 1941–42 by WPA workers.

LAKE CARLOS STATE PARK WPA/RUSTIC STYLE HISTORIC DISTRICT (7/2/92)
off Minn. Hwy. 29 (Lake Carlos State Park), Carlos Twp.
Buildings and water tower of split stone with rough siding, built in 1938–42 by WPA workers in park developed to serve region's summer resort trade.

KNUTE NELSON HOUSE (4/13/77)
1219 S. Nokomis St., Alexandria
Residence (1872) of two-term Minnesota governor and five-term U.S. senator, the first Scandinavian immigrant elected to Congress.

Knute Nelson House

AUGUST TONN FARMSTEAD (9/25/85)
off Co. Rd. 65, Carlos Twp.
Seven log buildings, including house, barns, and granaries, on subsistence farm built ca. 1875–90 by immigrant farm family.

NOAH P. WARD HOUSE (8/23/85)
422 7th Ave. W., Alexandria
Large, ornate Victorian residence built ca. 1903 for prominent grocer and civic leader.

FARIBAULT COUNTY

ADAMS H. BULLIS HOUSE (5/23/80)
Delavan Twp.
Italianate residence of local brick built ca. 1875 on large farm of noted cattle breeder and state legislator.

CENTER CREEK ARCHAEOLOGICAL DISTRICT (9/15/76)
Verona Twp.
Extensive, late Precontact Period habitation sites with tools and storage pits suggesting horticultural economy.

**CHICAGO MILWAUKEE ST. PAUL AND
PACIFIC DEPOT AND LUNCHROOM** (5/23/80)
89-100 1st St. N.W., Wells
Brick depot built in 1903 to serve passengers and crews in busy railroad townsite.

CHURCH OF THE GOOD SHEPHERD (EPISCOPAL) (5/23/80)
Moore and 8th Sts., Blue Earth
Small Gothic Revival board-and-batten church built in 1872 by the Rev. Solomon S. Burleson under direction of Bishop Henry Whipple.

DISTRICT NO. 40 SCHOOL (5/23/80)
Minn. Hwy. 109, Walnut Lake Twp.
Rural frame school (1896) with sunburst motif.

Church of the Good Shepherd

ANDREW C. DUNN HOUSE (5/23/80)
133 S. Main St., Winnebago
Large Queen Anne/Classical Revival residence built in
1901 by one of town founders and civic leaders.

FARIBAULT COUNTY COURTHOUSE (4/11/77)
415 N. Main St., Blue Earth
Richardsonian Romanesque public building erected in
1891–92 according to designs by C. A. Dunham.

FIRST NATIONAL BANK (5/23/80)
Main St. and Cleveland, Winnebago
Small Classical Revival stone bank designed by F. H.
Ellerbe and built in 1917.

PETER KREMER HOUSE (5/23/80)
Main and 4th Sts., Minnesota Lake
Large brick residence with limestone trim built in 1906
for town promoter and commercial developer.

MURET N. LELAND HOUSE (5/23/80)
410 2nd Ave. S.W., Wells
Queen Anne residence (1883) owned by leading merchant and politician.

MEMORIAL LIBRARY (12/20/88)
6th St. and Ramsey Ave., Blue Earth
Classical Revival brick library (1904) funded by local
banker and philanthropist W. E. C. Ross to honor his
late wife, Etta C. Ross.

JAMES B. WAKEFIELD HOUSE (5/23/80)
405 E. 6th St., Blue Earth
Italianate brick residence built in 1868 by town founder
and prominent political figure.

WALTERS JAIL (5/23/80)
3rd and Main Sts., Walters
False-front brick detention facility constructed in 1906;
served as occasional lodging for railroad workers.

FILLMORE COUNTY

ALLIS BARN (RELIANCE STOCK FARM) (4/27/82)
Co. Hwy. 17, Carrolton Twp.
Three-story, pegged-timber barn built ca. 1899 for Milwaukee's Allis family on stock farm for thoroughbred
cattle, swine, and horses.

Chatfield Public Library

FRANCIS H. BARTLETT HOUSE (5/24/84)
Gold and Pearl Sts., Wykoff
French Second Empire brick cottage built in 1876 for townsite founder and local government official.

BRIDGE NO. L-4770 (11/6/89)
Twp. Rd. 213 over Mahoney Creek, Fountain Twp.
Stone arch bridge type developed ca. 1915 by state highway commission for use in rural southeastern Minnesota.

CHATFIELD PUBLIC LIBRARY (4/27/82)
Main St., Chatfield
Carnegie-funded, Prairie School–style brick library designed in 1915 by Claude and Starck of Wisconsin.

COMMERCIAL HOUSE HOTEL (7/19/2001)
126 S. Broadway, Spring Valley
Brick hotel built in three phases (1876–1916) as town grew into railroad hub, regional trade center, and tourist destination.

DANIEL DAYTON HOUSE (RAVINE) (12/6/77)
off Co. Hwy. 17, Harmony Twp.
Greek Revival limestone house built in 1857 as overnight stop for travelers on St. Paul and Dubuque Stage Road.

SAMUEL T. DICKSON HOUSE (8/15/85)
225 S.W. 3rd St., Chatfield
Brick house built in 1863 for owner of several Root River area flour mills.

FILLMORE COUNTY JAIL AND CARRIAGE HOUSE (3/5/82)
Houston and Preston Sts., Preston
Italianate brick jail (1870) housing courtrooms, jail, sheriff's office, and residence, with adjacent ca. 1900 frame carriage house.

FORESTVILLE TOWNSITE (MEIGHEN STORE) (4/13/73)
Co. Road 12 (Forestville State Park), Forestville Twp.
Brick general store and attached residence (1856–57)
with wooden addition (ca. 1888), built for Felix
Meighen in small town at stagecoach crossroads.

GEORGE H. HAVEN HOUSE (11/19/82)
132 Winona St., Chatfield
Italianate brick residence built in 1874 by Maybury and
Son for prominent Chatfield businessman.

LANESBORO HISTORIC DISTRICT (9/2/82)
vicinity of Kirkwood, Coffee, and Parkway Sts., Lanesboro
Unified example of downtown commercial/industrial
areas in 19th-century town developed around waterpowered milling and rail transportation.

LENORA METHODIST EPISCOPAL CHURCH (11/19/82)
Co. Hwys. 23 and 24, Canton Twp.
Stone church (begun 1856, completed 1865) in pre-rail-
road townsite developed by area's first Methodist minister.

ELLEN M. LOVELL HOUSE (11/19/82)
218 Winona St., Chatfield
One of Minnesota's best examples of Shingle Style residential architecture, built in 1896.

NORWAY TOWNSHIP STONE HOUSE (4/27/82)
Co. Hwy. 10, Norway Twp.
Limestone residence built ca. 1870s in Norwegian im-
migrant settlement.

PARSONS BLOCK AND HALL (11/19/82)
112 S. Broadway, Spring Valley
Italianate building constructed in 1871 for real estate
investor Emilus Parsons as commercial, social, and theatrical center.

PIETENPOL WORKSHOP AND GARAGE (4/27/82)

Co. Hwy. 5, Forestville Twp.
Workshop (1921) where aircraft designer Bernard H.
Pietenpol built his prototype airplanes powered by
automobile engines.

PRESTON BREWERY (4/27/82)

Bluff St., Preston
Oldest known surviv-
ing industrial structure
in Fillmore County,
built ca. 1859.

QUICKSTAD FARM IMPLEMENT COMPANY

(4/27/82)
Mill St., Preston
Two-building complex
(1875, 1901) built to
house agricultural

1901 building, Quickstad Farm
Implement Company

equipment manufacturing company founded by
Norwegian immigrant Peter E. Quickstad.

RUSHFORD CITY MILL (4/27/82)

301 Winona St., Rushford
Stone mill built in 1875 to serve Minnesota's first significant wheat-growing and flour-milling region.

RUSHFORD WAGON AND CARRIAGE COMPANY (4/27/82)

Elm St. and Park, Rushford
Stone factory building where Rushford Wagons were
made; sole survivor of large manufacturing complex
built in 1872.

MICHAEL SCANLAN HOUSE (4/27/82)

708 Parkway Ave. S., Lanesboro
Large frame Queen Anne residence built ca. 1892 for
prominent businessman and state legislator.

SOUTHERN MINNESOTA DEPOT (6/20/86)
Elm St. and Pickle Alley, Rushford
Frame passenger depot and second-story stationmaster's quarters built in 1867; last vestige of Southern Minnesota Railroad still on original site.

SPRING VALLEY CARNEGIE LIBRARY (4/27/82)
201 S. Broadway, Spring Valley
Beaux Arts brick-and-stone building designed by H. J. Amlic; an early (1904) Carnegie-funded library in Minnesota.

SPRING VALLEY MAUSOLEUM (4/27/82)
Spring Valley Cemetery, Spring Valley
Massive stone building constructed in 1913–14 by Minnesota Mausoleum Company to represent community's progressive self-image.

William Strong House, Spring Valley

SPRING VALLEY METHODIST EPISCOPAL CHURCH (5/12/75)
221 W. Courtland St., Spring Valley
Late Gothic, polychrome brick-and-stone church built
in 1876–78, with large set of stained and painted glass
windows.

EPHRAIM STEFFENS HOUSE (4/27/82)
404 N. Broadway, Spring Valley
Victorian brick residence reflecting town's commercial
prosperity, built in 1877 for local entrepreneur, finan-
cier, and politician.

WILLIAM STRONG HOUSE (4/27/82)
Co. Hwy. 12, Carimona Twp. (Caromina)
Brick residence built in late 1850s; only surviving remnant of county's earliest settlement and one-time
county seat.

WILLIAM STRONG HOUSE (4/27/82)
508 N. Huron Ave., Spring Valley
French Second Empire brick residence built for prosperous
banker in 1879 during community's early boom years.

TUNNEL MILL (5/12/75)
off Co. Hwy. 1, Sumner Twp.
Waterpowered grist mill built in 1871 by local miller
J. A. Stout, who tunneled through bedrock to reroute
creek for power.

WALKER AND VALENTINE HOUSE (4/27/82)
504 High St., Rushford
Stone house built in 1859–61 by two of Rushford's
founders and milling entrepreneurs, Hiram Walker and
Roswell H. Valentine.

WYKOFF COMMERCIAL HISTORIC DISTRICT (8/5/94)
100 S. Gold–123 N. Gold Sts., Wykoff
Group of mostly brick commercial buildings in town's
compact commercial center, built largely after 1890s fire.

FREEBORN COUNTY

ALBERT LEA CITY HALL (5/17/84)
212 N. Broadway Ave., Albert Lea (also in
Albert Lea Commercial Historic District)
Romanesque Revival municipal building designed by E. F.
Warren in 1903 to house city offices, fire station, and jail.

ALBERT LEA COMMERCIAL HISTORIC DISTRICT (7/16/87)
vicinity of N. Broadway Ave. and
Water and E. Main Sts., Albert Lea
Concentration of late-19th- and early-20th-century
commercial buildings comprising city's central retail
and business district.

CHICAGO MILWAUKEE ST. PAUL AND
PACIFIC DEPOT (2/4/82)
606 S. Broadway, Albert Lea
Brick passenger/freight depot with open bay, built in
1914 to serve region's commercial and shipping center.

H. A. Paine House

CLARKS GROVE COOPERATIVE CREAMERY (3/20/86)
Main St. E. and Independence Ave., Clarks Grove
State-of-the-art brick creamery with meeting hall, built
in 1927 by state's first cooperative creamery association.

LODGE ZÁŘE ZAPÁDU NO. 44 (3/20/86)
Co. Hwy. 30, Hayward Twp.
Fraternal lodge building erected in 1909 to serve as social, cultural, and recreational center for community of Bohemian immigrants.

H. A. PAINE HOUSE (3/20/86)
609 W. Fountain St., Albert Lea
Queen Anne residence of Shavian type, built in 1898 with patterned masonry first story and half-timbered upper stories.

ALBERT C. WEDGE HOUSE (6/13/86)
216 W. Fountain St., Albert Lea
Shingle Style residence built ca. 1880 for early settler, leading physician, livestock breeder, and state legislator.

GOODHUE COUNTY

ALEXANDER P. ANDERSON ESTATE (TOWER VIEW) (4/13/77)
U.S. Hwy. 61, Red Wing
Georgian Revival residence, laboratory complex, and farm buildings built in 1916 for research botanist who originated puffed cereals.

BARN BLUFF (8/3/90)
U.S. Hwy. 61, Red Wing
Mississippi River bluff associated with Dakota legend; visual landmark for 19th-century explorers, travelers, and tourists.

BARTRON SITE (10/15/70)
Burnside Twp.
Large village site on Prairie Island occupied by Oneota peoples ca. 1000 A.D.

GEORGE BASLINGTON FARMHOUSE (2/12/80)
off U.S. Hwy. 52, Pine Island Twp.
Frame farmhouse for small subsistence farm, built around 1850s log cabin.

BRIDGE NO. 12 (11/6/89)
Twp. Rd. 43 over Bullard Creek, Hay Creek Twp.
Steel riveted pony truss designed in 1908, an early example of state government's attempt to standardize bridge design.

JACOB BRINGGOLD HOUSE (2/12/80)
314 S.W. 2nd St., Pine Island
Queen Anne frame residence built in 1906 for Swiss immigrant who introduced cheese-making to Pine Island.

CANNON FALLS COMMERCIAL HISTORIC DISTRICT (1/7/2000)
4th St. between Mill and Main Sts., Cannon Falls
Late-19th- and early-20th-century commercial buildings, many of local limestone, forming town's retail, service, and banking center.

CANNON FALLS ELEMENTARY SCHOOL (2/12/80)
115 W. Minnesota St., Cannon Falls
Two connected, Richardsonian Romanesque–inspired stone school buildings built in 1893 and 1912 to accommodate growing population.

GUSTAF A. CARLSON LIME KILN (9/27/76)
E. 5th St., Red Wing
Limestone-block kiln built in 1882 near Barn Bluff limestone quarry, one of then-numerous kilns that supplied materials for local construction.

CHICAGO GREAT WESTERN DEPOT (6/4/80)
Main St., Red Wing
Brick depot built in 1906 to serve as company's division headquarters after acquisition of local rail lines.

CHURCH OF THE REDEEMER (EPISCOPAL) (2/12/80)
123 N. 3rd St., Cannon Falls
Gothic church of locally quarried limestone, consecrated in 1867; one of area's first-generation Protestant churches.

CROSS OF CHRIST LUTHERAN CHURCH (2/12/80)
U.S. Hwy. 61, Welch Twp.
Gothic frame church with gabled steeple, built in 1878 as religious and cultural center for area's Swedish immigrants.

Dammon Round Barn

DAMMON ROUND BARN (2/12/80)
U.S. Hwy. 61, Wacouta Twp.
Round barn with central silo designed ca. 1914 for dairy farming, built on limestone base with clapboard upper story and conical roof.

DISTRICT NO. 20 SCHOOL (2/12/80)
Minn. Hwy. 58, Hay Creek Twp.
One-room brick schoolhouse with belfry, built in 1889 to serve as educational center for rural community.

ELLSWORTH HOUSE LIVERY STABLE (2/12/80)
4th St., Cannon Falls (also in Cannon Falls Commercial Historic District)
Limestone-rubble stable built ca. 1871 to serve hotel guests, primarily farmers from surrounding countryside.

FIREMEN'S HALL (2/12/80)
206 W. Mill St., Cannon Falls
Limestone firehouse and meeting hall for volunteer hose brigade, built in 1888 after business district was ravaged by fire.

FIRST CONGREGATIONAL CHURCH (2/12/80)
455 East Ave., Zumbrota
Greek Revival frame church built in 1862 by settlers from New England, modeled after New England meeting houses.

Florence Town Hall

FLORENCE TOWN HALL (7/20/2000)
33923 Hwy. 61 Blvd., Florence Twp. (Frontenac)
Italianate frame meeting hall built in 1875, with stage added in 1916, to serve as township governmental, social, and recreational center.

FORT SWENEY SITE (8/5/70)
Welch Twp.
Earthwork complex overlooking Cannon River, built
ca. 1000 A.D.

FRYK BARN (2/12/80)
off U.S. Hwy. 61, Hay Creek Twp.
Barn with limestone base and wooden superstructure,
built in 1872 to house and feed wheat-farm horse teams.

CHARLES GELLETT HOUSE (2/12/80)
311 N. 6th St., Cannon Falls
Greek Revival frame residence built in 1860 for sawmill
owner; later home of Joseph Peckham, founder of
state's teacher training system.

GLADSTONE BUILDING (11/14/79)
309 Bush St., Red Wing
Limestone commercial building erected in 1886 to
house local businesses, professional offices, and civic
organizations.

MARTIN T. GUNDERSON HOUSE (6/10/75)
107 Gunderson Blvd., Kenyon
Large Queen Anne frame residence built in 1896 for
mill owner who brought residential and commercial
electric lighting to Kenyon.

HAUGE LUTHERAN CHURCH (2/12/80)
off Minn. Hwy. 60, Kenyon Twp.
Small, spartan church of local limestone built in 1870s
and 1880s by members of Hauge Synod, a Norwegian
Lutheran reform movement.

HEWITT LABORATORY (11/15/79)
*216 Dakota St., Red Wing (also in Red
Wing Residential Historic District)*
Lab and office built in 1866 for Dr. Charles Hewitt,

a prominent physician/surgeon who pioneered in fields of public health and sanitation.

HOLDEN LUTHERAN CHURCH PARSONAGE (2/12/80)
Co. Hwy. 8, Wanamingo Twp.
Frame parsonage built ca. 1861 for state's first Church of Norway minister, the Rev. B. J. Muus, founder of St. Olaf College.

E. S. HOYT HOUSE (6/10/75)
300 Hill St., Red Wing (also in Red Wing Residential Historic District)
Prairie School brick-and-stucco residence (1913) designed by William G. Purcell, with ornament by George G. Elmslie.

IMMANUEL LUTHERAN CHURCH (2/12/80)
off Minn. Hwy. 58, Hay Creek Twp.
Steepled clapboard church with rose window, built in 1897 as religious and cultural center of German Lutheran community.

KAPPEL WAGON WORKS (11/14/79)
221 W. 3rd St., Red Wing
Commercial building with ornamental brickwork, built in 1875 for one of Red Wing's largest wagon manufactories.

KEYSTONE BUILDING (11/14/79)
409 Main St., Red Wing
Italianate commercial building with ornamental brickwork, designed and built in 1867 by Daniel C. Hill.

JAMES L. LAWTHER HOUSE (5/21/75)
927 W. 3rd St., Red Wing (also in Red Wing Residential Historic District)
Octagonal brick house with cupola, built in 1857 for prominent civic leader and real estate dealer.

MENDOTA TO WABASHA MILITARY ROAD:
CANNON RIVER SECTION (2/7/91)
Cannon River Rd., Red Wing
Portion of military road surveyed by U.S. Army Corps
of Topographical Engineers in 1850s.

HARRISON MILLER FARMHOUSE (5/22/78)
Minn. Hwy. 19, Stanton Twp.
Large farmhouse built in 1869 blending three architec-
tural styles—Greek Revival, Gothic, and Italianate.

JOHN MILLER FARMHOUSE (2/12/80)
Co. Hwy. 1, Leon Twp.
T-shaped clapboard house with elaborate portico, built
in 1860s by prosperous wheat farmer and state legislator.

MINNESOTA STONEWARE COMPANY (12/26/79)
1997 W. Main St., Red Wing
Manufacturing complex (1901) that produced stoneware
crocks, jugs, and other pottery from local clay; forerunner
of Red Wing Potteries.

James L. Lawther House, 1975

NANSEN AGRICULTURAL HISTORIC DISTRICT (11/15/2000)
vicinity of Minn. Hwy. 56 and County Hwys.
14 and 49, Holden and Warsaw Twps.
Group of 30 small to mid-sized farms in Sogn Valley,
settled by Norwegian immigrants in mid-19th century.

JULIA B. NELSON HOUSE (11/15/79)
219 5th St., Red Wing
Boardinghouse (ca. 1880), owned by noted educator and
leader in women's suffrage and temperance movements.

General Israel Garrard House, Old Frontenac Historic District, ca. 1965

OLD FRONTENAC HISTORIC DISTRICT (6/4/73)
Co. Hwy. 2, Florence Twp.
Mid-19th-century village and resort community on
Lake Pepin established by Garrard family of Ohio.

OPERA HOUSE BLOCK (2/12/80)
222 Main St., Pine Island
Ornate brick commercial/recreational facility built in
1895 by entrepreneur Loomis F. Irish.

OXFORD MILL RUIN (2/12/80)
off Co. Road 24, Stanton Twp.
Remains of four-story 1878 limestone flour mill

destroyed by fire in 1905, part of once-prosperous Cannon River Valley milling industry.

PINE ISLAND CITY HALL AND FIRE STATION (2/12/80)
Main and 3rd Sts., Pine Island
Brick municipal building with clock tower, constructed in 1909 to house city council chambers, jail, fire station, and meeting hall.

PRATT-TABER HOUSE (11/14/79)
706 W. 4th St., Red Wing (also in Red Wing Residential Historic District)
Italianate brick residence built ca. 1875 during peak period of town growth and prosperity.

RED WING CITY HALL (11/14/79)
W. 4th St., Red Wing
Renaissance Revival masonry building constructed in 1905–06 at height of town's City Beautiful Movement to house city government.

RED WING IRON WORKS (11/14/79)
401 Levee St., Red Wing
Machine and pattern shop (1874) that made and re-paired engines and machinery for Red Wing's early industries.

RED WING MALL HISTORIC DISTRICT (1/8/80)
vicinity of East and West Aves. and Broadway, Red Wing
Concentration of large-scale public and institutional buildings, including courthouse, library, post office, schools, and churches.

RED WING RESIDENTIAL HISTORIC DISTRICT (4/15/82)
vicinity of Dakota, Cedar, W. 5th, and 3rd Sts., Red Wing
Late-19th- and early-20th-century residences in variety of architectural styles, associated with leaders in all aspects of community life.

ROSCOE BUTTER AND CHEESE FACTORY (2/12/80)
Co. Hwy. 11, Roscoe Twp.
Small brick factory built in 1896 by farmers' cooperative to process products from local dairy farms.

ST. JAMES HOTEL COMPLEX (1/8/82)
Bush and Main Sts., Red Wing
Italianate brick hotel designed in 1874 by Edward P. Bassford.

THEODORE B. SHELDON HOUSE (6/7/76)
805 W. 4th St., Red Wing (also in Red Wing Residential Historic District)
French Second Empire residence (built in 1875, later altered) of prominent grain dealer, banker, transportation magnate, and civic leader.

SPRING CREEK PETROGLYPHS (11/14/96)
Red Wing
Indian rock-art site with depictions of animal, bird, snake, and human forms carved into St. Peter sandstone.

STATE TRAINING SCHOOL HISTORIC DISTRICT (6/4/73)
E. 7th St., Red Wing
Quadrangle of Richardsonian Romanesque buildings of local stone and brick after design by Warren B. Dunnell, constructed to house and educate delinquent youth; dedicated in 1889.

T. B. SHELDON MEMORIAL AUDITORIUM (6/3/76)
443 W. 3rd St., Red Wing (also in Red Wing Mall Historic District)
Renaissance Revival municipal playhouse designed by Lowell Lamoreaux and built in 1904 as a gift to the city from the estate of Theodore B. Sheldon.

THIRD STREET BRIDGE (11/6/89)
3rd St. over Cannon River, Cannon Falls

Steel, single-span, riveted through truss (1909) associated with Minneapolis bridge builder A. Y. Bayne, of a type unusual in Minnesota.

TOWNE-AKENSON HOUSE (11/15/79)
1121 W. 3rd St., Red Wing (also in Red Wing Residential Historic District)
Italianate frame residence built in 1875, a period marking town's commercial growth and prosperity.

VASA HISTORIC DISTRICT (5/30/75)
off Minn. Hwy. 19, Vasa Twp.
Small rural Swedish agricultural community founded in 1850s under leadership of the Rev. Eric Norelius, with 1869 church as focal point.

FRED WALLAUER FARMHOUSE (2/12/80)
Minn. Hwy. 58, Hay Creek Twp.
Italianate brick farmhouse built in 1882 to replace earlier frame dwelling.

YALE HARDWARE STORE (2/12/80)
139 N. 4th St., Cannon Falls (also in Cannon Falls Commercial Historic District)
Brick commercial building with Italianate, pressed-metal false front, built in 1887 for one of town's first hardware dealers.

St. James Hotel Complex, ca. 1870

DARWIN E. YALE HOUSE (2/12/80)
421 N. 6th St., Cannon Falls
Italianate frame residence with elaborate porch, built in 1879 for prominent hardware dealer.

ZUMBROTA COVERED BRIDGE (2/20/75)
West Ave. over north fork of Zumbro River, Zumbrota
Minnesota's last remaining covered bridge, built in 1869 to accommodate stagecoach traffic.

GRANT COUNTY

FORT POMME DE TERRE SITE (5/23/74)
Pelican Lake Twp.
Now-vacant location of defensive structure built on site of stage line station in 1863 for use as refuge after the Dakota War of 1862; reverted to relay station in 1866.

GRANT COUNTY COURTHOUSE
(9/5/85)
10 2nd St. N.E., Elbow Lake
Beaux Arts/Renaissance Revival 1905 courthouse designed by architects Bell and Detweiler, with murals by Odin J. Oyen of La Crosse, Wis.

Grant County Courthouse

ROOSEVELT HALL (8/23/85)
Hawkins Ave. and Front St., Barrett
Frame building that served as community auditorium and high school gymnasium, completed in 1934 under the CWA.

HENNEPIN COUNTY

ADVANCE THRESHER BUILDING/EMERSON–NEWTON IMPLEMENT COMPANY (9/20/77)
700-704 S. 3rd St., Minneapolis
Adjoining Louis Sullivanesque, brick-and-terra-cotta manufacturing/assembly plants designed in 1900 and 1904 by Kees and Colburn.

AMES-FLORIDA HOUSE (10/16/79)
8131 Bridge St., Rockford
Connected Greek Revival house, summer kitchen, and barn built in 1856 by mill owner and Rockford founder George F. Ames.

ANOKA-CHAMPLIN MISSISSIPPI RIVER BRIDGE (12/31/79)
U.S. Hwy. 52 over Mississippi River, Champlin
(also in Anoka County)
Continuous arch, reinforced-concrete bridge designed by C. M. Babcock and built in 1929 by Minneapolis Bridge Company.

ARCHITECTS AND ENGINEERS BUILDING (2/23/84)
1200 2nd Ave. S., Minneapolis
Italian Renaissance stone office block designed in 1920 by Hewitt and Brown as showcase for city's leading architects and designers.

GEORGE W. BAIRD HOUSE (3/27/80)
4400 W. 50th St., Edina
Queen Anne brick residence designed by Charles S. Sedgwick in 1886 for noted sheep breeder, Grange leader, and village founder.

BARDWELL-FERRANT HOUSE (8/9/84)
2500 Portland Ave. S., Minneapolis
Frame residence built in 1883, transformed with Moorish ornament in 1890 by architect Carl F. Struck.

RILEY L. BARTHOLOMEW HOUSE (11/28/78)
6901 Lyndale Ave. S., Richfield
Federal-style residence built in 1853 for early political
figure and framer of state constitution.

BASILICA OF ST. MARY (CATHOLIC) (3/26/75)
88 N. 17th St., Minneapolis
Classical/Baroque basilica of Vermont granite designed
by Emmanuel L. Masqueray, dedicated in 1913.

BENNETT-MCBRIDE HOUSE (9/19/77)
*3116 3rd Ave. S., Minneapolis (also in Healy
Block Residential Historic District)*
Queen Anne frame residence with stock millwork, built
in 1891 by architect-builder T. P. Healy.

CHARLES H. BURWELL HOUSE (5/2/74)
Co. Hwy. 5 and McGinty Rd., Minnetonka
Frame residence built in 1883 by manager/owner of
Minnetonka Mills Company, with earlier mill-worker's
cottage and mill office.

BUTLER BROTHERS COMPANY (3/11/71)
*100 N. 6th St., Minneapolis (also in Minneapolis
Warehouse Historic District)*
Brick wholesale warehouse and office building designed
by Harry Wild Jones in Gothic Revival style, built in
1906–08.

CAHILL SCHOOL (10/9/70)
Eden Ave. at Minn. Hwy. 100, Edina
One-room frame schoolhouse built in 1864 in one of
state's early school districts.

CAPPELEN MEMORIAL BRIDGE (11/28/78)
E. Franklin Ave. over Mississippi River, Minneapolis
Groundbreaking reinforced-concrete, continuous arch
bridge designed by Frederick W. Cappelen and Kristoffer
Olsen Oustad and built in 1919–23.

Riley L. Bartholomew House, 1886

ELBERT L. CARPENTER HOUSE (9/13/77)
314 Clifton Ave., Minneapolis
Georgian Revival brick residence designed by William
Channing Whitney and built in 1906 for organizer of
Minneapolis Symphony Orchestra.

EUGENE J. CARPENTER HOUSE (9/13/77)
300 Clifton Ave., Minneapolis
Georgian Revival residence (1906 remodeling) by
Edwin H. Hewitt for prominent lumberman and patron
of Minneapolis Institute of Arts.

CEDAR AVENUE BRIDGE (11/6/89)
10th Ave. over Mississippi River, Minneapolis
Reinforced-concrete, continuous arch bridge, the longest
and highest in city when built in 1929; designed by
Kristoffer Olsen Oustad.

LOREN L. CHADWICK COTTAGES (2/9/84)
617 W. 40th St., Minneapolis
Two small summer cottages with screened porches built
in 1902 as rental properties, sited between then-outlying
city lakes.

**CHAMBER OF COMMERCE BUILDING
(GRAIN EXCHANGE)** (11/23/77)
400 S. 4th St., Minneapolis
Three adjoining buildings by prominent architects Kees
and Colburn (main building, 1902), Long, Lamoreaux,
and Long (east building, 1909), and Bertrand and
Chamberlain (north building, 1928).

**CHICAGO MILWAUKEE ST. PAUL AND
PACIFIC DEPOT** (11/25/69)
37th St. and Brunswick Ave., St. Louis Park
Frame passenger and freight depot built ca. 1887 to serve
newly incorporated village.

**CHICAGO MILWAUKEE ST. PAUL AND PACIFIC DEPOT,
FREIGHT HOUSE, AND TRAIN SHED** (11/28/78)
201 3rd Ave. S., Minneapolis
Renaissance Revival station with clock tower and rare
surviving long-span, truss-roof train shed (1897–99);
1879 Italianate freight house.

CHRIST CHURCH LUTHERAN (6/20/2001)
*3244 34th Ave. S.,
Minneapolis*
International-style
brick church de-
signed in 1948 by
Eliel Saarinen, with
1962 addition by
Eero Saarinen.

**CHURCH OF ST.
STEPHEN (CATHOLIC)**
(8/15/91)
*2201 Clinton Ave. S.,
Minneapolis*
Stone church com-
bining Richardsonian

Christ Church Lutheran

Romanesque and Romanesque Revival styles, designed by Frederick G. Corser and built in 1889–91.

AMOS B. COE HOUSE (1/12/84)
1700 3rd Ave. S., Minneapolis
Eastlake-style brick residence built in 1884 for real estate developer; Shingle Style carriage barn added in 1886.

COMO-HARRIET STREETCAR LINE AND TROLLEY (10/17/77)
W. 42nd St. at Queen Ave. S., Minneapolis
Working section of once-extensive public transportation system operated 1884–1954; restored 1908 electric streetcar.

COUNTRY CLUB HISTORIC DISTRICT (4/26/82)
vicinity of W. 45th St., Arden Ave., W. 50th St., and Browndale Ave., Edina
Early suburban development planned by Samuel Thorpe, with variety of Period Revival–style homes built primarily 1924–31.

CRANE ISLAND HISTORIC DISTRICT (8/5/91)
Crane Island in Lake Minnetonka, Minnetrista
Summer community of private residential cottages and communal amenities for middle-class Christian families, built largely before 1915.

JOHN R. CUMMINS FARMHOUSE (9/2/82)
13600 Pioneer Trail, Eden Prairie
Brick farmhouse built in two phases (1879, 1910) and two styles (Greek Revival, Italianate) by noted horticulturist.

B. O. CUTTER HOUSE (1/30/76)
4th St. S.E. at 10th Ave. S.E., Minneapolis
Elaborate Gothic Cottage residence built in 1856 by master carpenter Cutter; enlarged in 1870s by later owner, prominent attorney John B. Gilfillan.

EAST LAKE BRANCH LIBRARY (5/26/2000)
2916 E. Lake St., Minneapolis
One of 13 Minneapolis Public Library branches built
under head librarian Gratia Countryman, leading proponent of public-library movement; constructed in 1924.

EXCELSIOR SCHOOL (11/13/80)
261 School Ave., Excelsior
Georgian Revival brick school with bell tower built in
1899–1901 near central business district to serve growing community.

FARMERS AND MECHANICS SAVINGS BANK (1/12/84)
115 S. 4th St., Minneapolis
Beaux Arts/Classical bank designed in 1891–92 by Long
and Kees, remodeled and enlarged in 1908 by William
M. Kenyon.

FIRE STATION NO. 19 (1/14/82)
2001 University Ave. S.E., Minneapolis
Queen Anne brick firehouse built in 1893 for horse-
drawn equipment; birthplace of kittenball, forerunner
of modern softball.

FIRST CHURCH OF CHRIST SCIENTIST (6/20/86)
614-620 E. 15th St., Minneapolis
Scaled-down example of Beaux Arts classicism, designed
in 1897 by S. J. Bowler; first Christian Science church
in Upper Midwest.

FIRST CONGREGATIONAL CHURCH (1/15/79)
500 8th Ave. S.E., Minneapolis
Richardsonian Romanesque church with Gothic spire,
designed by Warren H. Hayes and completed in 1886;
first use in Minnesota of Akron Plan.

WOODBURY FISK HOUSE (10/6/83)
424 5th St. S.E., Minneapolis

Round Tower, Fort Snelling Historic District

Italian Villa–style brick residence built in 1870 for partner in Pillsbury, Crocker, and Fisk milling company.

FLOUR EXCHANGE (8/29/77)
301 4th Ave. S., Minneapolis
City's first high-rise brick commercial building, designed by Long and Kees and constructed in two phases (1892, 1909).

FORT SNELLING HISTORIC DISTRICT (10/15/66)
(National Historic Landmark, 12/19/60)
Minn. Hwys. 55 and 5 (Ft. Snelling State Park), Ft. Snelling Military Reservation (also in Dakota County)
Minnesota's first military post, established in 1819 at the confluence of the Mississippi and Minnesota Rivers to protect U.S. interests.

FORT SNELLING–MENDOTA BRIDGE (10/15/66)
Minn. Hwy. 55 over Minnesota River, Fort Snelling Military Reservation (also in Dakota County)
Reinforced-concrete, continuous arch bridge built in 1925–26 according to plans by Walter Wheeler and C. A. P. Turner.

FOSHAY TOWER (9/20/78)
821 Marquette Ave., Minneapolis
Art Deco, 32-story skyscraper with obelisk shape and
construction method patented by Wilbur B. Foshay and
Gottlieb Magney and built in 1927–29.

**LAWRENCE A. AND MARY
FOURNIER HOUSE** (5/18/95)
*3505 Sheridan Ave. N.,
Minneapolis*
Bungalow residence blending
Prairie School and Craftsman
styles, designed in 1909 by
Lawrence Fournier.

Lawrence A. and Mary Fournier House

**FOWLER METHODIST
EPISCOPAL CHURCH** (1/30/76)
2011 Dupont Ave. S., Minneapolis
Romanesque church of Sioux quartzite, begun in 1894
by Warren H. Hayes, completed in 1906 by Harry Wild
Jones; Scottish Rite Temple since 1915.

FRANKLIN BRANCH LIBRARY (5/26/2000)
1314 W. Franklin Ave., Minneapolis
Renaissance Revival, Carnegie-funded public library
(1914); one of 13 branches built under leadership of
city's head librarian, Gratia Countryman.

FREDRIKA BREMER SCHOOL (1/31/78)
1214 Lowry Ave. N., Minneapolis
Early public school of Chaska brick with Romanesque
details; 1886 portion by Walter Pardee, later additions
by Stebbins and Hacksbee; named for Swedish author
and traveler.

GETHSEMANE EPISCOPAL CHURCH (3/8/84)
901-905 4th Ave. S., Minneapolis
Gothic Revival limestone church with bell tower, designed by Edward S. Stebbins and completed in 1884.

PETER GIDEON FARMHOUSE (9/17/74)
24590 Glen Rd., Shorewood
Site of horticultural experiments (1854–99) by the developer of the winter-hardy Wealthy apple, named for Gideon's wife.

GLEN LAKE CHILDREN'S CAMP (8/5/99)
6350 Indian Chief Rd., Eden Prairie
Summer camp funded by private philanthropists George and Leonora Christian for children with tuberculosis, developed in 1925 by Sund and Dunham.

JOHN G. AND MINNIE GLUEK HOUSE AND CARRIAGE HOUSE (2/9/90)
2447 Bryant Ave. S., Minneapolis
Georgian Revival clapboard residence designed for prominent brewer in 1902 by William M. Kenyon; carriage house by Boehme and Cordella.

GRACE EVANGELICAL LUTHERAN CHURCH (1/9/97)
324 Harvard St. S.E., Minneapolis
Gothic Revival brick church designed by Chapman and Magney and built in 1915–17 by Swedish Lutheran congregation to serve university students.

GREAT NORTHERN DEPOT (7/7/81)
402 E. Lake St., Wayzata
Small-town, one-story, frame combination depot built lakeside in 1906 to serve commuter and resort traffic.

JONATHAN T. GRIMES HOUSE (3/16/76)
4200 W. 44th St., Edina
Gothic Revival residence built in 1869 for mill owner and noted horticulturist who introduced gingko and catalpa trees to Minnesota.

HANOVER BRIDGE (BRIDGE NO. 92366) (12/11/79)
off Co. Hwy. 19 over Crow River, Hanover
(also in Wright County)

Pratt through truss metal bridge built in 1885 by Morse Bridge Company of Youngstown, Ohio.

HEALY BLOCK RESIDENTIAL HISTORIC DISTRICT (5/27/93)
3101-3145 2nd Ave. S. and 3116-3124
3rd Ave. S., Minneapolis
Group of frame houses in Queen Anne/Classical Revival styles designed and built in 1886–98 by contractor T. P. Healy.

HENNEPIN COUNTY LIBRARY, ROBBINSDALE BRANCH (10/2/78)
4915 42nd Ave. N., Robbinsdale
One-story frame community library built in 1925 through efforts of Robbinsdale Library Club.

HENNEPIN THEATRE (1/19/96)
910 Hennepin Ave., Minneapolis
Beaux Arts theater with ornate interior designed by Kirchhoff and Rose of Milwaukee, built in 1921 as part of Orpheum vaudeville circuit.

EDWIN H. HEWITT HOUSE (4/6/78)
126 E. Franklin Ave., Minneapolis
Large brick-and-stucco Tudor Revival residence designed in 1906 by owner, a prominent architect.

HINKLE-MURPHY HOUSE (9/20/84)
619 S. 10th St., Minneapolis
First Georgian Revival house in Minnesota, designed in 1886 by William Channing Whitney; home successively to business and civic leaders William H. Hinkle and William J. Murphy.

INTERCITY BRIDGE (FORD BRIDGE) (11/6/89)
Ford Pkwy. over Mississippi River,
Minneapolis (also in Ramsey County)
Monumental urban, reinforced-concrete, continuous-

arch bridge designed by engineer Martin S. Grytbak and built in 1925–27.

INTERLACHEN BRIDGE (11/6/89)
William Berry Dr., Minneapolis
Early concrete arch bridge built in 1900 by William S. Hewett using patented Melan reinforcing system.

HARRY WILD JONES HOUSE (ELMWOOD) (9/20/84)
5101 Nicollet Ave., Minneapolis
Shingle Style residence designed in 1887 by Jones, one of city's most prominent architects.

LAKEWOOD CEMETERY MEMORIAL CHAPEL (10/20/83)
3600 Hennepin Ave., Minneapolis
Byzantine-style chapel of St. Cloud granite designed by Harry Wild Jones and built in 1908–10, with interior mosaics by Venetian artisans.

HARRY F. LEGG HOUSE (6/3/76)
1601 Park Ave., Minneapolis
Queen Anne frame residence built in 1887 by tract developer George H. Hoit and Company.

Intercity Bridge (Ford Bridge), 1927

LINDEN HILLS BRANCH LIBRARY (5/26/2000)
2900 W. 43rd St., Minneapolis
Tudor Revival library (1913) designed by Bard and
Vanderbilt, one of 13 branches built under leadership
of city's head librarian, Gratia Countryman.

LITTLE SISTERS OF THE POOR HOME FOR THE AGED (9/21/78)
215 N.E. Broadway, Minneapolis
Brick building with attached chapel designed in 1895
by Frederick G. Corser; 1905 wing by Corser, 1914 wing
by Kees and Colburn.

JOHN LOHMAR HOUSE (4/18/77)
1514 Dupont Ave. N., Minneapolis
Large Queen Anne frame residence built in 1898 by
contractor Peter Jeub for well-to-do merchant.

LUMBER EXCHANGE (5/19/83)
425 Hennepin Ave. and 10 S. 5th St., Minneapolis
Richardsonian Romanesque commercial block (1885,
1890), an early fire-resistant design by Long and Kees,
built as center for state's lumber trade.

CHARLES J. MARTIN HOUSE (4/26/78)
1300 Mount Curve Ave., Minneapolis
City estate of milling company executive, with Renaissance Revival brick residence designed by William
Channing Whitney and built in 1903.

MASONIC TEMPLE (9/5/75)
528 Hennepin Ave., Minneapolis
Richardsonian Romanesque merchandise block and
Masonic headquarters designed by Long and Kees and
completed in 1888.

MATERNITY HOSPITAL (3/27/80)
300 Queen Ave. N., Minneapolis
Women's hospital complex founded in 1887 by social

reformer and women's rights advocate Dr. Martha G. Ripley and managed exclusively by women.

MILWAUKEE AVENUE HISTORIC DISTRICT (5/2/74)

vicinity of Milwaukee and E. Franklin Aves. and E. 24th St., Minneapolis

Planned workers' community of small brick homes on quarter lots, platted in 1883 and developed for sale by real-estate agent William Ragan.

MINNEAPOLIS ARMORY (9/26/85)

500-530 S. 6th St., Minneapolis

PWA Moderne-style quarters for Minnesota National Guard designed by P. C. Bettenburg and built in 1935–36.

MINNEAPOLIS BREWING COMPANY (6/21/90)

Marshall St. and 13th Ave. N.E., Minneapolis

Brewery complex with Richardsonian Romanesque brew house (1891–92) by Wolff and Lehle, office (1893, 1910) by Carl F. Struck; home of Grain Belt beer.

MINNEAPOLIS CITY HALL–HENNEPIN COUNTY COURTHOUSE (12/4/74)

400 4th Ave. S., Minneapolis

Richardsonian Romanesque municipal block with clock tower designed by Long and Kees and built in 1889–1905 of pink Ortonville granite.

Milwaukee Avenue Historic District

MINNEAPOLIS PIONEERS AND SOLDIERS MEMORIAL CEMETERY (LAYMAN'S CEMETERY) (6/6/2002)
2925 Cedar Ave. S., Minneapolis
City's oldest surviving cemetery, established in 1858; focus of 1920s preservation movement to protect sites significant to local history.

MINNEAPOLIS PUBLIC LIBRARY, NORTH BRANCH (12/7/77)
1834 Emerson Ave. N., Minneapolis
Chateauesque brick library designed in 1893 by Frederick G. Corser; an early open-shelf branch library.

MINNEAPOLIS WAREHOUSE HISTORIC DISTRICT (11/3/89)
vicinity of 1st Ave. N., N. 1st St., 10th Ave. N., and N. 6th St., Minneapolis
Thirty-block area of late-19th- and early-20th-century commercial buildings, many architect-designed, in city's wholesaling district.

MINNEAPOLIS YMCA CENTRAL BUILDING (11/29/95)
96 S. 9th St., Minneapolis
Late Gothic Revival, stone-and-brick high-rise designed by Long, Lamoreaux, and Long and built in 1917–19.

MINNEHAHA GRANGE HALL (10/9/70)
Eden Ave. at Minn. Hwy. 100, Edina
Frame quarters of Minnesota's oldest subordinate Grange, organized 1873 in Edina Mills settlement.

Minnehaha Grange Hall, 1948

MINNEHAHA HISTORIC DISTRICT (11/25/69)
vicinity of Hiawatha and Minnehaha Aves. and Godfrey Rd., Minneapolis

Early city park and recreation area containing natural sites, 1870s rail station, and historic houses.

MINNESOTA SOLDIERS' HOME HISTORIC DISTRICT (3/2/89)
vicinity of Minnehaha Ave., Godfrey Pkwy.,
and Mississippi River, Minneapolis
Care center for disabled veterans and families established in 1887; master plan by Horace W. S. Cleveland, first buildings by Warren B. Dunnell.

MOLINE, MILBURN AND STODDARD COMPANY (2/20/75)
250 3rd Ave. N., Minneapolis (also in
Minneapolis Warehouse Historic District)
Limestone factory/salesroom built in 1886 for leading farm machinery manufacturer, designed by Joseph Haley in Chicago Commercial style.

ELISHA JR. AND LIZZIE MORSE HOUSE (7/28/95)
2325-2327 Pillsbury Ave. S., Minneapolis
Italian Villa residence with cupola and wood siding simulating cut stone, constructed in 1874 for successful grocery merchant.

NEW MAIN, AUGSBURG SEMINARY (10/6/83)
731 21st Ave. S., Minneapolis
Classical brick-and-stone building designed by Omeyer and Thori and built in 1901 as center for campus activity.

GEORGE R. NEWELL HOUSE (9/15/77)
1818 LaSalle Ave., Minneapolis
Ornate Richardsonian Romanesque residence designed by Charles S. Sedgwick and built in 1888 for pioneering wholesale food distributor.

NOKOMIS KNOLL RESIDENTIAL HISTORIC DISTRICT (8/5/99)
vicinity of Bloomington Ave. S., E. 52nd St., W. Lake
Nokomis Pkwy., and E. 54th St., Minneapolis
Middle-class residential development, a concentration

of Period Revival–style houses with detached garages built largely in 1920s and 1930s.

NORTH EAST NEIGHBORHOOD HOUSE (7/19/2001)
1929 2nd St. N.E., Minneapolis
Georgian Revival settlement house (1919), run by reformers Robbins and Catheryne Gilman to serve immigrants and the underprivileged.

NORTHERN IMPLEMENT COMPANY (9/13/77)
616 S. 3rd St., Minneapolis
Louis Sullivan–influenced, seven-story brick commercial block designed by Kees and Colburn and built in 1910.

NORTHWESTERN KNITTING COMPANY FACTORY (6/3/83)
718 Glenwood Ave., Minneapolis
Group of five brick buildings (1904–15) constituting manufacturing plant for pioneering Munsingwear-brand underwear.

OGDEN APARTMENT HOTEL (1/13/92)
66-68 S. 12th St., Minneapolis
Renaissance Revival brick multiple dwelling designed by Adam Lansing Dorr and built in 1910 to provide afford-able, middle-class, downtown housing.

FLOYD B. OLSON HOUSE (12/31/74)
1914 W. 49th St., Minneapolis
Brick-and-stucco 1922 bungalow residence of three-term governor, political reformer, and Farmer-Labor party leader.

OSCAR OWRE HOUSE (3/8/84)
2625 Newton Ave. S., Minneapolis
Prairie School frame house designed by Purcell, Feick, and Elmslie and built in 1912, with 1917 garage by Purcell and Elmslie.

CHARLES AND GRACE PARKER HOUSE (6/11/92)

4829 Colfax Ave. S., Minneapolis
Prairie School frame house with ornamental entry
designed by Purcell, Feick, and Elmslie and built
in 1913.

PEAVEY-HAGLIN EXPERIMENTAL CONCRETE GRAIN
ELEVATOR (12/19/78) (National Historic Landmark, 12/21/81)

Minn. Hwys. 7 and 100, St. Louis Park
First circular reinforced-concrete grain elevator, engineered in 1899–1900 by Charles F. Haglin for grain
merchant Frank H. Peavey.

PILLSBURY A MILL (11/13/66)

(National Historic Landmark, 11/13/66)
*301 Main St. S.E., Minneapolis (also in
St. Anthony Falls Historic District)*
Six-story limestone flour mill designed by LeRoy S.
Buffington; largest and most advanced mill in world
when completed in 1881.

GIDEON H. POND HOUSE (7/16/70)

401 E. 104th St., Bloomington
House of brick made on site, built in 1856 by mission-
ary who worked with Dakota Indians and developed
"Pond alphabet" of Dakota language.

PROSPECT PARK WATER TOWER AND TOWER HILL PARK

(11/13/97)
*55 Malcolm Ave. S.E.,
Minneapolis*
Concrete water tower
with conical roof engi-
neered in 1913 by Fred-
erick W. Cappelen, built
in public park at city's
highest elevation.

Prospect Park Water Tower and
Tower Hill Park, 1937

WILLIAM G. PURCELL HOUSE (10/29/74)
2328 Lake Place, Minneapolis
Prairie School residence designed in 1913 by partner
in firm of Purcell and Elmslie, leading interpreters of
"organic" architecture.

QUEEN AVENUE BRIDGE (11/6/89)
W. Lake Harriet Blvd., Minneapolis
Early reinforced-concrete, single-span, barrel-arch
bridge designed by Charles Shepley and built in 1905.

RAND TOWER (4/14/94)
527-529 Marquette Ave., Minneapolis
Moderne-style, 26-story stepped skyscraper designed by
Holabird and Root of Chicago and built by C. F. Haglin
and Sons Company in 1928–29.

ROOSEVELT BRANCH LIBRARY (5/26/2000)
4026 28th Ave. S, Minneapolis
One of 13 Minneapolis Public Library branches built
under head librarian Gratia Countryman, leading proponent of public-library movement; constructed in 1927.

ST. ANTHONY FALLS HISTORIC DISTRICT (3/11/71)
*vicinity of Mississippi River between Plymouth
Ave. N. and 10th Ave. S., Minneapolis*

Pillsbury A Mill and Stone Arch Bridge, St. Anthony Falls Historic District, ca. 1890

Hydropower industrial area supporting development of lumber and flour milling central to the growth of Minneapolis.

SAM S. SHUBERT THEATRE (10/31/95)
515 Hennepin Ave., Minneapolis
Classical Revival two-balcony theater with terra cotta façade designed by William Albert Swasey and built in 1910 for Shubert brothers chain.

ANNE C. AND FRANK B. SEMPLE HOUSE (2/26/98)
100-104 W. Franklin Ave., Minneapolis
Renaissance Revival stone-and-brick mansion and carriage house designed by Long and Long and built in 1899–1901 for a prosperous hardware merchant and his wife.

H. ALDEN SMITH HOUSE (3/16/76)
1403 Harmon Place, Minneapolis
Large Richardsonian Romanesque residence of rusticated stone, designed in 1887 by William Channing Whitney for businessman Smith.

LENA O. SMITH HOUSE (9/26/91)
3905 5th Ave. S., Minneapolis
Home (from 1927 to 1940) of prominent African American civil rights lawyer, a founder of Minneapolis Urban League and head of legal redress for local NAACP chapters.

STATION 28 MINNEAPOLIS FIRE DEPARTMENT (11/12/93)
2724 W. 43rd St., Minneapolis
Brick 1914 fire station, the first in Minneapolis built solely for motorized equipment.

STEVENS SQUARE HISTORIC DISTRICT (7/1/93)
vicinity of E. 17th St., 1st Ave. S., W. Franklin Ave., and 3rd Ave. S., Minneapolis

High-density residential area of three-story brick apartment buildings framing small public park, built in 1912–26 for middle-class housing.

STEWART MEMORIAL PRESBYTERIAN CHURCH (11/28/78)
116 E. 32nd St., Minneapolis
Rare Prairie School church designed by Purcell and Feick; auditorium built in 1909–10, Sunday School wing in 1920s.

SUMNER BRANCH LIBRARY (5/26/2000)
611 Emerson Ave. N., Minneapolis
Tudor Revival Carnegie library (1915) designed by Chapman and Magney, one of 13 branches built under leadership of city's head librarian, Gratia Countryman.

SWINFORD TOWNHOUSES AND APARTMENTS (10/25/90)
1213-1221 and 1225 Hawthorne Ave., Minneapolis
Renaissance Revival brick-and-stone luxury housing; 1886 townhouses designed by Hodgson and Stem, 1897 apartments by Harry Wild Jones.

THIRTY-SIXTH STREET BRANCH LIBRARY (5/26/2000)
347 E. 36th St., Minneapolis
Tudor Revival Carnegie library (1916) designed by Henry D. Whitfield, one of 13 branches built under leadership of city's head librarian, Gratia Countryman.

THOMPSON SUMMER HOUSE (1/15/98)
3012 Shoreline Dr., Minnetonka Beach
Frame seasonal residence with open porches, built in 1887 in affluent lake resort community for prominent attorney and civic leader Charles Telford Thompson and his wife, Kate.

Thompson Summer House

SWAN TURNBLAD HOUSE (8/26/71)
2600 Park Ave., Minneapolis
Chateauesque mansion (1903–10) designed by Boehme and Cordella for newspaper publisher and founder of the American Swedish Institute.

TWIN CITY RAPID TRANSIT COMPANY
STEAM POWER PLANT (11/25/94)
12-20 6th Ave. S.E., Minneapolis
Renaissance Revival masonry power plant designed by Sargent and Lundy and built in 1903 to supply electricity to metropolitan streetcar system.

UNIVERSITY OF MINNESOTA OLD
CAMPUS HISTORIC DISTRICT (8/23/84)
vicinity of University and 15th Aves. S.E. and Pillsbury Dr. S.E., Minneapolis
Thirteen masonry buildings built in 1886–1907 in various styles by noted architects, constituting first major expansion of university.

HORATIO P. VAN CLEVE HOUSE (3/16/76)
603 5th St. S.E., Minneapolis
Greek Revival residence (1858) of a Civil War general and the commander of the Second Minnesota Infantry Regiment and his wife, Charlotte, author, humanitarian, and worker for women's suffrage.

GEORGE W. AND NANCY B. VAN DUSEN HOUSE (5/18/95)
1900 LaSalle Ave., Minneapolis
Richardsonian Romanesque/French Renaissance residence of Sioux quartzite (1893), designed by Edgar E. Joralemon for a grain-trade pioneer and his wife.

WALKER BRANCH LIBRARY (5/26/2000)
2901 Hennepin Ave. S., Minneapolis
Classical Revival library (1911) designed by Jerome P. Jackson, one of 13 branches built under leadership of city's head librarian, Gratia Countryman.

WASHBURN A MILL COMPLEX (3/11/71)
(National Historic Landmark, 5/4/83)
S. 1st St. at Portland Ave., Minneapolis
(also in St. Anthony Falls Historic District)
Complex of flour mills, grain elevators, and offices dating from 1878; site of innovative milling technology, birthplace of General Mills.

WASHBURN–FAIR OAKS MANSION
HISTORIC DISTRICT (2/17/78)
vicinity of 1st Ave. S., Stevens Ave., and
E. 22nd St., Minneapolis
Seven residences bordering public park, built in 1884–1912 in various styles by noted architects for prominent businessmen and civic leaders.

WASHBURN PARK WATER TOWER (10/6/83)
401 Prospect Ave., Minneapolis
Domed concrete water tower designed by Harry Wild Jones, engineered by William S. Hewett, and built in 1931–32; statuary by John K. Daniels.

WESLEY METHODIST EPISCOPAL CHURCH (2/9/84)
101 E. Grant St., Minneapolis
Richardsonian Romanesque church with tower designed by Warren H. Hayes on variant of Akron plan and built of Sioux quartzite in 1890–91.

White Castle Building No. 8

WESTMINSTER PRESBYTERIAN CHURCH (6/26/98)
83 S. 12th St., Minneapolis
Stone church with twin towers built in 1896–97 for
reform-minded congregation, designed jointly by
Charles S. Sedgwick and Warren H. Hayes.

WHITE CASTLE BUILDING NO. 8 (10/16/86)
3252 Lyndale Ave. S., Minneapolis
Example of fast-food chain's signature prefabricated,
white enamel-over-steel, portable-style hamburger
stand, built in 1936.

MALCOLM WILLEY HOUSE (2/23/84)
255 Bedford St. S.E., Minneapolis
Brick-and-wood residence designed in 1934 by Frank
Lloyd Wright, a bridge between his Prairie School and
Usonian styles; built for a University of Minnesota
administrator.

THEODORE WIRTH HOUSE/ADMINISTRATION
BUILDING (6/7/2002)
3954 Bryant Ave. S., Minneapolis
Residence/office built in 1910 for superintendent of
Minneapolis park system, a national leader in field of
landscape architecture.

ALLEMARINDA AND JAMES WYER HOUSE (4/18/77)
201 Mill St., Excelsior
Eastlake-style, two-story summer cottage built ca. 1880
in lakeside community.

HOUSTON COUNTY

BRIDGE NO. L-4013 (7/5/90)
Twp. Rd. 126 over Riceford Creek, Black Hammer Twp.
Stone arch bridge designed in 1915 by State Engineer
Alfred J. Rasmussen; became the standard for other
counties.

CHRISTIAN BUNGE JR. STORE (4/6/82)
Iowa Ave. and Main St., Eitzen
Commercial building constructed in 1890 by stone-mason Christian Krueger for early postmaster who named town after his German birthplace.

CALEDONIA COMMERCIAL HISTORIC DISTRICT (8/5/94)
101-205 E. Main and 101-108 S. Kingston, Caledonia
Brick commercial buildings with stone and metal trim (1872–1906) that served as area's business and retail center, anchored by 1902 Sprague Bank.

DANIEL CAMERON HOUSE (4/6/82)
429-435 7th St., La Crescent
Italianate frame residence with cupola built in 1871 for prosperous farmer, property owner, and state senator.

CHURCH OF THE HOLY COMFORTER (EPISCOPAL) (6/2/70)
Main St., Brownsville
Gothic-style, board-and-batten frame church (1850s); also used as a town hall and school.

EITZEN STONE BARN (4/6/82)
Iowa Ave., Winnebago Twp.
Rubblestone barn with pegged-timber framing, built ca. 1870s–80s by German immigrant stonemasons.

HOUSTON COUNTY COURTHOUSE AND JAIL (3/18/83)
304 S. Marshall St., Caledonia
Romanesque stone courthouse (1883) and Italianate stone jail and sheriff's residence (1875) designed by Maybury and Son.

JEFFERSON GRAIN WAREHOUSE (11/25/94)
off Minn. Hwy. 26, Jefferson Twp.
Rare Minnesota example of riverside limestone ware-house, built in 1868 to store grain awaiting shipment by steamboat.

JOHNSON MILL (4/6/82)
Co. Rds. 5 and 23, Winnebago Twp.
Waterpowered frame flour and grist mill built in 1877
at crossroads for local wheat farmers.

PORTLAND PRAIRIE METHODIST EPISCOPAL CHURCH (4/6/82)
off Minn. Hwy. 76, Winnebago Twp.
Eastlake-style frame church built in 1876 to serve Old-
Stock American settlers.

Schech Mill

SCHECH MILL (1/31/78)
off Co. Rd. 10 (Beaver Creek Valley State Park),
Caledonia Twp.
Waterpowered grist mill built of stone in 1875–76, containing original millstones and equipment for high-
grinding milling.

ROBERT D. AND ELLSWORTH A. SPRAGUE HOUSES (4/6/82)
204 and 224 W. Main, Caledonia
Georgian Revival brick residences built in 1900–05 for
family of bankers who founded county's first bank.

WILLIAMS HOTEL (4/6/82)
Main and Marshall St., Caledonia
Brick hotel with decorative wood trim built ca. 1870s.

YUCATAN FORT (11/14/96)
Black Hammer Twp.
Small earthwork complex of enclosure type, dating to late Precontact or early Contact Periods.

HUBBARD COUNTY

HUBBARD COUNTY COURTHOUSE (3/8/84)
3rd and Court Sts., Park Rapids
Classical Revival brick courthouse designed by M. E. Beebe and built in 1900 to house county government offices.

East Contact Station, Itasca State Park, ca. 1938

ITASCA STATE PARK (5/7/73)
off U.S. Hwy. 7, Clover and Lake Alice Twps.,
(also in Becker and Clearwater Counties)
Minnesota's oldest state park (est. 1891), site of Mississippi headwaters, with Rustic-style log and stone buildings/structures built in 1905–42.

LOUIS J. MOSER HOUSE (4/17/79)
off Co. Rd. 90 (Louie's Point), Thorpe Twp.
Vertical-log house built ca. 1907 by homesteader who operated it as one of area's first fishing camps.

PARK RAPIDS JAIL (10/27/88)
205 W. 2nd St., Park Rapids
Brick jail designed by Fremont D. Orff and built in 1901 for joint village and county use.

SHELL RIVER PREHISTORIC VILLAGE AND MOUND DISTRICT (6/19/73)
Crow Wing Lake Twp.
Village site and mounds at junction of two major travel routes, dating to Precontact Period (A.D. 900–1650).

ISANTI COUNTY

DISTRICT NO. 1 SCHOOL (7/24/80)
off Co. Hwy. 7, Spencer Brook Twp.
Frame school with bell tower built in 1874; rare surviving building associated with community settled by New Englanders in 1850s.

EDWARD ERICKSON FARMSTEAD (7/24/80)
Co. Hwy. 56 and Minn. Hwy. 65, Athens Twp.
Large farmstead with Classical Revival frame farmhouse, rainbow-roofed barn, and outbuildings built ca. 1915 for prosperous potato farmer.

Edward Erickson Farmstead

FARMERS COOPERATIVE MERCANTILE COMPANY OF WEST STANFORD (7/24/80)
Co. Hwy. 7, Stanford Twp. (Crown)
False-front frame store built in 1924 in village of Crown as mercantile cooperative run by and for area farmers.

ISANTI COUNTY COURTHOUSE (7/24/80)
237 2nd Ave. S.W., Cambridge
Brick-clad frame courthouse built in 1887 in local interpretation of French Second Empire style.

LINDEN BARN (7/24/80)
Co. Hwy. 19, Isanti Twp.
Round, concrete-block dairy barn with adjacent wood silo built in 1914 for Swedish immigrant farmer Olof Linden.

OSCAR OLSON HOUSE (7/24/80)
309 Beechwood Ave. N., Braham
Colonial Revival frame residence (1914) owned by prominent banker and civic leader.

ST. JOHN'S LUTHERAN CHURCH (7/24/80)
Co. Hwy. 5, Bradford Twp.
Greek Revival frame church built in 1882 by German Lutheran homesteaders.

SVENSKA MISSION KYRKA I SODRE MAPLE RIDGE (SWEDISH MISSION CHURCH OF SOUTH MAPLE RIDGE) (7/24/80)
Co. Hwy. 1, Maple Ridge Twp.
Gothic Revival frame church built in 1897 by reform-minded Swedish congregation.

WEST RIVERSIDE SCHOOL (7/24/80)
Co. Hwy. 14, Cambridge Twp.
One-room brick schoolhouse with bell tower (1898) that doubled as community center.

ITASCA COUNTY

BOVEY VILLAGE HALL (8/15/91)
402 2nd St., Bovey
Baroque Revival municipal building (1934), one of first Minnesota projects funded by the PWA.

CENTRAL SCHOOL (8/16/77)
N. Pokegama and 4th Sts., Grand Rapids
Brick-and-stone, Richardsonian Romanesque school containing town's first library, designed in 1895 by F. W. Hollister.

CHURCH OF THE GOOD SHEPHERD (EPISCOPAL) (8/11/80)
Cole and Olcott Aves., Coleraine
Log church built in 1908 by the U.S. Steel Corporation for use by supervisory and management personnel.

COLERAINE CARNEGIE LIBRARY (7/17/80)
Clemson and Cole Aves. S., Coleraine
Classical Revival brick public library designed by Kinney and Halden and built in 1912.

COLERAINE CITY HALL (6/18/92)
302 Roosevelt Ave., Coleraine
Renaissance Revival brick-and-stone municipal building designed in 1910 by Frank W. Kinney.

Coleraine Carnegie Library

COLERAINE METHODIST EPISCOPAL CHURCH (4/22/82)
Gayley and Cole Aves., Coleraine
Shingle Style church designed by Frank Young and built
in 1908–09; also housed YMCA recreational center.

CUT FOOT SIOUX RANGER STATION (8/7/74)
Minn. Hwy. 46 (Chippewa National Forest),
unorganized territory
One-room log building constructed in 1904 on Turtle
Mound portage in Minnesota's first national forest.

FRANK GRAN FARMSTEAD (4/22/82)
Co. Hwy. 10, unorganized territory
Large-scale dairy and potato farm in logged-over land,
with 1916 Queen Anne farmhouse built by prosperous
Finnish immigrant farmer.

HARTLEY SUGAR CAMP (4/22/82)
off Co. Hwy. 10, Trout Lake Twp.
Complex of log structures built in 1904–05 by Finnish
settlers for Duluth business leader Guilford G. Hartley's
maple syrup operation.

Oliver Iron Mining Company Buildings: Oliver Boarding House

HILL ANNEX MINE (8/1/86)

off U.S. Hwy. 169 (Hill Annex Mine State Park),
Greenway Twp.
State-owned, open-pit Mesabi Range iron mine operated 1912–79, with intact buildings and equipment used to process ore.

ITASCA LUMBER COMPANY
SUPERINTENDENT'S RESIDENCE (4/22/82)

506 5th St. S.E., Deer River
Log house built in 1904 for chief local administrator of region's foremost logging operation.

MARCELL RANGER STATION (5/19/94)

Minn. Hwy. 38 (Chippewa National Forest), Marcell Twp.
Rustic-style log residence with fieldstone fireplace and log outbuildings built in 1934–35 by CCC workers for the U.S. Forest Service.

OLIVER IRON MINING COMPANY BUILDINGS:
CANISTEO DISTRICT GENERAL OFFICE (4/22/82)

200 Cole Ave., Coleraine
Brick office building built in 1907–08 for model community of Coleraine; type used by mining company in other company towns on Mesabi Range.

OLIVER IRON MINING COMPANY BUILDINGS:
GENERAL SUPERINTENDENT'S RESIDENCE (4/22/82)

Cole Ave., Coleraine
Large frame residence with gabled roof (1911) of type used across Mesabi Range as management-level housing for company employees.

OLIVER IRON MINING COMPANY BUILDINGS:
OLIVER BOARDING HOUSE (4/22/82)

Jessie St., Marble
Two-story frame housing (ca. 1909) of type built by mining company for single immigrant workers in Mesabi Range communities.

SCENIC STATE PARK CCC/RUSTIC STYLE
HISTORIC DISTRICT (6/8/92)
off Co. Hwy. 7 (Scenic State Park), unorganized territory
Log buildings/structures in public-use area of park built
in 1934–35 by CCC workers, with Rustic-style furniture
and artwork by local artisans.

SCENIC STATE PARK CCC/RUSTIC STYLE
SERVICE YARD (6/8/92)
off Co. Hwy. 7 (Scenic State Park), unorganized territory
Log residence and service buildings noted for exceptional craftsmanship, built in 1934–35 by the CCC.

TURTLE ORACLE MOUND (8/27/74)
unorganized territory (Chippewa National Forest)
Earthwork, in the shape of a turtle, that commemorates
18th-century territorial battles between the Dakota and
Ojibwe.

WHITE OAK POINT SITE (10/18/72)
Morse Twp. (Chippewa National Forest)
Village and mound site dating from 5000 B.C. through
historic Ojibwe occupation.

WINNIBIGOSHISH LAKE DAM (5/11/82)
Co. Hwy. 9 at Mississippi River, unorganized territory
(also in Cass County)
Reinforced-concrete dam built in 1900 by the U.S. Army
Corps of Engineers as part of reservoir system to stabi-
lize Mississippi River flow.

JACKSON COUNTY

CHURCH OF THE SACRED HEART (CATHOLIC) (3/20/89)
9th St. and 4th Ave., Heron Lake
Classical Revival/Baroque, brick-faced church built in
1920–21 on basilica plan, designed by Wisconsin architects Parkinson and Dockendorff.

DISTRICT NO. 92 SCHOOL (10/27/88)
off Co. Hwy. 6, Middletown Twp.
Frame rural school built in 1906 on octagonal plan.

JACKSON COMMERCIAL HISTORIC DISTRICT (12/17/87)
2nd St. between Sheridan and White Sts., Jackson
Cohesive group of commercial buildings built in
1880–1944, largely brick with stone trim, that comprise
town's retail and business center.

JACKSON COUNTY COURTHOUSE (4/13/77)
413 4th St., Jackson
Classical Revival stone courthouse (1908) designed by
Buechner and Orth, with murals by Odin J. Oyen of La
Crosse, Wis.

GEORGE M. MOORE FARMHOUSE (1/7/87)
off Co. Hwy. 4, Middletown Twp.
Craftsman-style bungalow, office building, and garage
built in 1917 for prosperous farm family active in civic
affairs.

ROBERTSON PARK SITE (8/1/80)
Minneota Twp.
Multiple-component, stratified habitation site dating
from Precontact Period (ca. 100 B.C.–A.D. 800).

Jackson Commercial Historic District

KANABEC COUNTY

ANN RIVER LOGGING COMPANY FARM (8/18/80)
Minn. Hwy. 23, Arthur Twp.
Farmstead built in 1880s by Stillwater lumberman Isaac Staples; later used for summering animals and raising food for logging operations.

KANABEC COUNTY COURTHOUSE (4/11/77)
18 N. Vine St., Mora
Romanesque Revival brick-and-stone courthouse with tower, built in 1894 after designs by Buechner and Jacobson.

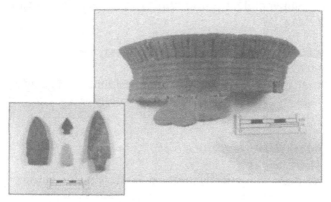

Artifacts from Knife Lake Prehistoric District

KNIFE LAKE PREHISTORIC DISTRICT (1/21/74)
Knife Lake Twp.
Habitation sites, mound groups, and wild-ricing sites dating from Precontact Period (200 B.C.–A.D. 1000) into the 1800s.

OGILVIE WATER TOWER (8/18/80)
Anderson St., Ogilvie
Early reinforced-concrete water tower built in 1918 by Circular Concrete Company of Minneapolis.

CHARLES E. WILLIAMS HOUSE (8/18/80)
206 E. Maple Ave., Mora
Large Queen Anne frame residence built in 1902; long-time home of leading businessman, banker, and civic leader.

ZETTERBERG COMPANY (8/18/80)
630 E. Forest, Mora
False-front agricultural implement dealership built in 1912 near depot on outskirts of town.

KANDIYOHI COUNTY

A. LARSON & CO. (3/2/89)
539 W. Pacific Ave., Willmar
Attached Italianate brick buildings constructed in 1876 and ca. 1885 for dry goods and grocery businesses in fledgling commercial district.

JOHN BOSCH FARMSTEAD (4/23/87)
Co. Hwy. 4, Lake Elizabeth Twp.
Home of national leader of Farmers' Holiday Association, a protest movement that sought government support for farmers during the Great Depression of the 1930s.

ANDREAS AND JOHANNA BROMAN AND FRANK E. AND ANNA BROMAN FARMSTEAD (2/28/91)
off Co. Rd. 8, Kandiyohi Twp.
Nineteenth-century farmstead settled by Swedish immigrant family.

DISTRICT NO. 55 SCHOOL (4/16/87)
Co. Hwy. 3, Whitefield Twp.
Rural school and meeting hall, Minnesota birthplace of Farmers' Holiday Association, a radical, agrarian protest movement during the Great Depression of the 1930s.

Hotel Atwater, 1914

GURI AND LARS ENDRESON HOUSE (7/24/86)
off Co. Hwy. 5, Dovre Twp.
Log home built ca. 1858 by settlers involved in the
Dakota War of 1862.

HOTEL ATWATER (6/13/86)
322 Atlantic Ave., Atwater
Brick hotel (1904), a center of commercial and community activity built through organized effort of local
business leaders.

SIBLEY STATE PARK CCC/RUSTIC STYLE
HISTORIC DISTRICT (1/22/92)
off U.S. Hwy. 71 (Sibley State Park), Lake Andrew Twp.
Buildings and structures of split stone erected in
1935–38 in park's public use area and service yard by
CCC workers.

JOHN M. SPICER HOUSE (8/13/86)
515 7th St. N.W., Willmar
Home (ca. 1873) of prominent businessman and railroad
official who helped develop town's railway connections.

JOHN M. SPICER SUMMER HOUSE AND FARMSTEAD (8/6/86)
11600 Indian Beach Rd., Green Lake Twp.
Summer home complex and model farm built in
1880s–1913 in resort area by leading real estate and
townsite developer.

WILLMAR AUDITORIUM (8/9/91)
311 6th St. S.W., Willmar
Moderne-style, brick-faced public building with cast-
stone motifs and WPA murals, built in 1935–38 under
state and federal work relief programs.

Administration Building (center), Willmar Hospital Farm for Inebriates Historic District

WILLMAR HOSPITAL FARM FOR
INEBRIATES HISTORIC DISTRICT (8/13/86)
off U.S. Hwy. 71, Willmar
State hospital complex with residential cottages built
in 1912–33, designed by State Architect Clarence H.
Johnston Sr. in variety of revival styles.

KITTSON COUNTY

LAKE BRONSON SITE (5/22/78)
Norway and Percy Twps.
Indian habitation site and mound group dating from
Precontact Period (ca. A.D. 100–1500).

LAKE BRONSON STATE PARK WPA/RUSTIC STYLE HISTORIC RESOURCES (10/25/89)

off Co. Hwy. 28 (Lake Bronson State Park),
east of Lake Bronson, Percy Twp.
Concrete dam and split-stone facilities for park and group camp, including water tower with observation deck, developed by WPA workers in 1936–40.

St. Nicholas Orthodox Church

ST. NICHOLAS ORTHODOX CHURCH (3/8/84)

Co. Hwy. 4, Caribou Twp.
(Caribou)
Small frame church with onion domes built in 1905 by community of Ukrainian immigrants.

KOOCHICHING COUNTY

BRIDGE NO. 5721 (7/13/98)

Minn. Hwy. 65 over Little Fork River, unorganized territory
Wrought-iron camelback through truss built ca. 1890, remodeled with steel approach spans in 1937.

ERNEST C. OBERHOLTZER RAINY LAKE ISLANDS HISTORIC DISTRICT (6/16/2000)

Mallard, Hawk, and Crow Islands in Rainy Lake, unorganized territory
Island home (1922–77) of conservation activist and leader of landmark movement to preserve Quetico-Superior wilderness area.

Big House, Ernest C. Oberholtzer
Rainy Lake Islands Historic District

FINSTED'S AUTO MARINE SHOP (1/27/83)

Sand Bay between Oak Ave. and Spruce St., Ranier
Concrete-block boat works built in 1911 to serve
seasonal residents, tourists, and commercial fishing
industries in Rainy Lake area.

GOLD MINE SITES HISTORIC DISTRICT (5/6/77)

off Minn. Hwy. 11 in Voyageurs National Park,
Island View, and unorganized territory
Mine shafts and test pits constituting scene of short-
lived 1894 gold rush that led to settlement of Rainy
Lake region.

KOOCHICHING COUNTY COURTHOUSE (9/15/77)

715 4th St., International Falls
Renaissance Revival brick-and-stone courthouse with
domed cupola, designed by Charles E. Bell and built in
1909–10, with murals by E. Sonderberg of La Crosse, Wis.

LAUREL MOUNDS (1/20/72)

unorganized territory
Village site and mound group (including Grand Mound)
associated with Laurel culture, which flourished ca.
200 B.C. TO A.D. 1000.

LITTLE AMERICAN MINE (4/16/75)

off Minn. Hwy. 11 in Voyageurs National Park and
Island View (also in Gold Mine Sites Historic District)
Only gold mine in Minnesota known to have produced
a profit during its operation (1893–98).

MCKINSTRY MOUNDS AND VILLAGE SITE (12/18/78)

unorganized territory
Habitation site and mound group from Precontact
Period (5000 B.C.–A.D. 1300).

NETT LAKE PETROGLYPHS (12/20/74)
unorganized territory
Rock carvings on Spirit Island depicting human, animal, and geometric forms made by Indians in late Precontact or Contact Periods.

SS. PETER AND PAUL RUSSIAN ORTHODOX CHURCH (1/27/83)
Minn. Hwy. 65, unorganized territory
Frame church with double onion dome built in 1915–18 by Russian homesteaders.

FRANCIS WHITE FARMHOUSE (1/27/83)
off U.S. Hwy. 71, unorganized territory
Log house built ca. 1901 by homesteader who later founded Koochiching County Farm Bureau.

LAC QUI PARLE COUNTY

CAMP RELEASE STATE MONUMENT (3/14/73)
U.S. Hwy. 212, Camp Release Twp.
Site of trials for surrendered and captured Dakota Indians following the Dakota War of 1862; first property added to state park system (1889).

COMMERCIAL BANK (1/28/82)
6th St., Dawson
Richardsonian Romanesque brick building, with polished granite trim, built in 1892 by entrepreneur and town founder Christopher M. Anderson.

DAWSON ARMORY AND COMMUNITY BUILDING (5/18/95)
676 Pine St., Dawson
Brick armory built in 1923 for joint use as Minnesota National Guard training center and civic recreational facility.

DAWSON CARNEGIE LIBRARY (8/15/85)
677 Pine St., Dawson

Classical Revival brick building designed by A. H. Foss and built in 1917–18.

LAC QUI PARLE COUNTY COURTHOUSE (8/15/85)
600 6th St., Madison
Romanesque Revival brick-and-stone courthouse with tower, designed by Buechner and Jacobson and built in 1899 after a 17-year battle over the county seat.

LAC QUI PARLE MISSION SITE (3/14/73)
Co. Hwy. 13, La qui Parle Twp. (also in Chippewa County)
Protestant mission established in 1835 at site of Fort Renville fur-trading center to serve Dakota Indians; church reconstructed in 1940s.

LAC QUI PARLE STATE PARK WPA/RUSTIC STYLE HISTORIC DISTRICT (8/19/91)
Co. Hwy. 33 (Lac qui Parle State Park), Lac qui Parle Twp.
Three buildings of split-stone construction built in 1938–41 in park developed by WPA workers as part of larger flood control project.

LOUISBURG SCHOOL (6/20/86)
1st St. and 3rd Ave., Louisburg
Brick schoolhouse built in 1911 to serve elementary and secondary grades; site of local prohibition effort.

Lac qui Parle County Courthouse

MADISON CARNEGIE LIBRARY (8/23/85)
401 6th Ave., Madison
Classical Revival brick library with limestone trim and polygonal dome, designed by Ralph D. Church, built in 1905–06.

MADISON CITY HALL (8/23/85)
404 6th Ave., Madison
Classical Revival brick building with limestone trim, designed by Buechner and Orth, built in 1902–03 to house city offices and an opera house.

LAKE COUNTY

BRIDGE NO. 3589 (6/29/98)
U.S. Hwy. 61 over Stewart River, Silver Creek Twp.
Reinforced-concrete arch bridge with Classical Revival detailing, built in 1924 on popular tourist route; widened in 1939.

DISTRICT NO. 4 SCHOOL (6/18/92)
Co. Hwy. 61, unorganized territory (Larsmont)
Small frame school built in 1914 to serve as educational, religious, recreational, and cultural center of Swede-Finn community.

DULUTH AND IRON RANGE DEPOT (2/24/83)
6th St., Two Harbors
Brick passenger/freight depot constructed in 1906–07 to serve region's lumber and iron mining operations.

GOOSEBERRY FALLS STATE PARK CCC/RUSTIC STYLE HISTORIC RESOURCES (10/25/89)
off U.S. Hwy. 61 (Gooseberry Falls State Park),
Silver Creek Twp.
Group of 88 log and stone buildings/structures built by CCC workers, featuring designs executed by Italian stonemasons in locally quarried granite.

HESPER SHIPWRECK (4/14/94)
vicinity of Silver Bay, Lake Superior
Wood-hulled, bulk-freight steamer that towed schooner barges for iron ore industry and grain trade; launched in 1890 and lost in 1905.

JOHN DWAN OFFICE BUILDING (6/11/92)
201 Waterfront Dr., Two Harbors
Birthplace of Minnesota Mining and Manufacturing Company (3M), founded in 1902 to mine and manufacture abrasives.

LAKE COUNTY COURTHOUSE (2/24/83)
601 3rd Ave., Two Harbors
Beaux Arts brick-and-stone courthouse with dome, designed by James Allen McLeod and built in 1906.

MADEIRA SHIPWRECK (7/23/92)
vicinity of Split Rock Lighthouse, Lake Superior
Schooner barge built in 1900 to carry bulk cargoes of grain, lumber, and iron ore; 1905 loss spurred construction of Split Rock Lighthouse.

Duluth and Iron Range Depot, 1982

EDWARD AND LISA MATTSON
HOUSE AND FISH HOUSE (8/9/90)
off U.S. Hwy. 61, Beaver Bay Twp.
Log residence (ca. 1902) and half-log fish house (ca. 1930) used for small-scale, family-managed commercial fishing operation.

NIAGARA SHIPWRECK (4/14/94)
vicinity of Knife River, Lake Superior
Early example of large wooden log-rafting tug, a type developed for Great Lakes logging industry; launched in 1872 and lost in 1904.

ONOKO SHIPWRECK (7/23/92)
vicinity of Knife River, Lake Superior
First iron-hulled steam freighter on Great Lakes, prototype for modern bulk freighters; launched in 1882 and sunk in 1915.

SAMUEL P. ELY SHIPWRECK (6/18/92)
vicinity of Two Harbors, Lake Superior
Schooner barge of type built to carry bulk cargo of iron ore; launched in 1869 and lost in 1896.

SPLIT ROCK LIGHTHOUSE (6/23/69)
U.S. Hwy. 61 (Split Rock Lighthouse State Park),
Beaver Bay Twp.
Brick light tower and keeper's residence erected in 1909–10 by the U.S. Lighthouse Service on a Lake Superior cliff to guide ore ships past the rocky coast.

TETTEGOUCHE CAMP (1/17/89)
off Co. Hwy. 4 (Tettegouche State Park), Beaver Bay Twp.
Rustic-style log and half-log buildings remaining from private sport and recreation club established ca. 1910 by group of Duluth businessmen.

TUGBOAT EDNA G. (6/5/75)
Agate Bay, Two Harbors

Last coal-fired, steam-powered tugboat operated on Lake Superior, built in 1896 to guide ore carriers to and from Two Harbors docks.

TWO HARBORS CARNEGIE LIBRARY (7/31/86)
4th Ave. and Waterfront, Two Harbors
Classical Revival, brick-and-stone building designed by Austin Terryberry, built in 1909 as permanent home for community library.

TWO HARBORS LIGHT STATION (7/19/84)
Agate and Burlington Bays, Two Harbors
Brick keeper's house with attached tower completed 1892 by the U.S. Coast Guard to guide ore shipments through then-primary Lake Superior port.

Split Rock Lighthouse, 1939

LAKE OF THE WOODS COUNTY

FORT ST. CHARLES (4/8/83)
Magnusons Island, unorganized territory
Archaeological remains of French outpost active from 1732 to mid-1750s as center for French exploration, trade, diplomacy, and missionary work.

Norris Camp

NORRIS CAMP (9/19/94)
off Norris-Roosevelt Forest Rd., unorganized territory
One of two surviving CCC work camps in Minnesota,
built in 1935 to house workers on Beltrami Island
Project, a pioneering federal resettlement effort.

NORTHWEST POINT (2/23/73)
Northwest Angle
Isolated stretch of land added to United States in 1818
to settle British-American land dispute and establish international boundary.

LE SUEUR COUNTY

JOHN R. ANDREWS HOUSE (10/10/78)
Co. Hwy. 19, Kasota Twp.
Residence (built ca. 1860) of family of performers
known as Andrews Opera Company, which toured
nationally in last decades of 19th century.

BRIDGE NO. 4846(1) (2/17/81)
Co. Hwy. 102 over Minn. Hwy. 22, Kasota Twp.
Minnesota's oldest known metal Pratt through truss
highway bridge, built in 1875.

BROADWAY BRIDGE (8/5/99)
Minn. Hwy. 99 over Minnesota River,

Oshawa Twp. (also in Nicollet County)
Two-span metal through truss bridge (1931) with ornamentation designed to enhance skewed configuration
necessitated by river current.

CARSON N. COSGROVE HOUSE (3/15/82)
228 S. 2nd St., Le Sueur
Elaborate Victorian home built ca. 1895 for civic leader
and founder of Minnesota Valley Canning Company,
forerunner of Green Giant.

ARTHUR DEHN HOUSE (11/19/82)
Herbert St., Waterville
Home base (1914–30) of Minnesota-born artist Adolf
Dehn, mid-20th-century American regionalist print-
maker and watercolorist.

ELYSIAN SCHOOL (2/17/81)
4th and Frank Sts., Elysian
Two-story, four-room brick school with bell tower
designed by George Pass and built in 1895.

FIRST NATIONAL BANK (3/15/82)
112 E. Main, New Prague
Renaissance Revival building with intricate, glazed terra
cotta façade, designed by Frederick Klawiter and built
in 1922.

GELDNER SAWMILL (6/11/75)
Co. Hwy. 13, Elysian Twp.
County's last surviving sawmill (built ca. 1860, moved
1876), with attached power shed housing stationary
steam engine.

GERMAN EVANGELICAL SALEM CHURCH (3/15/82)
Co. Rd. 156, Tyrone Twp.
Small Greek Revival frame church built in 1870 by Ger-
man immigrants who settled and farmed northwestern
Le Sueur County.

Hilltop Hall

HILLTOP HALL (3/15/82)
206 1st St., Montgomery
Buff-colored brick commercial building with second-floor dance hall built ca. 1892 as social center of downtown business district.

HOTEL BROZ (3/15/82)
212 W. Main, New Prague
Georgian Revival, "first class" brick hotel built in 1898; served as community's social center.

KASOTA TOWNSHIP HALL (2/17/81)
Hill and Rice Sts., Kasota
Brick building with Kasota stone trim, constructed in 1889 as public meeting space and site of township government.

KASOTA VILLAGE HALL (2/17/81)
Cherry and Webster Sts., Kasota
Two-story Queen Anne brick municipal building with Kasota stone trim and one-story fire department wing, built in 1898.

LE SUEUR COUNTY COURTHOUSE AND JAIL (2/17/81)
88 and 130 S. Park Ave., Le Center
Richardsonian brick courthouse with Kasota stone trim designed by Louis M. Curry of Chicago, built in 1896; 1914 brick jail by Albert Schippel.

WILLIAM W. MAYO HOUSE (11/25/69)
118 N. Main St., Le Sueur
Home and medical office built in 1859 by physician who, with his sons, William J. and Charles H., later established Rochester's Mayo Clinic.

NEEDHAM-HAYES HOUSE (3/15/82)
off Railroad St., Ottawa Twp.
Large brick residence trimmed with locally quarried Ottawa stone, built ca. 1870 by early settler and merchant Charles Needham.

OTTAWA STONE BUILDINGS:
Methodist Episcopal Church (3/15/82)
Liberty and Whittier Sts., Ottawa Twp. (Ottawa)
Ottawa Township Hall (3/15/82)
Buchanan and Bryant Sts., Ottawa Twp. (Ottawa)
David Patten House (3/15/82)
Liberty St., Ottawa Twp. (Ottawa)
John Rinshed House (3/15/82)
Sumner and Whittier Sts., Ottawa Twp. (Ottawa)
Charles Schwartz House and Barn (3/15/82)
off Co. Hwy. 23, Ottawa Twp. (Ottawa)
Trinity Chapel (Episcopal) (3/15/82)
Sumner and Exchange Sts., Ottawa Twp. (Ottawa)
Small-scale buildings constructed between 1859 and ca. 1870 of Ottawa limestone from local quarries that constituted town's principal industry.

SMITH-COSGROVE HOUSE (3/15/82)
228 S. Main St., Le Sueur
French Second Empire brick residence built ca. 1878 by banker Edson Smith; later purchased by harness shop owner James A. Cosgrove.

GEORGE W. TAYLOR HOUSE (9/5/75)
103 S. 2nd St., Le Sueur
Large Eastlake-style residence built in 1890 for a prominent merchant and his wife, Lodusky, a national presi-

dent of the Woman's Relief Corps, auxiliary of the
Grand Army of the Republic.

UNION HOTEL (3/15/82)
201 Paquin St., Waterville
Italianate brick hotel built in 1888 to accommodate vis-
itors to booming commercial center and vacation spot.

WESTERMAN LUMBER COMPANY
OFFICE AND RESIDENCE (3/15/82)
201 1st St. S., Montgomery
Two-story building (1895) enlarged and veneered in
locally manufactured brick by sawmill and lumber
company owner Henry E. Westerman.

LINCOLN COUNTY

DANEBOD (6/30/75)
Danebod St., Tyler
State's oldest Danish settlement, comprising Folk School
(built in 1888, rebuilt in 1917), Stone Hall (1889), Cross
Church (1893), and Gym Hall (1904).

DRAMMEN FARMERS' CLUB (12/12/80)
Co. Hwy. 13, Drammen Twp.
Social club and community center built in 1921 to serve
rural residents of sparsely settled agricultural county.

LAKE BENTON OPERA HOUSE AND
KIMBALL BUILDING (4/22/82)
Benton St., Lake Benton
Brick performance hall with adjacent commercial space
built in 1896 to host community cultural activities and
traveling theatrical troupes.

LINCOLN COUNTY COURTHOUSE (12/12/80)
319 N. Rebecca St., Ivanhoe
Classical Revival brick courthouse with Kasota stone

trim, designed by C. Howard Parsons and built in 1919 after a long county-seat dispute.

LINCOLN COUNTY FAIRGROUNDS (12/12/80)
Strong and Marsh Sts., Tyler
Cohesive fairgrounds complex built in 1920s–40s by local builders and WPA workers to provide social and professional meeting place for farm families.

Drammen Farmers' Club, ca. 1921

ERNEST OSBECK HOUSE (12/12/80)
106 S. Fremont, Lake Benton
Queen Anne frame house built in 1896–97 for prominent grocery merchant and community developer.

TYLER SCHOOL (12/12/80)
Strong St., Tyler
Renaissance Revival/Romanesque brick school with stone trim and four-story bell tower, designed by Andrew J. Van Deusen and built in 1903.

LYON COUNTY

J. S. ANDERSON HOUSE (3/15/82)
402 E. 2nd, Minneota
Queen Anne/Classical Revival residence with octagonal tower built ca. 1896 for real estate speculator.

BRIDGE NO. 5083 (6/29/98)
Minn. Hwy. 19 over Redwood River, Marshall
Two-span concrete deck-girder bridge of ornamental
urban design type with Classical Revival light stan-
dards, built in 1931.

BRIDGE NO. 5151 (6/29/98)
Minn. Hwy. 19 over Redwood River, Marshall
Two-span concrete deck-girder bridge of ornamental
urban design type with Classical Revival light stan-
dards, built in 1931.

O. G. Anderson and Co. Store, 1922–23

CAMDEN STATE PARK CCC/WPA/RUSTIC STYLE
HISTORIC DISTRICT (4/19/91)
Minn. Hwy. 23 (Camden State Park),
Lynd and Lyons Twps.
National Park Service landscape design and split-stone
park buildings/structures developed by CCC and WPA
workers in 1934–38.

FIRST NATIONAL BANK (3/15/82)
101 3rd St., Tracy
Romanesque Revival bank of Sioux quartzite from
Jasper Stone Company quarry, built in 1897.

WILLIAM F. GIESKE HOUSE (3/15/82)
601 W. Lyon, Marshall
Large Stick Style residence (ca. 1900–05) of developer
and president of Marshall Milling Company.

KIEL AND MORGAN HOTEL (3/15/82)
off Co. Hwy. 5, Lynd Twp. (Lynd)
Frame hotel built ca. 1871; served as first county courthouse in newly organized county.

MASONIC TEMPLE (3/15/82)
325 W. Main, Marshall
Egyptian Revival brick lodge hall designed by F. H.
Ellerbe and built in 1917.

MARTIN NORSETH HOUSE (3/15/82)
86 E. Main, Cottonwood
Georgian-style frame residence (ca. 1898) of townsite
developer, lumber company executive, and Cottonwood mayor.

O. G. ANDERSON AND CO. STORE (3/15/82)
Jefferson St., Minneota
Commercial Queen Anne brick mercantile store with
second-story opera house designed by Henry G. Gerlach
and built in 1901.

ST. PAUL'S EVANGELICAL LUTHERAN CHURCH (3/15/82)
412-414 E. Lyon St., Minneota
Gothic frame church with three-story bell tower (1895)
and parsonage (1891) built by members of Icelandic
immigrant community.

MAHNOMEN COUNTY

MAHONMEN CITY HALL (12/22/88)
104 W. Madison Ave., Mahnomen
Multipurpose municipal building with fire-bell tower

designed by George H. Carter and built in 1937 of fieldstone hand-cut by WPA workers.

Mahnomen City Hall

MAHNOMEN COUNTY COURTHOUSE (2/16/84)
311 N. Main St., Mahnomen
Classical Revival brick courthouse designed by Kinney
and Halden and built in 1909 for new county within
boundaries of White Earth Indian Reservation.

MAHNOMEN COUNTY FAIRGROUNDS
HISTORIC DISTRICT (3/2/89)
off Minn. Hwy. 200, Pembina Twp.
Buildings/structures, some of hand-cut fieldstone, designed by George H. Carter, built in 1936 by WPA
workers to house annual agricultural fair.

MARSHALL COUNTY

K. J. TARALSETH COMPANY (9/6/2002)
427 N. Main St., Warren
Brick commercial building built in 1911 to house community's major vendor, a family-owned department
store; second-floor Masonic lodge.

LARSON MILL (6/4/73)
Co. Hwy. 39 (Old Mill State Park), Foldahl Twp.
Steam-powered frame grist mill built in 1889 by John
Larson on family farm, moved in 1897 and restored
with original machinery in 1950s.

OLD MILL STATE PARK WPA/RUSTIC STYLE
HISTORIC RESOURCES (10/25/89)
off Co. Hwy. 39 (Old Mill State Park), Foldahl Twp.
Buildings/structures of split-stone construction, including one of only two suspension bridges in state park
system, built in 1937–41 by WPA workers.

K. J. Taralseth Company

MARTIN COUNTY

ORVILLE P. AND SARAH CHUBB HOUSE (5/18/95)
209 Lake Ave., Fairmont
Greek Revival residence of brick from town's first brick-
yard, built in 1867 for an Old-Stock American townsite
developer/Fairmont's first physician and his wife.

FAIRMONT OPERA HOUSE (7/2/80)
Downtown Plaza and Blue Earth Ave., Fairmont
Classical Revival brick performing arts center with Mankato stone trim designed by C. A. Dunham, built in 1901.

FIRST CHURCH OF CHRIST SCIENTIST (5/19/88)
222 Blue Earth Ave. E., Fairmont
Richardsonian Romanesque church of Sioux quartzite with limestone trim
designed by Harry Wild
Jones, built in 1898 for
early Christian Science
congregation.

FOX LAKE SITE (4/8/94)
Fox Lake Twp.
Habitation site with
pottery remains defin-
ing Precontact cultures,
500 B.C.–A.D. 1650.

Fairmont Opera House, 1928

MARTIN COUNTY COURTHOUSE (9/22/77)
201 Lake Ave., Fairmont
Renaissance/Baroque stone courthouse with domed
tower designed by Charles E. Bell, built in 1906–07;
interior murals by local artist F. Rorbeck.

SHERBURN COMMERCIAL HISTORIC DISTRICT (8/3/87)
Main St. N. between Front and 2nd Sts., Sherburn
Victorian commercial buildings, largely two-story with
decorative brickwork, built between 1898 and ca. 1908
in railroad town's trade and service center.

GEORGE WOHLHETER HOUSE (6/20/75)
320 Woodland Ave., Fairmont
Ornate Queen Anne/Classical Revival frame mansion
built in 1899 by prominent grain merchant and civic
leader.

MCLEOD COUNTY

MERTON S. GOODNOW HOUSE (8/15/85)
446 S. Main St., Hutchinson
Prairie School brick-and-stucco residence designed by
William G. Purcell of Purcell, Feick, and Elmslie, built
in 1913.

HUTCHINSON CARNEGIE LIBRARY (12/12/77)
Main St., Hutchinson
Classical Revival, brick-and-limestone building designed
by Edward S. Stebbins and built in 1904.

MCLEOD COUNTY COURTHOUSE (8/23/84)
830 11th St. E., Glencoe
Beaux Arts brick-and-
stone courthouse de-
signed by Frank W.
Kinney and built in
1909 in front of 1876
brick courthouse de-
signed by Bisbee and
Bardwell.

Winsted City Hall

WINSTED CITY HALL
(8/19/82)
181 1st St. N., Winsted
Queen Anne brick municipal building with bell tower,
constructed in 1895 to house city government, fire department, and second-floor social hall.

MEEKER COUNTY

HENRY AMES HOUSE (8/9/84)
Minn. Hwy. 24, Darwin Twp.
Residence built in 1888–89 of cream-colored Litchfield
brick from contractor Ames's on-site Litchfield Brickyard.

BRIDGE NO. 5388 (6/26/98)
Minn. Hwy. 24 over north fork of Crow River, Forest City Twp.
Steel Warren pony truss bridge with curved top chord,
built in 1935; longest span of its type in Minnesota.

BRIDGE NO. 90980 (1/25/97)
Co. Rd. 190 over north fork of Crow River, Kingston Twp.
Early Minnesota example of steel Pratt through truss,
built in 1899 by Hewett Bridge Company of Minneapolis.

Bridge No. 90980

BRIGHTWOOD BEACH COTTAGE (5/22/78)
S. Ripley Dr., Litchfield Twp.
Octagonal board-and-batten cottage with conical roof,
built in 1889 as part of resort complex designed by
G. B. Phelps.

DISTRICT NO. 48 SCHOOL (1/25/97)
off Co. Hwy. 8, Collinwood Twp.
One-room frame rural schoolhouse with belfry built
shortly after Collinwood Village was platted in 1870.

GRAND ARMY OF THE REPUBLIC HALL (5/21/75)
370 N. Marshall St., Litchfield
Medieval fortress–like meeting hall built of Litchfield
brick in 1885 as memorial to local Civil War veterans.

LITCHFIELD COMMERCIAL HISTORIC DISTRICT (3/1/96)
N. Sibley Ave. between Depot and 3rd Sts., Litchfield
Late-19th- and early-20th-century commercial buildings, many of Litchfield brick, constituting main business district of agricultural trade center.

LITCHFIELD OPERA HOUSE (10/4/84)
126 N. Marshall Ave., Litchfield
Renaissance Revival polychrome brick meeting/performance hall, with terra cotta and cut-stone trim, designed by W. T. Towner and completed in 1900.

TRINITY EPISCOPAL CHURCH (6/20/75)
400 N. Sibley Ave., Litchfield
Gothic-style board-and-batten church built in 1871.

UNIVERSAL LABORATORIES BUILDING (3/1/96)
901 1st St. N., Dassel
Processing plant built in 1937 by company that became major U.S. supplier of ergot, a fungus used by pharmaceutical firms to manufacture medicines.

MILLE LACS COUNTY

BRIDGE NO. 3355 (6/29/98)
U.S. Hwy. 169 over Whitefish Creek, Kathio Twp.
Concrete-slab roadway (1921) expanded by National Park Service in 1939 with ornamental, rock-faced granite stonework by CCC workers.

COOPER SITE (9/22/70)
Mille Lacs-Kathio State Park, Kathio Twp.
(also in Kathio Historic District)
Precontact habitation site and mound group and Contact Period village site of Mdewakanton Dakota Indians.

ROBERT C. DUNN HOUSE (8/29/85)
708 S. 4th St., Princeton

Robert C. Dunn House

Colonial Revival brick residence (1902) designed by Louis Lockwood for newspaper publisher active in state/local government and Good Roads Movement.

EPHRIAM C. GILE HOUSE (8/29/85)
311 8th Ave. S., Princeton
Gothic Revival house of brick from town's first brick-yard, with scrollwork and other pattern-book ornamen-tation, built ca. 1872 for physician Gile.

GREAT NORTHERN DEPOT (11/23/77)
101 S. 10th Ave., Princeton
Queen Anne/Jacobean passenger/freight depot of local brick with sandstone trim, built in 1902 to handle ship-ment of bricks and agricultural commodities.

KATHIO HISTORIC DISTRICT (10/15/66)
(National Historic Landmark, 7/19/64)
Mille Lacs-Kathio State Park, Kathio Twp.
Habitation sites and mound groups (3000 B.C.–A.D. 1750) important to documenting Dakota Indian culture and early Dakota-Ojibwe relationships.

MILACA CITY HALL (9/11/85)
145 Central Ave. S., Milaca
Fieldstone municipal hall designed by Louis Pinault

and built in 1936 by WPA workers; interior murals by
Andre Boratko.

MILLE LACS COUNTY COURTHOUSE (3/25/77)
635 2nd St. N.E., Milaca
Renaissance Revival/Classical Revival courthouse of Bedford stone designed by Croft and Boerner and built in
1923 using fireproof materials.

ONAMIA MUNICIPAL HALL (9/10/85)
Main and Birch Sts., Onamia
Arts and Crafts–inspired, multipurpose fieldstone hall
designed by Carl Buetow and built in 1935–36 by WPA
workers.

PETAGA POINT (9/22/70)
Mille Lacs-Kathio State Park, Kathio Twp.
(also in Kathio Historic District)
Earliest habitation site in Kathio Historic District, with
copper and stone tools dating to 3000–1000 B.C.

SAW MILL SITE (9/22/70)
Mille Lacs-Kathio State Park, Kathio Twp.
(also in Kathio Historic District)
Precontact village site spanning A.D. 400–1600.

VINELAND BAY SITE (9/22/70)
Mille Lacs-Kathio State Park, Kathio Twp.
(also in Kathio Historic District)
Precontact village site occupied ca. A.D. 800–1100.

MORRISON COUNTY

AYER MISSION SITE (6/18/73)
Belle Prairie Twp.
Site of farmhouse and mission school established in
1849 by Frederick and Elizabeth Ayer to serve Indian
children and other area families.

BELLE PRAIRIE VILLAGE SITE (8/14/73)
Belle Prairie Twp.
Precontact village site located at strategic spot along
Mississippi River.

BURTON-ROSENMEIER HOUSE (3/13/86)
606 1st St. S.E., Little Falls
Classical Revival frame residence (ca. 1900) owned successively by merchant Barney Burton and state senator/
attorney Christian Rosenmeier.

**C. A. LINDBERGH STATE PARK WPA/RUSTIC STYLE
HISTORIC RESOURCES** (10/25/89)
off Co. Hwy. 52 (C. A. Lindbergh State Park), Pike Creek Twp.
Log and stone buildings/structures constructed in
1938–39 by WPA workers on parkland donated in memory of U.S. Congressman Charles A. Lindbergh Sr. by his
family, including his son, Charles Jr., the famed aviator.

CHURCH OF OUR SAVIOR (EPISCOPAL) (7/17/80)
113 4th St. N.E., Little Falls
Second-generation Episcopal church (1903) with fieldstone foundation, mock half-timbering, and corner
tower, designed by John Lutcliff of Chicago.

CHURCH OF ST. JOSEPH (CATHOLIC) (9/5/85)
Main St., Pierz
Gothic Revival polychrome brick church built in
1886–88 to serve German Catholic community named
for missionary the Rev.
Francis Pierz.

CLOUGH TOWNSHIP HALL
(9/5/85)
Co. Rd. 206, Clough Twp.
Small Classical Revival rural
meeting hall clad in sheet
metal stamped to simulate
stone block, built in 1922
by A. O. Nelson and Son.

Church of St. Joseph, 1971

FORT DUQUESNE (11/15/84)

Green Prairie Twp.

Site of French wintering fort probably built ca. 1752 by Joseph Marin to control Mississippi headwaters trade and search for route to western sea.

FORT RIPLEY (9/10/71)

Minn. Hwy. 115, Camp Ripley Military Reservation

Minnesota's second military post, built in 1848–49 to keep peace among Dakota, Ojibwe, and Winnebago Indians.

Charles A. Lindbergh House

CHARLES A. LINDBERGH HOUSE (11/20/70)

(National Historic Landmark, 12/8/76)

Co. Hwy. 52 (C. A. Lindbergh State Park), Pike Creek Twp.

Frame summer house built in 1906–07 for U.S. Congressman Charles A. Lindbergh Sr.; occupied until 1920 by his son, Charles Jr., the famed aviator who in 1927 crossed the Atlantic Ocean in the *Spirit of St. Louis.*

LITTLE FALLS CARNEGIE LIBRARY (11/3/80)

108 3rd St. N.E., Little Falls

Craftsman-style brick-and-stone library designed by Fremont D. Orff and built in 1905.

LITTLE FALLS COMMERCIAL HISTORIC DISTRICT (7/22/94)
vicinity of 1st St. and Broadway, Little Falls
Commercial buildings (1887–1936), largely of local brick with granite trim, reflecting city's rise as lumbering, agricultural, and tourism center.

MORRISON COUNTY COURTHOUSE (12/5/78)
107 2nd St. S.E., Little Falls
Richardsonian Romanesque courthouse with clock tower designed by C. A. Dunham, built in 1890–91 of local cream-colored brick and gray granite.

NORTHERN PACIFIC DEPOT (9/5/85)
200 1st St. N.W., Little Falls
One of architect Cass Gilbert's last Minnesota works, a Shingle Style, one-story passenger depot built in 1899–1900 to serve major rail stop.

PELKEY LAKE SITE (10/2/73)
Belle Prairie Twp.
Precontact mound group dating from 5000 B.C. to A.D. 1700.

PINE TREE LUMBER COMPANY OFFICE (9/5/85)
735 1st St. N.E., Little Falls
Brick commercial building (1891), headquarters for region's major industry, founded by lumber magnate Frederick Weyerhaeuser.

RICE LAKE PREHISTORIC DISTRICT (10/2/73)
Little Falls Twp.
Indian habitation and mound groups dating from 1000 B.C. to A.D. 1700.

STANCHFIELD LOGGING CAMP (2/12/99)
Camp Ripley Military Reservation
Site of camp established by pioneering commercial logger David Stanchfield in winter of 1847–48 to harvest pine from Ojibwe-owned lands.

SWAN RIVER VILLAGE SITE (10/2/73)

Little Falls Twp.

Ojibwe village site on Mississippi River, occupied as late as 1836 when observed by French explorer Joseph N. Nicollet.

WILLIAM WARREN TWO RIVERS HOUSE SITE
AND PETER MCDOUGALL FARMSTEAD (12/4/74)

Co. Rd. 23, Bellevue Twp.

Site of ca. 1847 trading post of Warren, who authored first published history of Ojibwe Indians; 19th-century farmstead with English-style barn (1874).

CHARLES A. WEYERHAEUSER AND
RICHARD D. MUSSER HOUSES (9/5/85)

Highland Ave., Little Falls

Adjoining Shingle Style houses built in 1898 (expanded 1910–30) for second generation of families that ran area's lumbering operations.

ALMOND A. WHITE HOUSE (3/13/86)

Cleveland and Beaulieu Sts., Motley

Queen Anne frame house with four-story octagonal tower; built in 1902 for lumberman.

ZEBULON PIKE'S 1805–06 WINTERING HEADQUARTERS (7/11/88)

Swan River Twp.

Site of fortified winter camp built by a U.S. Army expeditionary force under Lieutenant Zebulon Pike, sent to survey northern reaches of the Louisiana Purchase.

Archaeological fieldwork, Zebulon Pike's Headquarters, 1985

MOWER COUNTY

COOK-HORMEL HOUSE (8/19/82)
208 4th Ave. N.W., Austin
Italianate brick house built in
1871 by Austin mayor John
Cook; altered in 1902 as stuc-
coed Classical Revival house by
meat-packer George Hormel.

Cook-Hormel House, ca. 1959

EXCHANGE STATE BANK (6/10/75)
Main and 1st Sts., Grand Meadow
Prairie School brick bank built in 1910; first major joint
project of William G. Purcell (building design) and
George G. Elmslie (ornamentation).

FIRST NATIONAL BANK OF ADAMS (3/20/86)
322 Main St., Adams
Prairie School brick bank by Purcell and Elmslie (1924)
that doubled as village council chambers; interior
mural by John Warner Norton of Chicago.

FIRST STATE BANK OF LE ROY (3/20/86)
Main St. and Broadway, Le Roy
Prairie School brick bank (1914) designed by Purcell
and Elmslie; due to budget constraints, the smallest
and most severe of their small-town banks.

FREUND STORE (4/24/86)
Co. Hwy. 7, Adams Twp.
Frame store, multipurpose hall, and house built in 1895
by Peter and Christina Freund; served as community's
social and commercial hub.

GRAND ARMY OF THE REPUBLIC HALL (6/13/86)
S. Main St. between 1st and 2nd Sts., Grand Meadow
Small frame meeting hall built in 1891 by fraternal
organization of Civil War veterans.

GRAND MEADOW QUARRY ARCHAEOLOGICAL DISTRICT (4/8/94)

Grand Meadow Twp.

Scattered pits where chert was quarried for stone tools ca. 8000 B.C.–A.D. 1600.

LE ROY PUBLIC LIBRARY (3/20/86)

Luella St. and Broadway, Le Roy

Classical Revival brick library with limestone trim, built in 1915 through volunteer efforts of the Ladies Book Club, a community organization.

Paramount Theater

PARAMOUNT THEATER (10/23/86)

125 4th Ave. N.E., Austin

Spanish Colonial Revival movie theater with "atmospheric" auditorium resembling a Spanish village, designed by Ellerbe and Company, built in 1929.

ARTHUR W. WRIGHT HOUSE (3/20/86)

300 4th Ave. N.W., Austin

Italianate frame residence (ca. 1866–74) owned by prominent businessman Wright; remodeled ca. 1905 with Classical Revival porch.

MURRAY COUNTY

AVOCA SCHOOL (10/16/79)
Cole Ave. and 2nd St., Avoca
Town's first public school, a two-story, four-room brick school with bell tower built in 1894.

CHICAGO MILWAUKEE ST. PAUL AND PACIFIC DEPOT (10/16/79)
St. Paul and Front Sts., Fulda
Frame passenger/freight depot with Stick Style second story for agent's quarters, built ca. 1901.

CHICAGO ST. PAUL MINNEAPOLIS AND OMAHA TURNTABLE (12/12/77)
Co. Hwy. 38, Currie
Manually operated, wood-and-steel turntable built in 1901 by American Bridge Company of Chicago to turn locomotives at western end of branch line.

DINEHART-HOLT HOUSE (12/7/82)
2812 Linden Ave., Slayton
Queen Anne/Stick Style frame house designed by Frank Thayer and built in 1891 for banker

Kitchen shelter, Lake Shetek State Park, Historic District

and Slayton mayor Christopher Dinehart.

FIRST NATIONAL BANK (12/7/82)
115 N. St. Paul Ave., Fulda
Beaux Arts bank building of brick with terra cotta ornamentation, built in 1918–19 by Lytle Company of Sioux City, Iowa.

LAKE SHETEK STATE PARK WPA/RUSTIC STYLE
GROUP CAMP (7/2/92)
off Co. Hwy. 37 (Lake Shetek State Park),
Murray and Shetek Twps.
Board-and-batten recreation building and mess hall with
split-stone fireplaces, built for public use in 1940–41 by
WPA workers.

LAKE SHETEK STATE PARK WPA/RUSTIC STYLE
HISTORIC DISTRICT (7/2/92)
off Co. Hwy. 37 (Lake Shetek State Park),
Murray and Shetek Twps.
Buildings/structures, mostly of split-stone construction,
and island causeway, all built in 1938–41 by WPA
workers in park with extensively designed landscape.

NICOLLET COUNTY

ALEXANDER HARKIN STORE (6/4/73)
Co. Hwy. 21, West Newton Twp.
Rural store and post office built by Harkin in 1871 to
serve as commercial and social center of West Newton,
then a promising river town.

BRIDGE NO. 6422 (8/5/99)
Minn. Hwy. 99 over Washington Ave., St. Peter
Minnesota's first cantilevered concrete deck-girder
bridge, begun in 1942 and completed in 1948 after
wartime steel shortage ended.

BROADWAY BRIDGE (8/5/99)
Minn. Hwy. 99 over Minnesota River, St. Peter
(also in Le Sueur County)
Two-span metal through truss bridge (1931) with ornamentation designed to enhance skewed configuration
necessitated by river current.

CENTER BUILDING, MINNESOTA
HOSPITAL FOR THE INSANE (7/31/86)
Freeman Dr., St. Peter
Classical Revival main building of state's first mental
hospital, designed on Kirkbride plan by Samuel Sloan
of Philadelphia, built in 1867–78.

CHURCH OF THE HOLY
COMMUNION (EPISCOPAL) (5/19/83)
116 N. Minnesota Ave., St. Peter
Gothic Revival church of Kasota stone designed by
Henry Congdon of New York, built in 1869–70 for early
Episcopal congregation.

EUGENE ST. JULIEN COX HOUSE (11/20/70)
500 N. Washington Ave., St. Peter
Elaborate Early Gothic Revival, board-and-batten residence built in 1871 for St. Peter's first mayor.

FREDERICK A. DONAHOWER HOUSE (5/19/83)
720 S. Minnesota Ave., St. Peter
Italianate brick residence with limestone trim built ca.
1875 for prominent banker and civic leader.

FORT RIDGELY HISTORIC DISTRICT (12/2/70)
Minn. Hwy. 4 (Fort Ridgely State Park), Ridgely Twp.
Minnesota's third military post, established in 1853 to
watch over lands ceded by Dakota Indians; battle site
during the Dakota War of 1862.

FORT RIDGELY STATE PARK CCC/RUSTIC STYLE
HISTORIC RESOURCES (10/25/89)
off Co. Hwy. 30 (Fort Ridgely State Park), Ridgely Twp.
Group of 26 buildings and structures of Morton rainbow granite built in 1934–39 by CCC workers, who also
reconstructed Fort Ridgely's 1853 stone Commissary.

JOHN A. JOHNSON HOUSE (5/19/83)
418 N. 3rd St., St. Peter

John A. Johnson House

Frame residence of state's 15th governor, first native-born Minnesotan elected to the office; built in 1905 at beginning of first of his three terms.

SARAH AND THOMAS MONTGOMERY HOUSE (12/13/2000)
408 S. Washington Ave., St. Peter
Italianate brick residence built in 1874 for a prominent attorney and his wife.

NICOLLET COUNTY BANK (5/19/83)
224 S. Minnesota Ave., St. Peter
(also in St. Peter Commercial Historic District)
Queen Anne brick commercial building with Kasota limestone trim and corner oriel, built in 1886–87 to house town's second bank.

NICOLLET COUNTY COURTHOUSE AND JAIL (9/6/2002)
501 S. Minnesota Ave., St. Peter
Romanesque Revival brick courthouse (1880–81) designed by Edward P. Bassford; adjacent Queen Anne brick jail (1906–07) by Andrew J. Van Deusen.

NICOLLET HOTEL (5/12/75)
Minnesota Ave. and Park Row, St. Peter
(also in St. Peter Commercial Historic District)
Italianate brick hotel designed by Edward P. Bassford, built in 1873–74 with funds raised by enterprising citizens' group.

NORSELAND STORE (5/19/83)
Co. Hwy. 3, Lake Prairie Twp. (Norseland)
Frame general store with appendages, built ca. 1900 at rural crossroads to serve surrounding farming communities.

NORTH MANKATO SCHOOL (1/27/83)
442 Belgrade Ave., North Mankato
Queen Anne two-story, four-room school with bell tower, built in 1890 of local brick; 1904 addition designed by George Pass.

OLD MAIN, GUSTAVUS ADOLPHUS COLLEGE (5/12/76)
off College Ave., St. Peter
Italianate building of locally quarried Kasota stone blocks, designed by Edward P. Bassford and built in 1875–76 as focal point of campus.

Emily and Stephen Schumacher House

ST. PETER ARMORY (1/9/97)
419 S. Minnesota Ave., St. Peter
First state-owned National Guard armory in Minnesota (1912–13), a Gothic Revival brick building with Kasota limestone trim, designed by James Denson.

ST. PETER CARNEGIE LIBRARY (5/19/83)
429 S. Minnesota Ave., St. Peter
Classical Revival, brick-and-stone library designed by
Ralph D. Church and built in 1903–04 to house long-
established library.

ST. PETER COMMERCIAL HISTORIC DISTRICT (1/12/2001)
Minnesota Ave. between Broadway and Grace Sts., St. Peter
Late-19th- and early-20th-century commercial buildings,
largely brick with stone trim, constituting city's retail/
service/banking center.

EMILY AND STEPHEN SCHUMACHER HOUSE (12/13/2000)
202 3rd Street N., St. Peter
Elaborate Queen Anne brick residence designed by
Henry C. Gerlach, built in 1887–88 for dry-goods store
owner and his wife.

WILLIAM E. STEWART HOUSE (11/8/84)
733 Range St., North Mankato
House, barn, and carriage house of brick from adjacent
brickyard, designed by Henry C. Gerlach, built in 1910
for Mankato Brick and Tile Company founder.

HENRY A. SWIFT HOUSE (5/19/83)
820 S. Minnesota Ave., St. Peter
Federal/Italianate residence (built in 1857–58) of one of
St. Peter's founders and Minnesota's third governor.

TRAVERSE DES SIOUX (3/20/73)
U.S. Hwy. 169, Traverse Twp.
Site of 1851 treaty negotiations and signing by which
Dakota Indians ceded 24 million acres of land to the
U.S. government.

UNION PRESBYTERIAN CHURCH (5/19/83)
311 W. Locust St., St. Peter
Gothic Revival church of locally quarried Kasota stone
designed by A. M. Radcliff and built in 1871–72.

NOBLES COUNTY

ADRIAN STATE BANK (5/15/80)
Main St. and 2nd Ave., Adrian
Brick commercial block with corner tower and false-front
pediments, built in 1891 by Melius brothers, influential
land agents and developers.

CHURCH OF ST. ADRIAN (CATHOLIC) (5/15/80)
Main and Church Sts., Adrian
Romanesque Revival brick church built in 1900 for
congregation that had served as center of Bishop John
Ireland's Catholic colonization effort in Nobles County.

CHURCH OF ST. KILIAN (CATHOLIC) (3/31/98)
off Co. Hwy. 18, Wilmont Twp.
Late Gothic Revival frame church constructed in 1900
for German Catholic immigrant community.

CITIZENS NATIONAL BANK (3/18/82)
326 10th St., Worthington
Second-generation, brick-and-stone commercial block
designed by Henry C. Gerlach, built in 1901 to house
bank founded by local business leaders.

HOTEL THOMPSON (2/16/84)
300-310 10th St., Worthington
Georgian Revival brick hotel designed by W. E. E.
Greene, built in 1911–12 by entrepreneur and civic
leader Peter Thompson.

KILBRIDE CLINIC (11/23/77)
701 11th St., Worthington
Small frame hospital and clinic founded in 1927 by
general practitioner and coroner Dr. E. A. Kilbride.

SIEMER SILO AND BARN (5/15/80)
Co. Hwy. 19, Grand Prairie Twp.
Traditional gambrel-roofed, wood-frame barn (1918)

and rare late example of wood-hoop silo (1936).

SIOUX CITY AND ST. PAUL SECTION HOUSE (5/15/80)
Spencer and 1st Sts., Dundee
First dwelling constructed in Dundee, a two-story clapboard cottage built by railroad in 1879 to house depot employees.

Church of St. Kilian

SLADE HOTEL (6/30/75)
2nd Ave. and Main St., Adrian
Commercial Queen Anne brick hotel built in 1891, with attached frame building used as salesmen's sample room.

NORMAN COUNTY

ADA CONGREGATIONAL CHURCH (11/8/84)
E. 2nd Ave. N. and 1st St. E., Ada
Craftsman-style church of cream-colored Ada brick with Queen Anne belfry, designed by Ohio architect Charles Waterbury, built in 1900.

ADA VILLAGE HALL (2/26/98)
404 W. Main St., Ada
Combined city hall and fire hall designed by Omeyer and Thori in Classical Revival style, built of Ada brick in 1904.

CANNING SITE (6/19/86)
Hendrum Twp.
Winter bison-processing campsite used by Indians and dating to ca. 1500 B.C.

Norman County Courthouse

NORMAN COUNTY COURTHOUSE (5/9/83)
16 E. 3rd Ave., Ada
Romanesque Revival red brick courthouse with clock tower designed by Omeyer and Thori, built in 1904.

ZION LUTHERAN CHURCH (10/21/99)
off Co. Hwy. 3, Shelly Twp.
Victorian Gothic frame church built in 1883 as religious and cultural center for Norwegian Lutheran community.

OLMSTED COUNTY

AVALON HOTEL (3/19/82)
301 N. Broadway, Rochester
Brick hotel designed by Ellerbe Architects, built in 1919 to serve Mayo Clinic patients; later, first hotel in city open to black clientele.

JOHN G. BUSH HOUSE (7/2/80)
Center St., Dover
Italianate brick residence built ca. 1877 for prosperous farmer-turned-merchant.

CHATEAU DODGE THEATRE (7/17/80)
15 1st St. S.W., Rochester
Exotic Revival-style "atmospheric" theater with sunburst
marquee designed by Ellerbe Architects, built in 1927 as
live-performance and movie house.

COAN HOUSE (7/2/80)
118 W. 5th St., Eyota
Brick house with elaborate Eastlake-style wood trim,
built ca. 1888 in small agricultural shipping center.

EYOTA COOPERATIVE CREAMERY (7/2/80)
222 Washington Ave. S., Eyota
Brick creamery designed by Harold H. Crawford, built
in 1924 by cooperative association to improve dairy
products and boost farmer income.

FRANK'S FORD BRIDGE (7/8/80)
Co. Rd. 121 over south branch of Zumbro River, Oronoco Twp.
Early metal through truss highway bridge, built in 1895 by
Horace E. Horton of Chicago Bridge and Iron Company.

CHRISTOPH KRAUSE FARMSTEAD (10/10/80)
Co. Hwy. 30, Dover Twp.
Well-preserved farmstead (Italianate brick farmhouse,
gambrel-roofed barn, and outbuildings) built in 1870s
by prosperous German immigrant farmer.

WILLIAM J. MAYO HOUSE (3/26/75)
*701 4th St. S.W., Rochester (also in Pill Hill Residential
Historic District)*
Tudor Revival residence of physician who, with brother
Charles H. Mayo, developed private medical-clinic con-
cept; designed by Ellerbe Architects and built in 1916–17.

MAYOWOOD HISTORIC DISTRICT (3/31/82)
3720 Mayowood Rd. S.W., Rochester
Estate of Dr. Charles H. Mayo, cofounder of Mayo Clinic,
and son Charles W. Mayo: main house (1910–11) with
lodge, farm, and greenhouse complexes (1908–20s).

1914 Building (center) and Plummer Building (right), Mayo Clinic, 1932

1914 BUILDING AND PLUMMER BUILDING, MAYO CLINIC
(8/11/69) (National Historic Landmark, 8/11/69)
102 and 110 2nd Ave. S.W., Rochester
Nation's first medical clinic for private group practice, a
research and diagnostic facility designed by Dr. Henry S.
Plummer with Ellerbe and Company.

ORONOCO SCHOOL (7/2/80)
Co. Hwy. 18, Oronoco
Italianate two-story brick school constructed in 1875
during flour milling community's boom years.

PIERCE HOUSE (7/21/80)
426 2nd Ave. S.W., Rochester
Italianate brick hotel constructed in 1877.

PILL HILL RESIDENTIAL HISTORIC DISTRICT (11/29/90)
*vicinity of 3rd and 9th Sts. and 7th and
10th Aves. S.W., Rochester*
Fashionable residential neighborhood developed in

early decades of 20th century largely for medical professionals at Mayo Clinic.

PLEASANT GROVE MASONIC LODGE (10/10/80)
off Co. Hwy. 1, Pleasant Grove Twp.
Oldest known Minnesota building in continuous use as Masonic lodge, built in 1868 as social center of community.

HENRY S. PLUMMER HOUSE (QUARRY HILL) (5/21/75)
1091 Plummer Lane, Rochester
English Tudor mansion and grounds designed in 1917–24 by Dr. Plummer, visionary clinician and diagnostician at Mayo Clinic.

ROCHESTER ARMORY (12/2/80)
121 N. Broadway, Rochester
Romanesque Revival brick Minnesota National Guard armory built in 1915.

ROCHESTER PUBLIC LIBRARY (7/2/80)
226 2nd St. S.W., Rochester
Jacobean-style, Kasota stone library designed by Harold H. Crawford, built in 1937 by PWA workers.

ST. MARY'S HOSPITAL DAIRY FARMSTEAD (7/2/80)
Co. Hwy. 104, Cascade Twp.
Clay-tile barns and milk house of dairy farm built by hospital in 1923 to supply pasteurized milk to patients.

GEORGE STOPPEL FARMSTEAD (5/12/75)
Co. Hwys. 25 and 122, Rochester
Immigrant farmstead with limestone house (ca. 1861), barn, and two-story shed/smokehouse with cupola.

TOOGOOD BARNS (6/26/75)
16th St. S.W., Rochester
Three stone livestock barns (ca. 1870) reflecting Old-Stock American heritage of farmer William F. Toogood.

VIOLA COOPERATIVE CREAMERY (11/12/99)
10500 Viola Rd. N.E., Viola Twp.
Brick creamery designed by Harold H. Crawford, built in 1924 as part of farmer-owned cooperative movement to improve dairy products and boost farm income.

MILO WHITE HOUSE (HAZELWOOD) (3/19/82)
122 Burr Oak St., Chatfield
Elaborate Queen Anne brick residence built in 1883–84 for U.S. Congressman White.

TIMOTHY A. WHITING HOUSE (12/4/80)
225 1st Ave. N.W. (Central Park), Rochester
Italianate frame house built in 1875 by Whiting, a prosperous grain merchant.

OTTER TAIL COUNTY

BARNARD MORTUARY (8/13/86)
119 N. Union Ave., Fergus Falls
Mission Revival funeral home designed by Walter R. Dennis, built in 1930 for business owner and civic leader Edward T. Barnard.

O. A. E. BLYBERG HOUSE (2/16/84)
22 5th Ave. S.W., Pelican Rapids
Italianate brick residence built in 1884 for land speculator Blyberg, town's first merchant and postmaster.

CHARLES C. CLEMENT HOUSE (8/13/86)
608 N. Burlington Ave., Fergus Falls
Stick Style frame house with Eastlake ornament attributed to Charles N. Daniels and built in 1882 for developer Clement.

DISTRICT NO. 182 SCHOOL (8/9/91)
off Co. Hwy. 35, Sverdrup Twp.

Moderne-style split-stone school designed by E. O. Broaten and built in 1939–40 by WPA workers.

ELIZABETH VILLAGE HALL AND JAIL (2/16/84)
Broadway Ave., Elizabeth
Multipurpose municipal building with ornamental brickwork (1898) that housed village government and fire hall; attached brick jail.

FERGUS FALLS CITY HALL (5/10/84)
112 W. Washington Ave., Fergus Falls
Independence Hall–inspired, Georgian Revival munici-pal building (1928) designed by William M. Ingemann to house city offices, fire department, and city garage.

Fergus Falls State Hospital Complex, ca. 1915

FERGUS FALLS STATE HOSPITAL COMPLEX (6/26/86)
Minn. Hwy. 297, Fergus Falls
Minnesota's only state institution retaining complete Kirkbride-plan hospital design, created by architect Warren B. Dunnell, built in 1888–1907.

HOTEL KADDATZ (2/24/83)
111-113 W. Lincoln Ave., Fergus Falls
City's first major hotel, a Renaissance Revival building
by George Hancock, built in 1914–15 by merchant
Charles Kaddatz to house U.S. District Court officials.

MAPLEWOOD SITE (12/18/78)
Maplewood Twp.
Precontact habitation site with two periods of occupation (A.D. 650–900 and 1450–1650) in forest/prairie
transitional zone.

JOHN W. MASON HOUSE (8/13/86)
205 W. Vernon Ave., Fergus Falls
Italianate frame house built ca. 1881 for city's first mayor.

MORRISON MOUNDS (6/4/73)
Everts Twp.
Mound group dating to middle Precontact Period
(ca. 500–200 B.C.).

ORWELL SITE (12/4/74)
Orwell Twp.
Mound group within earthen enclosure dating to late
Precontact Period.

OTTER TAIL COUNTY COURTHOUSE (5/10/84)
121 W. Junius Ave., Fergus Falls
Beaux Arts brick-and-limestone courthouse designed by
Buechner and Orth, built in 1921–22 to replace earlier
building.

PARK REGION LUTHER COLLEGE (11/8/84)
715 W. Vernon Ave., Fergus Falls
Romanesque brick-and-sandstone main building of
Norwegian Lutheran Synod college, designed by
Omeyer and Thori, built in 1901.

Perham Village Hall and Fire Station

PERHAM VILLAGE HALL AND FIRE STATION (7/31/86)
153 E. Main, Perham
Brick municipal building with corner tower designed by
Fremont D. Orff, built in 1906 to house village council,
fire station, jail, and social hall.

PHELPS MILL (2/24/75)
Co. Hwy. 45, Maine Twp. (also in Phelps Mill Historic District)
Four-story frame, waterpowered flour mill built in 1889
(expanded in 1895) to produce commercial-grade flour
and grind feed, buckwheat, and rye.

PHELPS MILL HISTORIC DISTRICT (5/10/84)
Co. Hwy. 45, Maine Twp.
Crossroads agricultural service center comprising waterpowered flour mill (1889), store (1891), and Italianate
frame miller's house (1902).

RIVER INN (12/20/88)
133 Mill St. S., Fergus Falls
Georgian/Gothic Revival hotel designed by Vernon A.
Wright and built in 1929 at behest of local commercial
club to improve accommodations for U.S. District Court.

CHARLES J. WRIGHT HOUSE (11/30/78)
831 Mount Faith Ave. E., Fergus Falls
Large frame house designed in Stick Style variant of
Gothic Revival by LeRoy S. Buffington and built in
1881–82 for developer Wright.

PENNINGTON COUNTY

**MINNEAPOLIS ST. PAUL AND
SAULT STE. MARIE DEPOT** (7/14/95)
Third St. and Atlantic Ave., Thief River Falls
Only remaining first-class, architect-designed Soo Line
depot in Minnesota, a Craftsman-style, brick-and-lime-
stone building (1913) by Kenyon and Maine.

RED RIVER TRAIL: GOOSE LAKE SWAMP SECTION (2/6/91)
off Co. Hwy. 10, Polk Centre Twp.
Portion of overland route used for commercial trade ca.
1844–71.

THIEF RIVER FALLS PUBLIC LIBRARY (10/6/83)
102 N. Main Ave., Thief River Falls
Renaissance Revival, brick-and-limestone, Carnegie-
funded library designed by Joseph C. Lutz, built in
1914–15 as center for educational activities.

Red River Trail: Goose Lake Swamp Section

PINE COUNTY

BETHLEHEM LUTHERAN CHURCH (8/18/80)
Kirke Alle, Askov
Gothic-style brick church built in 1914–15 to serve as religious and cultural center of Danish settlement.

BRIDGE NO. 1811 (8/28/98)
Co. Hwy. 33 over Kettle River, Kettle River Twp.
Minnesota's longest remaining steel Pratt through truss, built in 1915–16 as part of state highway commission's effort to standardize bridge design.

CLOVERTON SCHOOL (8/18/80)
Co. Rd. 32, New Dosey Twp.
Two-story, polychrome brick school with cast-stone ornamentation, designed by E. S. Broomhall and built in 1920 during town's boom years.

District No. 74 School

DISTRICT NO. 74 SCHOOL
(6/25/92)
Co. Hwy. 22, Danforth Twp.
Rural, one-room log school built in 1899, with 1909 frame addition; also served as township hall for largely Swedish immigrant community.

JOHN DOBOSZENSKI FARMSTEAD (8/18/80)
off Co. Hwy. 43, Norman Twp.
Rare surviving subsistence farm (log-and-frame house, log barns) on logged-over land, homesteaded in 1894 by a Polish-born Russian immigrant.

HINCKLEY FIRE RELIEF HOUSE (8/18/80)
Court Ave. and 6th St., Sandstone
Small frame house with lean-to, a type built by state commission to aid survivors of 1894 forest fire.

HINCKLEY STATE LINE MARKER (9/6/2002)
Minn. Hwy. 48, Omega Twp.
Rustic-style sandstone monument, a federal relief construction project erected in 1941–42 to welcome vehicles entering Minnesota from Wisconsin.

LOUIS HULTGREN HOUSE AND SAND PIT (8/18/80)
Minn. Hwy. 23, Kerrick
Log-and-frame house built ca. 1896 by Swedish immigrant who operated adjacent moulding sand pit, an early Pine County industry.

KETTLE RIVER BRIDGE (BRIDGE NO. 5718) (6/29/98)
Minn. Hwy. 123 over Kettle River, Sandstone
Steel deck truss designed in 1941 and completed in 1948 after wartime materials shortage.

KETTLE RIVER SANDSTONE COMPANY QUARRY (7/18/91)
off Minn. Hwy. 123, Sandstone
Site of state's most extensive sandstone quarry operation (1885–1919), which led to platting of town of Sandstone.

PETER P. KILSTOFTE FARMSTEAD (8/18/80)
6443 Hans Christian Andersen Alle, Askov
Dairy farm established in 1913 by prominent building contractor; notable for bungalow-style house and rubble work on barn and silo.

MINNEAPOLIS TRUST COMPANY BUILDING (8/18/80)
Main and 4th Sts., Sandstone
Commercial building of Kettle River sandstone constructed shortly after 1894 forest fire by development company that helped rebuild town.

NORTH WEST COMPANY POST (8/7/72)
Pokegama Twp.
Reconstructed winter trading post with log living quarters and surrounding stockade, built in 1804–05 by North West Company fur traders.

NORTHERN PACIFIC DEPOT (8/18/80)
Front St. at Finland Ave., Finlayson
Board-and-batten combination depot built in 1909
to serve growing agricultural trade center on logged-
over land.

NORTHERN PACIFIC DEPOT (5/7/73)
Old U.S. Hwy. 61 and 1st St. S.E., Hinckley
Frame depot built in 1895 from plans of original depot
lost in 1894 fire, featuring dining room and second-story
stationmaster's quarters.

JOHN A. OLDENBURG HOUSE (12/13/78)
Minn. Hwy. 18, Finlayson
French Second Empire frame residence built ca. 1896
by prominent merchant and developer; a community
gathering place.

PARTRIDGE TOWNSHIP HALL (8/18/80)
Kobmagergade, Askov
False-front frame public building built in 1901 to serve
township's political, social, educational, and religious
needs.

North West Company Post

RED CLOVER LAND COMPANY
DEMONSTRATION FARM (8/18/80)
off Co. Rd. 32, New Dosey Twp.
Small farm with house, barn, and machine shed developed as showplace by land speculators ca. 1915 to attract prospective settlers.

ST. CROIX RECREATIONAL DEMONSTRATION AREA
(1/31/97) (National Historic Landmark, 9/25/97)
off Minn. Hwy. 48 (St. Croix State Park), Crosby, Clover, Ogema, Munch, and Chengwatana Twps.
33,000-acre recreational area developed by the U.S. government (1934–43); master plan by National Park Service, rustic stone/log facilities built by CCC and WPA workers.

SANDSTONE SCHOOL (2/7/79)
Commercial Ave. between 5th and 6th Sts., Sandstone
Romanesque/Classical Revival public school (1901, enlarged in 1910), built of Kettle River sandstone by local craftsmen.

ARNOLD SCHWYZER SUMMER HOUSE
AND FARMSTEAD (8/18/80)
Co. Rd. 17, Dell Grove Twp.
Lakeside summer retreat developed in 1901–1920s for family of prominent St. Paul physician; dairying operation established in 1915.

Craft building, St. Croix Recreational Demonstration Area

STUMNE MOUNDS
(6/20/72)
Royalton Twp.
Linear and conical mound group with pottery fragments dating to ca. A.D. 600

WILLOW RIVER RUTABAGA WAREHOUSE AND PROCESSING PLANT (6/21/90)

off Co. Hwy. 61, Willow River

Only known Minnesota facility (built in 1935) designed for storing and processing rutabagas, an important cash crop for area farmers.

PIPESTONE COUNTY

BAUMAN HALL (3/3/80)

201 W. Wall St., Jasper

Commercial block of Sioux quartzite built as hotel in 1891 in nearby North Sioux Falls, S.D.; moved to Jasper in 1893 for use as community hall.

CALUMET HOTEL (3/16/76)

104 S. Hiawatha, Pipestone (also in Pipestone Commercial Historic District)

Richardsonian Romanesque hotel/bank building of local pink and red Sioux quartzite, constructed in 1888.

GERBER HOSPITAL (3/3/80)

120 E. Wall St., Jasper

Hospital building of locally quarried Sioux quartzite, built ca. 1913.

IHLEN MERCANTILE COMPANY (3/3/80)

Holman St. and Sherman Ave., Ihlen

Town's first business establishment, occupying adjoining frame buildings constructed in 1892.

PIPESTONE COMMERCIAL HISTORIC DISTRICT (5/2/77)

vicinity of Main St., 2nd Ave. N.W. and S.W., and 2nd Ave. N.E. and S.E., Pipestone

Concentration of Sioux quartzite buildings constructed primarily in 1890s by local tradesmen, with decorative stonework in contrasting colors.

PIPESTONE COUNTY COURTHOUSE (3/3/80)

416 S. Hiawatha Ave., Pipestone

Beaux Arts courthouse with tower (1900), built of locally quarried, rock-faced Sioux quartzite.

PIPESTONE INDIAN SCHOOL
SUPERINTENDENT'S RESIDENCE (4/5/93)

off N. Hiawatha Ave., Pipestone

House of Sioux quartzite built in 1907 on campus of U.S. government–run Indian boarding school, in operation 1892–1953.

Pipestone National Monument (Cannomoke), ca. 1893

PIPESTONE NATIONAL MONUMENT
(CANNOMOKE) (10/15/66)

off Hiawatha Ave., Pipestone

Site of quarries yielding red pipestone, or catlinite, used largely for ceremonial purposes by Indian peoples from late Precontact Period to present.

PIPESTONE PUBLIC LIBRARY (3/3/80)

S. Hiawatha Ave. and 3rd St. S.E., Pipestone

Gothic Revival/Richardsonian library of red and pink

Sioux quartzite, designed by Joseph Schwartz of Sioux Falls and built with Carnegie funds in 1904.

PIPESTONE WATER TOWER (3/3/80)
2nd St. N.E. and 6th Ave. S.E., Pipestone
Innovative concrete structure for municipal water storage based on design by engineer L. P. Wolff and built in 1920.

ROCK ISLAND DEPOT (3/3/80)
400 N. Hiawatha Ave., Pipestone
Brick passenger/freight depot with locally quarried Sioux quartzite trim, built ca. 1915.

JOHN ROWE HOUSE (3/3/80)
200 E. 2nd St., Jasper
Common bungalow type (built ca. 1905) expressed in uncommon material—locally quarried Sioux quartzite.

SPLIT ROCK BRIDGE (11/6/89)
Co. Rd. 54 over Split Rock Creek, Eden Twp.
Longest single-span, stone arch highway bridge in Minnesota, built in 1937–38 of locally quarried Sioux quartzite by WPA workers.

STORDAHL BUILDING (3/3/80)
119 W. Wall St., Jasper
Commercial building of locally quarried Sioux quartzite, built in 1894.

POLK COUNTY

CATHEDRAL OF THE IMMACULATE CONCEPTION (CATHOLIC) (10/1/98)
N. Ash St. at 2nd Ave., Crookston
Gothic Revival brick cathedral with triple spires, designed by Bert Keck and built in 1912–16 for newly established Diocese of Crookston.

Crookston Commercial Historic District, ca 1905

CHURCH OF ST. PETER (CATHOLIC) (8/19/82)
off U.S. Hwy. 2, Gentilly Twp.
Gothic Revival brick church, with central bell tower,
built in 1914–15 to serve French-Canadian Catholic
community; adjacent frame rectory (1902).

CROOKSTON CARNEGIE PUBLIC LIBRARY (5/10/84)
N. Ash St. and 2nd Ave., Crookston
Classical Revival, yellow-brick building with stone trim,
designed by Bert Keck and built in 1907–08.

CROOKSTON COMMERCIAL HISTORIC DISTRICT (11/23/84)
vicinity of Main, Fletcher, and
2nd Sts. and Broadway, Crookston
Late-19th- and early-20th-century commercial buildings,
largely brick with stone trim, constituting railroad
town's central business district.

ELLERY C. DAVIS HOUSE (5/10/84)
406 Grant St., Crookston
Italianate residence of yellow brick made on site, built
in 1879–80 for Crookston homesteader, railroad contractor, merchant, and first mayor.

HAMM BREWING COMPANY BEER DEPOT (9/20/84)
401 Demers Ave., East Grand Forks
Trackside brick refrigerated warehouse built in 1907 by
St. Paul–based brewery to serve its expanding market.

SORLIE MEMORIAL BRIDGE (7/19/99)
west end of Demers Ave., East Grand Forks
Metal Parker through truss bridge with abutments
adapted to clay banks of Red River, built in 1929 as
joint Minnesota–North Dakota project.

POPE COUNTY

ANN BICKLE HOUSE (3/28/97)
226 Minnesota Ave. E., Glenwood
Residence (built in 1913) of community organizer and
volunteer notable for contributions to health care and
World War II civilian defense efforts.

**FREMAD ASSOCIATION BUILDING/
POPE COUNTY STATE BANK** (4/1/82)
18-20 S. Franklin, Glenwood
Brick commercial building (1893) and Classical Revival
bank (1908) built by mercantile cooperative as town's
commercial hub.

GLENWOOD PUBLIC LIBRARY (4/1/82)
108 S.E. 1st Ave., Glenwood
Classical Revival, Carnegie-funded brick library designed
by A. H. Foss and built in 1908 as county's first public
library.

URJANS IVERSON HOUSE (2/11/82)
off Minn. Hwy. 104, Gilchrist Twp.
One-room log cabin built in 1866 by Norwegian settler;
from 1869 used as area's first schoolhouse and church.

LAKESIDE PAVILION (12/4/98)
S. Lakeshore Dr. and First Ave. S.W., Glenwood
Dance pavilion (built in 1909) that introduced popular music to area residents and growing lake-resort tourist trade.

MINNEWASKA HOSPITAL (4/1/82)
Wollan and 5th Sts., Starbuck
County's first medical facility, a 14-bed, Georgian Revival frame hospital built ca. 1900 for Dr. C. R. Christenson's expanding medical practice.

NORTHERN PACIFIC DEPOT (10/6/83)
off Washington Ave., Villard
Frame depot built in 1882 to serve shipping and supply needs of newly platted village named for railroad president Henry Villard.

Terrace Mill Historic District, 1904

DANIEL PENNIE HOUSE (4/1/82)
Co. Hwy. 27, Leven Twp.
Residence of grout construction scored to imitate stone, built ca. 1870s–80s by Scottish mason Pennie, an organizer of Pope County.

POPE COUNTY COURTHOUSE (4/1/82)
130 E. Minnesota Ave., Glenwood
Beaux Arts courthouse of buff-colored brick and limestone designed by Nairne Fisher and built in 1930 to replace earlier building.

SUNSET BEACH HOTEL (2/11/82)
Co. Hwy. 17, Glenwood Twp.
Early lake resort, a group of three Craftsman-style frame buildings (1915, 1927, 1930) built by Henry P. Peters family.

TERRACE HISTORIC DISTRICT (4/1/82)
off Minn. Hwy. 104, Chippewa Falls Twp.
Small rural community (residences, store, school/town hall, church, flour mill), established ca. 1870, that grew up around local milling operation.

TERRACE MILL HISTORIC DISTRICT (7/17/79)
off Minn. Hwy. 104, Chippewa Falls Twp.
(also in Terrace Historic District)
Rural milling complex: frame, waterpowered flour mill (1903); fieldstone miller's house (1930); mill dam (ca. 1882); and stone arch bridge (1903).

RAMSEY COUNTY

JOHN M. ARMSTRONG HOUSE (1/27/83)
225 Eagle Pkwy., St. Paul
Double brick house designed in Queen Anne style by Edward P. Bassford, built in 1886 as rental property.

ASSUMPTION SCHOOL (3/26/75)
68 W. Exchange St., St. Paul
Italian Villa–style limestone parochial school built in 1864 to serve German-speaking children of parishioners.

WARD BEEBE HOUSE (8/29/77)
2022 Summit Ave., St. Paul (also in
West Summit Avenue Historic District)
Prairie School stucco residence designed in 1912 by
Purcell, Feick, and Elmslie for veterinarian and presi-
dent of Beebe Laboratories.

BLAIR FLATS (7/18/75)
165 Western Ave., St. Paul (also in Historic Hill District)
Victorian sandstone-and-brick apartment house designed
in 1887 by Hermann Kretz and William H. Thomas,
converted to residential hotel in 1893.

BRIDGES NO. L-5853 AND 92247 (11/6/89)
Lexington Ave. in Como Park, St. Paul
Early reinforced-concrete, barrel-arch bridges (1904)
designed by William S. Hewett using patented Melan
system.

EDWARD SR. AND MARKELL BROOKS
HOUSE (EASTCLIFF) (6/15/2000)
176 N. Mississippi River Blvd., St. Paul
Colonial Revival main house (1921–22, expanded 1930),
bathhouse, and five-stall garage designed by firm of
Clarence H. Johnston Sr.; the urban estate of a prominent lumberman and his wife.

BENJAMIN BRUNSON HOUSE (5/12/75)
485 Kenny Rd., St. Paul
Federal-style brick residence built in 1855 for surveyor
of the city of St. Paul and an early civic leader.

CASIVILLE BULLARD HOUSE (1/9/97)
1282 Folsom St., St. Paul
Foursquare brick residence built in 1909–10 by Bullard,
one of few black masons then working in building trades.

BURBANK-LIVINGSTON-GRIGGS HOUSE (10/15/70)
432 Summit Ave., St. Paul (also in Historic Hill District)

Italian Villa–style limestone mansion built in 1862–63 for businessman and civic leader James Burbank, expanded in 1925 by Mary Livingston Griggs.

PIERCE AND WALTER BUTLER HOUSE (4/22/82)

1345-1347 Summit Ave., St. Paul
(also in West Summit Avenue Historic District)
Double house designed in 1900 by Clarence H. Johnston Sr. for brothers Pierce, a U.S. Supreme Court justice, and Walter, head of family's construction firm.

CENTRAL PRESBYTERIAN CHURCH (2/10/83)

500 Cedar St., St. Paul
Richardsonian Romanesque brownstone-and-brick church with asymmetrical façade, designed by prominent church architect Warren H. Hayes, built in 1888–1900.

Central Presbyterian Church, ca. 1915

CHURCH OF ST. AGNES (CATHOLIC)
(11/19/80)
548-550 Lafond Ave.,
St. Paul
Baroque Revival stone church with onion dome designed by George Ries, built in 1901–12 for German-speaking Austro-Hungarian immigrant congregation.

CHURCH OF ST. BERNARD (CATHOLIC) (2/24/83)

197 W. Geranium Ave., St. Paul
Early reinforced-concrete, brick-and-stone-clad church designed by John Jager in mix of Prairie School and Art Nouveau styles, built in 1905–14.

CHURCH OF ST. CASIMIR (CATHOLIC) (3/31/83)
937 E. Jessamine Ave., St. Paul
Beaux Arts brick church with twin bell towers built in
1904 to serve Polish immigrant parish.

CHURCH OF THE ASSUMPTION (CATHOLIC) (2/10/75)
51 W. 9th St., St. Paul
Romanesque Revival limestone church with five-story
towers (1870–74), designed by German architect Joseph
Reidl based on Munich's Ludwigskirche.

CYRUS B. COBB HOUSE (4/14/83)
2199 1st St., White Bear Lake
Year-round residence (1885) built of brick in Queen
Anne style for prominent businessman in lakeside
resort community.

COLORADO STREET BRIDGE (7/5/90)
east side of S. Wabasha St. near Terrace Park, St. Paul
Skewed single-span, stone arch bridge designed by
engineer Andreas W. Munster, built in 1888 by O'Brien
Brothers.

COMO PARK CONSERVATORY (11/19/74)
Como Park, St. Paul
Horticultural facility of iron/steel truss construction
with ribbed glass domes, built in 1914–15 under direction of park superintendent Frederick Nussbaumer.

Como Park Conservatory, ca. 1950

CSPS HALL (2/17/77)
381-383 Michigan St., St. Paul
Brick commercial building built in 1887 by Czecho Slovak
Protective Society, a Czech fraternal organization, as a cultural center, shared by St. Paul Sokol gymnastics society.

DAIRY BUILDING, GRANARY/ROOT CELLAR, AND
AUXILIARY BUILDINGS, NORTH OAKS FARM (9/10/99)
Red Barn Rd. at Hill Farm Circle, North Oaks
Facilities remaining from railroad magnate James J.
Hill's experimental crop and livestock farm, developed
in 1884–90 to promote agricultural diversification.

WILLIAM DAVERN HOUSE (10/6/83)
1173 S. Davern St., St. Paul
Italianate frame farmhouse built ca. 1862 for early settler
and member of first territorial legislature.

DERHAM HALL AND OUR LADY OF VICTORY CHAPEL,
COLLEGE OF ST. CATHERINE (10/31/85)
2004 Randolph Ave., St. Paul
Oldest hall (1903–04) at state's first Catholic women's
college, designed by John Wheeler; 1923 Romanesque
Revival chapel by Herbert A. Sullwold.

FINCH, VAN SLYCK, AND MCCONVILLE
DRY GOODS COMPANY (2/1/82)
366 Wacouta St., St. Paul (also in Lowertown Historic District)
Classical Revival, reinforced-concrete-and-brick headquarters for pioneering wholesaler; 1911 portion by
James Denson, 1923 addition by Clarence H. Johnston Jr.

FIRST BAPTIST CHURCH (2/24/83)
499 Wacouta St., St. Paul
Gothic Revival Kasota stone church designed by William
W. Boyington of Chicago, built in 1874–75 for Minnesota's oldest Baptist congregation.

FIRST NATIONAL BANK OF WHITE BEAR (2/24/83)
4744 Washington Square, White Bear Lake
Classical Revival, brick-and-stone bank with red tile roof designed in 1921 by Clark E. Van Kirk for growing resort community.

F. SCOTT FITZGERALD HOUSE (11/11/71)
(National Historic Landmark, 11/11/71)
599 Summit Ave., St. Paul (also in Historic Hill District)
Brownstone row house (1889) where Fitzgerald lived in 1919–20 while writing his first published novel, *This Side of Paradise.*

FITZPATRICK BUILDING (7/19/90)
465-467 N. Wabasha St., St. Paul
Queen Anne brick commercial building with pressed metal bays and corner turret, built in 1890 in city's main retail/office district.

FOSS HOUSE (5/19/83)
321 Silver Lake Rd., New Brighton
Victorian brick house with tower, built ca. 1896 by early settlers Ingebor and Peder Foss in a then-rural area.

GERMANIA BANK BUILDING (12/6/77)
6 W. 5th St., St. Paul
Richardsonian Romanesque sandstone office tower designed by J. Walter Stevens, built in 1889 during downtown building boom.

HEMAN GIBBS FARMSTEAD (4/23/75)
2097 Larpenteur Ave., Falcon Heights
Farmstead settled in 1849, with 1854 frame farmhouse and 1910 barn.

GIESEN-HAUSER HOUSE (5/19/83)
827 Mound St., St. Paul
Queen Anne brick residence designed in 1891 by Albert

Zschocke for bookbinder/publisher Peter Giesen; later owned by contractor Eric Hauser.

S. EDWARD HALL HOUSE (4/16/91)
996 Iglehart Ave., St. Paul
Residence (1889) of black businessman and community activist in human, economic, and civil rights who helped organize St. Paul Urban League.

HAMM BUILDING (5/30/97)
408 St. Peter St., St. Paul
Steel-frame commercial building clad in ornate structural terra cotta tile, designed by Toltz, King, and Day and built in 1915–20.

HARRIET ISLAND PAVILION (7/10/92)
75 Water St., St. Paul
Moderne-style park building of Kasota stone built in 1941 by WPA workers; designed by Clarence W. Wigington, nation's first black municipal architect.

HIGHLAND PARK TOWER
(7/17/86)
1570 Highland Pkwy., St. Paul
Municipal water tower of brick and Kasota stone (1928) designed by Clarence W. Wigington.

Highland Park Tower, ca. 1940

JAMES J. HILL HOUSE (10/15/66)
(National Historic Landmark, 11/5/61)
240 Summit Ave., St. Paul (also in Historic Hill District)
Richardsonian Romanesque mansion with art gallery, designed for railroad magnate Hill by Peabody and Stearns of Boston, built in 1889–91.

James J. Hill House, Historic Hill District

JACOB HINKEL HOUSE (1/3/78)
531 Brainerd Ave., St. Paul
Italian Villa–style frame residence with cupola, built in
1872 as country home of wealthy businessman Hinkel.

HISTORIC HILL DISTRICT (8/13/76)
Summit Hill, St. Paul
Minnesota's largest concentration of late-19th- and
early-20th-century, architect-designed homes for upper-
and upper-middle-class residents.

ENGELBRECHT H. HOBE HOUSE (SOLHEIM) (5/19/83)
5590 W. Bald Eagle Blvd., White Bear Lake Twp.
Victorian frame mansion designed by Carl F. Struck,
built in 1897 for longtime Norwegian consul Hobe.

HOLMAN FIELD ADMINISTRATION BUILDING (8/15/91)
644 Bayfield St., St. Paul
Modern-style, WPA-funded, Kasota stone airport control
tower (1938–41) designed by Clarence W. Wigington,
nation's first black municipal architect.

INTERCITY BRIDGE (FORD BRIDGE) (11/6/89)
Ford Pkwy. over Mississippi River, St. Paul
(also in Hennepin County)
Monumental urban, reinforced-concrete, continuous-
arch bridge designed by engineer Martin S. Grytbak and
built in 1925–27.

HORACE IRVINE HOUSE
(GOVERNOR'S RESIDENCE) (12/16/74)
1006 Summit Ave., St. Paul (also in Historic Hill District)
English Tudor brick mansion designed by William
Channing Whitney and built in 1911 for lumberman
Irvine; donated to state in 1965.

IRVINE PARK HISTORIC DISTRICT (11/27/73)
vicinity of Ryan Ave. and Chestnut, Sherman,
and W. 7th Sts., St. Paul
Exclusive residential neighborhood platted by realtor
John R. Irvine in 1849 near Upper Levee steamboat
landing, with homes dating from 1849 to 1890.

FRANK B. KELLOGG HOUSE (11/6/74)
(National Historic Landmark, 12/8/76)
633 Fairmount Ave., St. Paul (also in Historic Hill District)
Home (built in 1889) of statesman, diplomat, and
Nobel Peace Prize winner who, as U.S. secretary of state
(1925–29), signed Kellogg-Briand Pact outlawing war.

KRANK MANUFACTURING COMPANY (2/24/83)
1855 W. University Ave., St. Paul
Brick cosmetics factory with elaborate terra cotta ornament designed by Toltz, King, and Day, built in 1926 in
expanding Midway industrial area.

LAUER FLATS (6/5/75)
226 S. Western Ave., St. Paul
Apartment block of Mankato stone with ornamental
ironwork, designed and built in 1887 by stone contractors Henry and Charles Lauer.

OLAF LEE HOUSE (2/16/84)
955 N. Jessie St., St. Paul
Residence combining Swiss chalet and Craftsman
elements designed by Clarence H. Johnston Sr. and
built in 1905.

LOWERTOWN HISTORIC DISTRICT (6/21/83)

vicinity of Kellogg Blvd. and Jackson,
7th, and Broadway Sts., St. Paul
Concentration of brick commercial buildings
(1880s–1920s), many designed by noted architects, in
city's warehousing, wholesaling, and transportation
center.

DAVID LUCKERT HOUSE (5/12/75)

480 Iglehart Ave., St. Paul
Residence of locally quarried limestone built in 1850
by stonemason Luckert along old St. Anthony Road, an
overland stage route.

MANHATTAN BUILDING (7/13/88)

360 N. Robert St., St. Paul
Renaissance Revival brick-and-stone banking/office
building designed by Clarence H. Johnston Sr., built in
1890–91 during downtown boom.

ANDREW R. MCGILL HOUSE (12/31/74)

2203 Scudder Ave., St. Paul
Towered Queen Anne frame mansion built in 1888 for
state governor McGill.

MENDOTA ROAD BRIDGE (11/6/89)

Water St. over Pickerel Lake Outlet, St. Paul
Small single-span, stone arch highway bridge with ornamental use of locally quarried limestone, built in 1894.

MERCHANTS NATIONAL BANK (12/19/74)

366-368 Jackson St., St. Paul
Richardsonian Romanesque sandstone commercial
building designed by Edward P. Bassford and built in
1892 near mercantile wholesaling district.

MICKEY'S DINER (2/24/83)

36 W. 9th St., St. Paul
Only known Minnesota example of railroad car–inspired,

Art Deco diner, fabricated in 1937 by Jerry O'Mahoney Company in New Jersey and installed in 1939.

MINNESOTA BOAT CLUB BOATHOUSE (2/4/82)
1 S. Wabasha St., St. Paul
Spanish Colonial Revival quarters (designed by H. G. Carsley, built in 1910) for state's oldest athletic organization, a rowing club founded in 1870.

MINNESOTA HISTORICAL SOCIETY (3/20/73)
690 Cedar St., St. Paul
Classical Revival headquarters (built in 1915–18) of a society established in 1849; designed by State Architect Clarence H. Johnston Sr. and constructed of Minnesota materials.*

Minnesota State Capitol, ca. 1925

MINNESOTA STATE CAPITOL (2/23/72)
75 Rev. Dr. Martin Luther King Jr. Blvd., St. Paul
State's third capitol building, a Beaux Arts, art-filled,

---

* This building became the Minnesota Judicial Center at 25 Rev. Dr. Martin Luther King Jr. Blvd. after the Minnesota Historical Society moved in 1992 to its new Minnesota History Center at 345 Kellogg Blvd. W., St. Paul.

domed marble edifice designed by Cass Gilbert and built in 1896–1905.

ADOLPH MUENCH HOUSE (THE MANOR) (5/12/75)
653 E. 5th St., St. Paul
Queen Anne frame residence (mid-1880s) of lumber company owner and influential publisher of German-language newspaper.

NORTHERN PACIFIC RAILWAY COMPANY
COMO SHOPS HISTORIC DISTRICT (3/31/83)
vicinity of Energy Park Dr. and Bandana Blvd., St. Paul
Group of brick-and-stone buildings (1885–1920) remaining from industrial complex where railroad passenger cars were built, serviced, and modernized.

NORWAY LUTHERAN CHURCH (MUSKEGO) (5/12/75)
2375 Como Ave. W. (Luther Northwestern Theological Seminary), St. Paul
Early Norwegian Lutheran church, a two-story log meeting house built in 1843 (moved to present site in 1904).

CHARLES P. NOYES COTTAGE (RED CHALET) (12/12/76)
303 Lake Ave., White Bear Lake
Stick Style lakeside summer cottage built in 1879, exemplifying picturesque ideals popularized in house pattern books in the 1860s–1870s.

Pilgrim Baptist Church and congregation, 1928

OLD MAIN, MACALESTER COLLEGE (8/16/77)

1600 Grand Ave., St. Paul
Richardsonian Romanesque brick-and-stone campus
center designed by William H. Willcox and built in
1884–88.

PILGRIM BAPTIST CHURCH (4/16/91)

732 W. Central Ave., St. Paul
Romanesque Revival brick church built in 1928 for
St. Paul's oldest black congregation (founded ca. 1863),
led by social activist and community organizer the Rev.
L. W. Harris.

Ramsey County Poor Farm Barn

PIONEER AND ENDICOTT BUILDINGS (7/10/74)

4th and Robert Sts., St. Paul
Romanesque office tower (1889) designed by Solon
Spencer Beman and Renaissance palazzo office building
(1890s) by Cass Gilbert, connected in 1940s.

RAMSEY COUNTY POOR FARM BARN (9/22/77)

2020 White Bear Ave., Maplewood
Brick livestock barn with silos and milk house (1918),
designed by Buechner and Orth for government-owned
farm worked by county's welfare recipients.

ALEXANDER RAMSEY HOUSE (11/25/69)
265 S. Exchange St., St. Paul
(also in Irvine Park Historic District)
French Second Empire limestone residence designed by
Monroe Sheire and built in 1868–72 for territorial/state
governor and celebrated statesman.

JUSTUS RAMSEY HOUSE (5/6/75)
252 W. 7th St., St. Paul
One-room cottage built ca. 1855–57 of locally quarried
limestone and owned by brother and business partner
of territorial governor Alexander Ramsey.

RAU-STRONG HOUSE (6/18/75)
2 E. George St., St. Paul
Victorian house and carriage barn of local yellow limestone built in 1884–86 by stonecutter Adam Rau.

ROBERT STREET BRIDGE (11/6/89)
Robert St. over Mississippi River, St. Paul
Moderne-style, reinforced-concrete, multiple-arch highway bridge with monumental central rainbow arch,
built in 1924–26.

ROCHAT-LOUISE-SAUERWEIN BLOCK (11/19/80)
261-277 W. 7th St., St. Paul
Adjoining brick commercial buildings (1884, 1885,
1895) combining street-level storefronts with upper-
story residences.

ST. AGATHA'S CONSERVATORY OF MUSIC AND ARTS (5/25/89)
26 E. Exchange St., St. Paul
Beaux Arts conservatory with chapel wing (1908–10),
designed by John Wheeler for city's oldest arts school,
founded in 1884 by the Sisters of St. Joseph.

ST. JOSEPH'S ACADEMY (6/5/75)
355 Marshall Ave., St. Paul
Italianate yellow limestone Catholic boarding school
complex built in 1863–88 by the Sisters of St. Joseph.

ST. MATTHEW'S SCHOOL (11/8/84)
7 W. Robie St., St. Paul
Victorian brick school with mansard roof designed by
John F. Fischer and built in 1901–02 to serve German
immigrant community.

ST. PAUL CARNEGIE LIBRARIES:
Arlington Hills Branch Library (2/10/84)
1105 Greenbrier St., St. Paul
Riverview Branch Library (2/10/84)
1 E. George St., St. Paul
St. Anthony Park Branch Library (2/10/84)
2245 W. Como Ave., St. Paul
Beaux Arts brick-and-stone libraries built in 1916–17,
the earliest public buildings designed by City Architect
Charles A. Hausler.

ST. PAUL CATHEDRAL (CATHOLIC) (6/28/74)
Summit Ave. at Selby Ave., St. Paul (also in Historic Hill District)
Beaux Arts cathedral of St. Cloud granite, designed by Emmanuel L. Masqueray, begun in 1906 and consecrated in 1953.

St. Paul Cathedral, ca. 1918

ST. PAUL CITY HALL–RAMSEY COUNTY COURTHOUSE (2/11/83)
15 W. Kellogg Blvd., St. Paul
Moderne-style, skyscraper-type limestone municipal
building (1930–32) designed by Holabird and Root of
Chicago with Ellerbe and Company of St. Paul.

ST. PAUL MINNEAPOLIS AND MANITOBA RAILWAY COMPANY SHOPS HISTORIC DISTRICT (12/21/87)

Jackson St. and Pennsylvania Ave., St. Paul

Limestone machine shop, pattern shop, and storehouse built in 1882 by James J. Hill for Minnesota's first successful railroad company.

ST. PAUL PUBLIC LIBRARY/JAMES J. HILL REFERENCE LIBRARY (9/11/75)

80-90 W. 4th St., St. Paul

Renaissance Revival marble building housing two libraries, one endowed by railroad magnate Hill; designed by Electus D. Litchfield and built in 1914–17.

ST. PAUL UNION DEPOT (12/18/74)

214 E. 4th St., St. Paul

Classical Revival stone passenger terminal/freight depot designed by Charles Frost and built in 1917–23 by seven railroads serving St. Paul.

ST. PAUL WOMEN'S CITY CLUB (3/19/82)

305 St. Peter St., St. Paul

Moderne-style headquarters for prominent social club designed by Magnus Jemne and built in 1931 of Mankato stone; interiors by artist Elsa Jemne.

SALVATION ARMY WOMEN'S HOME AND HOSPITAL (2/10/83)

1471 W. Como Ave., St. Paul

Tudor Revival facility designed by Clarence H. Johnston Sr. and built in 1912–13 as home for unwed mothers and their children.

CHARLES W. SCHNEIDER HOUSE (2/16/84)

1750 E. Ames Place, St. Paul

Shingle Style frame residence with corner tower built in 1890 for *St. Paul Pioneer Press* bookkeeper.

SCHORNSTEIN GROCERY AND SALOON (8/21/84)

707 E. Wilson Ave. and 223 N. Bates Ave., St. Paul

Italianate/French Second Empire brick commercial building with upper-story residence and meeting hall, designed by Augustus F. Gauger and built in 1884.

SEVENTH STREET IMPROVEMENT ARCHES (11/6/89)
E. 7th St. over Burlington Northern right-of-way, St. Paul
Skewed, helicoidal, double-arch highway bridge of Mankato limestone, a rare, technically demanding type, completed in 1884.

FREDERICK SPANGENBURG HOUSE (6/22/76)
375 Mt. Curve Blvd., St. Paul
Early limestone farmhouse built in 1864–67 by German dairy farmer.

TRIUNE MASONIC TEMPLE (11/13/80)
1898 Iglehart Ave., St. Paul
Classical Revival brick Masonic lodge building designed by H. C. Struchen and built in 1910–11, with interior features symbolic of order's rituals.

St. Paul Women's City Club

UNITED CHURCH SEMINARY (10/31/85)
2481 Como Ave, St. Paul
Beaux Arts, temple-front brick building designed by Omeyer and Thori and built in 1900–01 as focal point for Norwegian Lutheran seminary.

UNIVERSITY HALL (OLD MAIN), HAMLINE UNIVERSITY (9/22/77)
1536 Hewitt Ave., St. Paul
Victorian Gothic brick-and-stone campus center designed by Warren H. Hayes and built in 1883.

U.S. POST OFFICE, COURTHOUSE, AND CUSTOMS HOUSE (LANDMARK CENTER) (3/24/69)

75 W. 5th St., St. Paul

Chateauesque granite building with clock towers and ornate interiors designed by Willoughby J. Edbrooke and built in 1894–1902.

VIENNA AND EARL APARTMENT BUILDINGS (4/10/84)

682-688 Holly Ave., St. Paul

Classical Revival brick apartment houses designed by Louis Lockwood and built in 1907 for developer Carl P. Waldon.

WALSH BUILDING (5/25/89)

189-191 E. 7th St., St. Paul

Romanesque brick commercial/residential block with stone, cast-iron, and pressed metal trim, designed by Edward P. Bassford and built in 1888.

WEST SUMMIT AVENUE HISTORIC DISTRICT (5/4/93)

Summit Ave. between Lexington Pkwy. and Mississippi River Blvd., St. Paul

Stately avenue of architect-designed, Period Revival homes (1885–1938) anchored by three college campuses; continuation of Historic Hill District.

WOODLAND PARK HISTORIC DISTRICT (5/12/78)

vicinity of Dale and Arundel Sts. and Marshall and Dayton Aves., St. Paul

Upper-middle-class neighborhood of single- and multiple-family residences representing major architectural styles for period 1880–1910.

ANTHONY YOERG SR. HOUSE (5/29/89)

215 W. Isabel St., St. Paul

French Second Empire frame residence designed by Monroe Sheire and built in 1875 for prominent brewery owner.

RED LAKE COUNTY

CLEARWATER EVANGELICAL LUTHERAN CHURCH (11/18/99)
off Co. Hwy. 10, Equality Twp.
Gothic frame church (1912) with bell tower (1923) built by Norwegian-American immigrants as community's religious, cultural, and social center.

RED LAKE COUNTY COURTHOUSE (5/9/83)
124 Langevin, Red Lake Falls
Beaux Arts brick-and-stone municipal building with corner pavilions, designed by Fremont D. Orff and built in 1910.

Clearwater Evangelical Lutheran Church

REDWOOD COUNTY

J. A. ANDERSON HOUSE (8/11/80)
402 4th Ave. S., Lamberton
Queen Anne frame residence built ca. 1900 for local druggist.

BANK OF REDWOOD FALLS (7/31/80)
2nd St. off Washington, Redwood Falls
Richardsonian Romanesque brick-and-stone commercial building constructed ca. 1885.

Lower Sioux Agency, 1897

BIRCH COULEE SCHOOL (4/12/90)
off Co. Hwy. 2, Lower Sioux Indian Community
One-story frame day school built in 1891 by the U.S. government to acculturate Dakota children through formal education.

CHICAGO NORTH WESTERN DEPOT (8/11/80)
1st St., Lucan
Small frame passenger/freight depot built in 1902 by railroad crew in townsite platted by Western Town Lot Company.

HENRY D. CHOLLAR HOUSE (8/11/80)
4th and Minnesota Sts., Redwood Falls
Italianate frame residence built ca. 1878 for manager of local rail-line lumberyard.

CITY BLACKSMITH SHOP (8/11/80)
Douglas St. and 2nd Ave., Lamberton
False-front frame blacksmith shop built ca. 1898 to serve surrounding agricultural community.

CLEMENTS STATE BANK (8/11/80)
1st and Pine Sts., Clements
Commercial Queen Anne brick-and-stone bank building constructed in 1902 by group establishing business operations in towns platted by railroad.

COMMERCIAL HOTEL (8/11/80)
Front and Main Sts., Wabasso
Trackside frame hotel built in 1901 at juncture of two rail lines serving townsite.

DELHI CORONET BAND HALL (5/17/84)
3rd St., Delhi
False-front frame hall with bell tower built in 1896 by local musical organization to house its activities and other community events.

DISTRICT NO. 8 SCHOOL (8/11/80)
Co. Rd. 70, New Avon Twp.
Frame school and outbuildings (1908) that served township's educational, governmental, and social functions.

GILFILLAN (8/11/80)
Hwy. 67, Paxton Twp.
Large farmstead settled in 1880s by Charles D. Gilfillan, a promoter of diversified farming.

HONNER-HOSKEN HOUSE (8/11/80)
North and Main Sts., North Redwood
Frame residence built ca. 1872 by early settler and civic leader J. S. G. Honner; later owned by stonecutter and quarry owner Thomas Hosken.

LAND AND LOAN OFFICE (8/11/80)
Main St., Belview
False-front frame commercial building constructed in 1892 as private land office to promote agricultural development.

LOWER SIOUX AGENCY (9/22/70)
Paxton Twp.
Stone warehouse (1861) remaining from U.S. government administrative center for Dakota Indian reservation; site where the Dakota War began in 1862.

MILROY STATE BANK (8/11/80)
Superior St. and Euclid Ave., Milroy
Commercial Queen Anne/Richardsonian brick-and-stone bank constructed in 1902 by group establishing business operations in towns platted by railroad.

MINNEAPOLIS AND ST. LOUIS DEPOT (8/11/80)
off Main St., Belview
Small frame passenger/freight depot built in 1892 after town was platted by private landowners.

ODEON THEATER (8/30/74)
Main St., Belview
Simplified Queen Anne frame performing arts hall constructed in 1901.

RAMSEY PARK SWAYBACK BRIDGE (8/11/80)
Ramsey Park, Redwood Falls
Ten-span bridge of concrete and locally quarried granite built over Redwood River Gorge in 1938 by WPA workers.

REDWOOD FALLS CARNEGIE LIBRARY (8/11/80)
334 S. Jefferson, Redwood Falls
Classical Revival brick library with locally quarried granite foundation and trim, designed by Rockey, Church, and Pass and built in 1904.

REVERE FIRE HALL (8/11/80)
2nd St., Revere
False-front frame fire station with bell tower built ca. 1900.

ST. CORNELIA'S EPISCOPAL CHURCH (10/11/79)
off Co. Hwy. 2, Lower Sioux Indian Community
Gothic Revival church of local granite, built largely by congregation in 1889–91 to serve Dakota Indians returning after the Dakota War of 1862.

SCENIC CITY COOPERATIVE OIL COMPANY (8/11/80)
2nd and Mill Sts., Redwood Falls

Automobile service station built ca. 1925 of rainbow-colored block manufactured by Artstone Company of New Ulm.

RENVILLE COUNTY

BIRCH COULEE BATTLE SITE (6/4/73)
off Co. Hwys. 18 and 2, Birch Coulee Twp.
Site of a major battle during the Dakota War of 1862.

JOSEPH R. BROWN HOUSE RUINS (8/3/86)
Co. Hwy. 15, Sacred Heart Twp.
Remains of large family home of former Indian agent Brown, burned at outbreak of the Dakota War of 1862.

HEINS BLOCK (8/8/2001)
102-104 N. 9th St., Olivia
City's most prominent commercial building, a brick Queen Anne structure built in 1896 to house P. W. Heins's bank and hardware store.

MINNEAPOLIS AND ST. LOUIS DEPOT (7/24/86)
Park St. and 2nd Ave. S., Fairfax
Small frame passenger/freight depot built ca. 1883 shortly after town was platted by railroad company.

Heins Block

RENVILLE COUNTY COURTHOUSE AND JAIL (6/13/86)
500 E. Depue, Olivia
Classical Revival, brick-and-stone courthouse (1902)
designed by Fremont D. Orff; 1904 brick jail by Frank W.
Kinney.

LARS RUDI HOUSE (7/24/86)
Co. Hwy. 15, Sacred Heart Twp.
Two-room log house built in 1868 by Norwegian immigrant farmer and lay preacher whose residence served
as community gathering spot.

RICE COUNTY

ADAM WEYER WAGON SHOP (7/12/90)
32 2nd St. N.E., Faribault
Vernacular limestone commercial building constructed
ca. 1874 to house wagon factory and blacksmith shop.

ADMINISTRATION BUILDING–GIRLS' DORMITORY, STATE SCHOOL FOR THE DEAF (11/6/86)
Minn. Hwy. 299, Faribault
Georgian Revival main building of public institution
opened in 1863, designed by State Architect Clarence H.
Johnston Sr., built in 1912–13 of locally quarried
limestone.

ALL SAINTS CHURCH (EPISCOPAL) (4/6/82)
Washington and 5th Sts., Northfield
Gothic Revival frame church built in 1866 under leader-
ship of Bishop Henry Whipple.

EDWARD T. ARCHIBALD HOUSE (6/17/76)
Hamilton and 2nd Sts., Dundas
Greek Revival frame residence (built in 1860s) of pio-
neering flour miller.

ARCHIBALD MILL (10/8/76)
Railway St., Dundas
Limestone remains (1857, 1879) of mill owned by J. S.
Archibald that manufactured patent flour.

AULT STORE (4/6/82)
2nd St., Dundas
Limestone commercial building built in 1866 in town's
original business district to house mercantile store,
library, and newspaper office.

BATCHELDER'S BLOCK (7/12/90)
120 Central Ave. N., Faribault
Italianate limestone commercial building (1868) housing George Batchelder's dry goods business; third-floor
labor union meeting hall.

ELIZABETH AND FRANK A. BERRY HOUSE (8/9/90)
319 3rd St. N.W., Faribault
Queen Anne/Classical
Revival frame residence
designed by Olof Hanson
and built in 1896 for an
entrepreneur and his wife.

Elizabeth and Frank A. Berry House

BLIND DEPARTMENT BUILDING AND DOW HALL, STATE SCHOOL FOR THE BLIND (7/25/90)
400 6th Ave. S.E., Faribault
Brick school/residence buildings (Blind Department,
1874; Dow Hall by Monroe Sheire, 1883) representing
earliest period of state-funded education for the blind.

TOSTEN BONDE FARMHOUSE (4/6/82)
Minn. Hwy. 246, Wheeling Twp.
Large limestone house built in 1875 by prominent
Norwegian immigrant farmer and civic leader.

BRIDGE NO. 8096 (6/26/98)
Minn. Hwy. 19 over Spring Creek, Northfield
Reinforced-concrete arch bridge (1918) reconstructed
in 1947 with limestone veneer and Gothic Revival
detailing.

CASSIUS BUCK HOUSE (BUCKEYE) (4/6/82)
124 1st Ave. S.E., Faribault
Classical Revival frame residence built in 1895 for
prominent banker and political leader.

EUCHARISTE AND LOUIS CARUFEL HOUSE (8/3/90)
425 3rd St. S.W., Faribault
Gothic Revival residence of locally quarried limestone
(1877) with Italianate modifications (1883), built for
flour mill owner and his wife.

**CATHEDRAL OF OUR MERCIFUL SAVIOUR
AND GUILD HOUSE (EPISCOPAL)** (2/19/82)
515 2nd Ave. N.W., Faribault
Gothic Revival limestone cathedral built in 1862–69
according to plans by James Renwick; brick-and-stone
Guild House added in 1894.

Cathedral of Our Merciful Savior, ca. 1870

CHAPEL OF THE GOOD SHEPHERD,
SHATTUCK SCHOOL (4/4/75)
off Shumway Ave., Faribault
(also in Shattuck Historic District)
English Gothic limestone church designed by Henry
Congdon of New York and built in 1871–73 for Episcopal congregation founded by Bishop Henry Whipple.

CHURCH OF ST. PATRICK (CATHOLIC) (4/6/82)
Minn. Hwy. 21, Shieldsville Twp. (Shieldsville)
Romanesque Revival limestone church built in 1888 for
state's first organized Irish colony, established in 1850s.

CHURCH OF THE ANNUNCIATION (CATHOLIC) (4/6/82)
Co. Hwy. 46, Webster Twp.
Craftsman-style church with ornamental corner tower
designed by John Wheeler and built in 1913.

CHURCH OF THE HOLY CROSS (EPISCOPAL) (4/6/82)
2nd St., Dundas
Gothic church of locally quarried stone built in 1868
under Bishop Henry Whipple, with land and funds
donated by mill owner J. S. Archibald.

CHURCH OF THE MOST HOLY
TRINITY (CATHOLIC) (11/13/97)
4938 N. Washington St., Wheatland Twp.
Romanesque limestone church designed by Clarence H.
Johnston Sr. and built in 1905 as center of religious,
cultural, and social life for Czech community.

GORDON AND KATE T. COLE HOUSE (8/3/90)
111 2nd St. N.W., Faribault
Italianate frame residence (ca. 1856, enlarged in 1867
and 1889) of a civic leader and his wife.

CONGREGATIONAL CHURCH OF FARIBAULT (5/12/77)
227 3rd St. N.W., Faribault
Romanesque Revival limestone church designed by

Monroe Sheire and built in 1867–69 for county's oldest congregation.

JOHN N. AND ELIZABETH C. COTTRELL HOUSE (8/3/90)
127 1st St. N.W., Faribault
Stick Style frame residence constructed in 1897 for a merchant and his wife.

DEN SVENSKA EVANGELISKA LUTHERSKA CHRISTDALA FORSAMLINGEN (CHRISTDALA EVANGELICAL SWEDISH LUTHERAN CHURCH) (5/18/95)
4695 Millersburg Rd., Forest Twp.
Late Gothic Revival frame church built in 1878 by Swedish immigrant congregation as religious, cultural, and social center.

REVEREND JAMES DOBBIN HOUSE/ ST. JAMES SCHOOL FOR BOYS (7/23/90)
1800 14th St. N.E., Faribault
Gothic Revival limestone cottage built in 1874, enlarged in 1901 and converted to boys' preparatory division of Shattuck School.

EDWIN S. DRAKE FARMHOUSE (4/6/82)
Co. Hwy. 22, Bridgewater Twp.
Brick farmhouse built ca. 1863 for a first-generation Rice County farmer.

EPISCOPAL RECTORY (8/9/90)
112 6th St. N.W., Faribault
Colonial Revival frame dwelling designed by Olof Hanson, commissioned by Bishop Henry Whipple in 1897.

FARIBAULT CITY HALL (4/6/82)
208 1st Ave. N.W., Faribault
Renaissance Revival brick-and-stone municipal building designed by Harry Wild Jones and constructed in 1894–97 to house city government and public library.

FARIBAULT COMMERCIAL HISTORIC DISTRICT (4/6/82)

Central Ave. between 2nd and 3rd Sts., Faribault
Concentration of late-19th-century commercial buildings in main business district of regional center for trade and manufacturing.

Alexander Faribault House

ALEXANDER FARIBAULT HOUSE (9/22/70)

12 N.E. 1st Ave., Faribault
County's first frame residence, a Greek Revival dwelling built in 1853 by fur trader Faribault; also served as a civic center, polling place, and church.

FARIBAULT VIADUCT (11/6/89)

Division St. over Straight River, Faribault
Multiple-span, reinforced-concrete bridge with Moderne-style ornamentation, built in 1937–39 to link institutional and commercial areas of city.

FARIBAULT WATER WORKS (4/6/82)

7th St. N.W., Faribault
Structures representing two periods of municipal improvements: 1883 brick pumping station and 1938 Moderne-style concrete facility built by WPA workers.

FARMER SEED AND NURSERY COMPANY (4/6/82)
818 4th St. N.W., Faribault
Limestone-and-frame warehouse built in phases ca.
1890–1920s, representing city's role as major agricultural processing and distribution center.

GOODSELL OBSERVATORY, CARLETON COLLEGE (5/12/75)
off 1st St. E., Northfield
Romanesque Revival
masonry astronomical
laboratory (1887) designed by J. Walter
Stevens; one of nation's
official time stations,
1887–1930s.

Lonsdale School

M. P. HOLMAN HOUSE (8/3/90)
107 3rd Ave. N.W., Faribault
Italianate brick residence with wraparound porch constructed ca. 1875.

HOSPITAL, STATE SCHOOL FOR THE FEEBLE MINDED (4/6/82)
off 6th Ave. S.E. (Faribault State Hospital), Faribault
Brick hospital (1900–04) by Clarence H. Johnston Sr.,
noted for psychology laboratories of A. R. T. Wiley,
pioneer in field of mental health research.

JOHN HUTCHINSON HOUSE (4/6/82)
305 2nd St. N.W., Faribault
Elaborate Queen Anne frame residence built in 1892 for
owner of Faribault Furniture Company.

JOHNSTON HALL, SEABURY DIVINITY SCHOOL (3/21/75)
1st St. S.E. and State Ave. S.E., Faribault
Limestone library/residence hall (1888) on campus of
divinity school established in 1860 by Episcopal Bishop
Henry Whipple.

LAURA BAKER SCHOOL (4/17/78)
211 Oak St., Northfield
School/residence for mentally retarded children, opened in 1898 by Baker, innovator in special education methodology.

VINCENT AND ELIZABETH LIEB HOUSE (7/23/90)
201 4th Ave. S.W., Faribault
Vernacular limestone residence built in 1862 by shoemaker Lieb.

LONSDALE SCHOOL (8/30/79)
3rd Ave. S.W., Lonsdale
Two-story frame school with cupola built in 1908 by local carpenter Patrick Sullivan.

DREW H. LORD HOUSE (4/6/82)
201 E. 3rd St., Northfield
Eastlake-style frame residence constructed in 1887 by one of town's leading builders.

WILLIAM MARTIN HOUSE (4/6/82)
Bridge and 1st Sts., Dundas
Greek Revival/Italianate frame residence built in 1869 by Archibald Milling Company treasurer.

CORMACK MCCALL HOUSE (8/3/90)
817 Ravine St. N.E., Faribault
Vernacular limestone dwelling built ca. 1871 by prominent stonecutter and mason McCall.

THOMAS MCCALL HOUSE (8/3/90)
102 4th Ave. S.W., Faribault
Italianate limestone residence built ca.1868 by master stonemason McCall (remodeled 1908).

THOMAS AND BRIDGET S. MCMAHON HOUSE (7/19/90)
603 Division St. E., Faribault

Vernacular limestone residence built in 1871 by a quarry owner and his wife.

NERSTRAND CITY HALL (4/6/82)
Main St., Nerstrand
Brick municipal building with bell tower designed by Thori, Alban, and Fisher and built in 1908 to house city offices, fire hall, jail, and library.

NORTHFIELD HISTORIC DISTRICT (6/11/79)
vicinity of Division, Water, 3rd, and 5th Sts., Northfield
Town center integrating civic, commercial, and industrial functions, with largely late-19th-century buildings of local brick and quarried stone.

NOYES HALL, STATE SCHOOL FOR THE DEAF (5/12/75)
off 6th Ave. N.E., Faribault
Classical Revival education building with domed rotunda designed by State Architect Clarence H. Johnston Sr. and built of locally quarried limestone in 1902–10.

ELIZABETH H. AND JONATHAN L. NOYES HOUSE (8/9/90)
105 1st Ave. N.W., Faribault
Queen Anne/Shingle Style frame residence (1896) designed by deaf architect Olof Hanson for the superintendent of the State School for the Deaf and his wife.

Nerstrand
City Hall

JOHN C. NUTTING HOUSE (10/15/70) ·
217 Union St., Northfield
Eastlake-style brick residence (1887–88) designed by J. E. Cooke for bank founder.

OLD MAIN, ST. OLAF COLLEGE (6/3/76)
off St. Olaf Ave., Northfield
Victorian Gothic brick campus center designed by Long and Haglin and built in 1877–78 for Norwegian Lutheran religious and educational institution.

OSMUND OSMUNDSON HOUSE (4/6/82)
off Minn. Hwy. 246, Nerstrand
Brick house (1880) of Norwegian immigrant homesteader, town founder, and civic promoter.

JOHN GOTTLIEB PFEIFFER HOUSE (8/3/90)
931 3rd Ave. N.W., Faribault
Dwelling of locally quarried limestone with Federal styling, built in 1868 by stonecutter Pfeiffer.

PHELPS LIBRARY, SHATTUCK SCHOOL (4/4/75)
off Shumway Ave., Faribault (also in Shattuck Historic District)
Early Gothic Revival limestone library built in 1869 for Seabury Divinity School, an Episcopal seminary founded by Bishop Henry Whipple.

RICE COUNTY COURTHOUSE AND JAIL (4/6/82)
218 3rd St. N.W., Faribault
Moderne-style stone courthouse (1932–34) designed by Nairne Fisher; Richardsonian Romanesque brick jail (1910) by Albert Schippel.

ROCK ISLAND DEPOT (4/6/82)
off 3rd St. and 1st Ave. N.E., Faribault
Brick-and-stone passenger depot built in 1902 on last major link of Faribault's rail connections.

O. E. ROLVAAG HOUSE (8/4/69)
(National Historic Landmark, 8/4/69)
311 Manitou St., Northfield
Residence (1912) of professor and author of *Giants in the Earth* and other works depicting the experiences of Norwegian immigrant settlers on the Midwestern frontier.

ST. MARY'S HALL (4/6/82)
4th St. N.E., Faribault
Gothic Revival limestone school (1926) designed by Clarence H. Johnston Sr. to house Episcopal girls' boarding school founded by Bishop Henry Whipple.

SCOVILLE MEMORIAL LIBRARY, CARLETON COLLEGE (4/6/82)
1st St. E. and College St., Northfield
Richardsonian Romanesque limestone library designed by Patton and Fisher of Chicago and built in 1896.

SCRIVER BLOCK (5/5/78)
Bridge Square and Division St., Northfield
(also in Northfield Historic District)
Limestone commercial block built ca. 1867 for merchant and civic leader Hiram Scriver; also housed bank robbed by James-Younger gang in 1876.

SHATTUCK HISTORIC DISTRICT (4/6/82)
off Shumway Ave., Faribault
Gothic Revival campus complex of boys' boarding school founded in 1864 by Episcopal Bishop Henry Whipple, shared until 1873 with Seabury Divinity School.

SHUMWAY HALL AND MORGAN REFECTORY, SHATTUCK SCHOOL (4/4/75)
off Shumway Ave., Faribault (also in Shattuck Historic District)
Romanesque/English Gothic limestone campus center and dining hall (1887, 1888) designed by Willcox and Johnston.

O. E. Rolvaag House, 1983

SKINNER MEMORIAL CHAPEL, CARLETON COLLEGE (4/6/82)
1st St. between Winona and College Sts., Northfield
Gothic Revival stone chapel designed by Patton, Holmes, and Flynn of Chicago and built in 1916 at college founded in 1866 by the Congregational church.

STEENSLAND LIBRARY, ST. OLAF COLLEGE (4/6/82)
off St. Olaf Ave., Northfield
Classical Revival, brick-and-stone library designed by Omeyer and Thori and built in 1902 during Norwegian Lutheran college's early development.

THEOPOLD MERCANTILE COMPANY
WHOLESALE GROCERY (4/6/82)
1st Ave. and 3rd St. N.E., Faribault
Brick warehouse built in 1893 by grocers F. A. and H. C. Theopold in regional trade and distribution center.

THOMAS SCOTT BUCKHAM MEMORIAL LIBRARY (4/6/82)
Central Ave. and Division St., Faribault
Moderne-style public library of Kasota stone (1930) designed by Charles Buckham of Vermont, gifted to city by widow of prominent judge.

TIMOTHY J. MCCARTHY BUILDING (8/3/90)
24 3rd St. N.W., Faribault
Italianate brick-and-stone commercial block with marble façade, built in 1884 by owner of Faribault Marble and Granite Works.

TRONDHJEM NORWEGIAN LUTHERAN CHURCH (9/7/2001)
8501 Garfield Ave., Webster and Wheatland Twps.
Greek Revival/Gothic Revival church built in 1899 as religious, educational, cultural, and social center for area's Norwegian Lutheran settlers.

VALLEY GROVE (4/6/82)
Co. Rd. 29, Wheeling Twp.
Two adjacent Lutheran churches: Gothic Revival frame edifice (1894) and earlier Greek Revival stone church (1862) retained as guild hall.

THOMAS VEBLEN FARMSTEAD (6/30/75)
(National Historic Landmark, 12/21/81)
Minn. Hwy. 246, Wheeling Twp.
Family home (built ca. 1875) of economist Thorstein Veblen, author of *The Theory of the Leisure Class* and other seminal works on modern society.

W. ROBY ALLEN ORAL HOME SCHOOL (7/12/90)
525 5th St. N.E., Faribault
Private boarding school opened in 1923 by Bessie Blaker Allen, pioneer in early childhood education and mainstreaming for deaf students.

WILLIS HALL, CARLETON COLLEGE (6/13/75)
College St., Northfield
College's first permanent facility, a French Second Empire stone building erected in 1868–72 (modified after 1879 fire).

HUDSON WILSON HOUSE (4/6/82)
104 1st Ave. N.W., Faribault

French Second Empire brick residence built in 1876 for prominent banker and civic leader.

ROCK COUNTY

BLUE MOUNDS STATE PARK WPA/RUSTIC STYLE HISTORIC RESOURCES (10/25/89)
off U.S. Hwy. 75, north of Luverne
(Blue Mounds State Park), Mound Twp.
Structures/building of Sioux quartzite built by WPA workers in 1938–42, including two stone dams creating recreational lakes.

BRIDGE NO. 1482 (6/25/92)
U.S. Hwy. 75, Luverne Twp.
One of Minnesota's few surviving steel, single-span, king-post pony-truss bridges, built in 1908 by Hewett Bridge Company of Minneapolis.

Lower Dam, Blue Mounds State Park

BRIDGE NO. L-2162
(11/6/89)
Co. Rd. 51 over Split Rock Creek, Rose Dell Twp.
Single-span reinforced-concrete bridge with Classical Revival detailing, built ca. 1907 by Perley N. Gillham of Luverne.

BRIDGE NO. L-2315 (11/6/89)
Twp. Rd. 89 over Rock River, Kanaranzi Twp.
Early single-span reinforced-concrete bridge with Classical Revival detailing, built ca. 1901 by Perley N. Gillham.

BRIDGE NO. L-2316 (11/6/89)
Twp. Rd. 89 over Rock River, Kanaranzi Twp.
Single-span reinforced-concrete bridge with Classical Revival detailing, built ca. 1906 by Perley N. Gillham.

Bridge No. L-4646

BRIDGE NO. L-4646 (11/6/89)
6th St. over Spring Brook, Beaver Creek
Single-span reinforced-concrete bridge with Classical
Revival detailing, built in 1911 by Perley N. Gillham.

FIRST NATIONAL BANK OF BEAVER CREEK (3/18/80)
1st Ave., Beaver Creek
Classical Revival brick bank with false-front sandstone
façade built in 1917.

J. W. GERBER HOUSE (3/18/80)
324 W. Main St., Luverne
Colonial Revival clapboard residence designed by W. E. E.
Greene and built in 1901 for prominent businessman
and civic leader.

RAY B. HINKLY HOUSE (6/10/75)
217 N. Freeman Ave., Luverne
Queen Anne residence of Sioux quartzite with advanced electrical, plumbing, and telephone systems,
built in 1892 by entrepreneurial businessman.

HOLY TRINITY CHURCH (EPISCOPAL) (3/18/80)
Cedar St. N. and Luverne St. E., Luverne
Gothic Revival church of Sioux quartzite built in 1891
by city's first Episcopal parish.

JASPER STONE COMPANY AND QUARRY (1/5/78)
off Sherman Ave., Jasper
Source of pink Sioux quartzite used since ca. 1890 in
building construction and since World War I as grinding media for industrial processing.

KENNETH SCHOOL (3/18/80)
230 1st Ave. W., Kenneth
Two-story frame school with bell tower built in 1901;
also used as town hall.

PIERCE J. KNISS HOUSE (3/18/80)
209 N. Estey St., Luverne
Italian Villa brick residence built in 1878–79 for town
founder and leading entrepreneur; remodeled in 1901
by architect W. E. E. Greene.

LUVERNE CARNEGIE LIBRARY (3/18/80)
205 N. Freeman Ave., Luverne
Beaux Arts brick library with Sioux quartzite trim
designed by W. E. E. Greene and built in 1904 for
Luverne Library Association.

MAPLEWOOD CHAPEL (3/18/80)
W. Warren St., Luverne
Gothic Revival shingled cemetery chapel designed by
W. E. E. Greene and built in 1895.

JACOB NUFFER FARMSTEAD (3/18/80)
Co. Rds. 53 and 57, Martin Twp.
Farm homesteaded in 1872, with 1880s barn and shed
built by Nuffer, 1890 brick farmhouse, and other buildings spanning farm's evolution.

OMAHA DEPOT (3/18/80)
E. Fletcher St. at Freeman Ave., Luverne
Standard-plan brick passenger/freight depot constructed in 1913.

PALACE THEATER (3/18/80)
Main St. and Freeman Ave., Luverne
Classical Revival brick performing arts hall designed by W. E. E. Greene and built in 1915 with elaborate Art Nouveau interior.

ROCK COUNTY COURTHOUSE AND JAIL (4/18/77)
204 E. Brown, Luverne
Richardsonian Romanesque buildings designed by T. D. Allen and built in 1887–90 of Sioux quartzite with Kasota stone trim.

ROSEAU COUNTY

CANADIAN NATIONAL DEPOT (4/6/82)
Main St., Warroad
Craftsman-style brick depot authorized by a U.S.-Canadian treaty, built in 1914 on only section of Canadian railway system to pass through United States.

Lodge Boleslav Jablonsky No. 219

LODGE BOLESLAV JABLONSKY NO. 219 (9/6/2002)
30033 110th St., Poplar Grove Twp.
Frame lodge hall built in 1916 by members of Czech freethinkers' fraternal organization to serve community's cultural and social needs.

ROSEAU COUNTY COURTHOUSE (8/15/85)
216 Center St. W., Roseau
Brick municipal building designed by Lignell and Loebeck and built in 1913–14.

ST. LOUIS COUNTY

AERIAL LIFT BRIDGE (5/22/73)
Lake Ave. over Duluth Ship Canal, Duluth
Aerial bridge built in 1901–05 at head of Great Lakes, modeled after bridge in Rouen, France; modified with vertical lift in 1929 by C. A. P. Turner.

ELIAS AND LISI AHO FARMSTEAD (4/9/90)
off Twp. Rd. 358, Waasa Twp.
Subsistence farm with house, barn, and outbuildings of traditional Finnish log construction, built in 1902–07 by immigrant homesteader.

ALANGO SCHOOL (7/17/80)
Co. Hwys. 25 and 22, Alango Twp.
Large rural brick-and-stucco consolidated school with second-floor teachers' quarters, built in 1927.

ANDREW G. ANDERSON HOUSE (12/4/80)
1001 E. Howard St., Hibbing
Georgian Revival residence with tile roof built in 1920 for founder of Mesaba Transportation Company, forerunner of Greyhound Bus Corporation.

ANDROY HOTEL (6/13/86)
592 E. Howard St., Hibbing (also in East Howard Street Commercial Historic District)

Renaissance Revival brick-and-stone hotel built by
Oliver Iron Mining Company in 1921 to serve city's
social and hostelry needs.

ARCHAEOLOGICAL SITE 21SL55 (7/8/88)
unorganized territory (Voyageurs National Park)
Campsite dating from Precontact Period (A.D. 700–1500).

ARCHAEOLOGICAL SITE 21SL73 (1/16/89)
unorganized territory (Voyageurs National Park)
Seasonal campsite dating from Precontact Period
(100 B.C.–A.D. 1500).

ARCHAEOLOGICAL SITE 21SL82 (2/17/88)
unorganized territory (Voyageurs National Park)
Campsite spanning Precontact, Contact, and Postcontact
Periods (ca. 3000 B.C.–A.D. 1900).

W. BAILEY HOUSE (8/27/80)
705 Pierce St., Eveleth
Queen Anne residence of rose-pigmented cement brick
with red stone trim, built in 1905 by manager of min-
ing-rights fee office.

W. T. BAILEY HOUSE (12/4/80)
816 S. 5th Ave., Virginia
Spanish Mission–style residence built ca. 1921 for lumber company founder.

BERGETTA MOE BAKERY (6/3/76)
716 E. Superior St., Duluth
Frame residence/store built ca. 1875 during city's first
period of construction.

B'NAI ABRAHAM SYNAGOGUE (8/18/80)
328 S. 5th St., Virginia
Brick synagogue built in 1909 to serve Iron Range's
Jewish immigrant community.

B'nai Abraham Synagogue

BRIDGE NO. 5757 (6/26/98)
Minn. Hwy. 23 over Mission Creek, Duluth
Two-span, multi-plate arch bridge with Gothic Revival
fieldstone veneer, built in 1937 as part of highway
beautification movement.

BRIDGE NO. L-6007 (11/6/89)
Skyline Pkwy. over Stewart Creek, Duluth
Single-span, stone arch highway bridge of locally quar-
ried gabbro, built ca. 1925

BRUCE MINE HEADFRAME (11/28/78)
U.S. Hwy. 169, Chisholm
Steel headframe built in 1925–26 to provide locomotion
for crew elevators and ore skips in underground mining
operation.

BUHL PUBLIC LIBRARY (2/10/83)
Jones Ave. and Frantz St., Buhl
Classical Revival, brick-and-stone library designed by
Holstead and Sullivan and built in 1917–18 with tax
revenues from mining operations.

BUHL VILLAGE HALL (2/10/83)
Jones Ave. and 4th St., Buhl
Beaux Arts brick-and-stone municipal building designed
by Keith Architectural Services and built in 1913 with
mine tax revenues.

BULL-OF-THE-WOODS LOGGING SCOW (2/12/99)
Morse Twp.
Underwater remains of paddle-wheeled, steam-powered
scow (ca. 1893) used to tow log rafts across lakes to mills
or railroad lines.

BURNTSIDE LODGE HISTORIC DISTRICT (6/23/88)
off Co. Hwy. 88, Morse Twp.
Region's earliest full-scale resort, with large collection
of log buildings constructed in 1914–37 by local,
primarily Finnish craftsmen.

Main Lodge, Burntside Lodge Historic District

EMMETT BUTLER HOUSE (12/4/80)
2530 3rd Ave. W., Hibbing
Colonial Revival residence built in 1916 by co-founder
of Butler Brothers Construction Company, innovator in
mining technology.

CHESTER TERRACE (11/19/80)
1210-1232 E. 1st St., Duluth
Romanesque Revival brick-and-stone row house designed by Oliver G. Traphagen and Francis Fitzpatrick and built in 1890.

CHURCH OF ST. JOHN THE BAPTIST (CATHOLIC) (8/27/80)
321 S. 3rd St., Virginia
Gothic Revival brick church built in 1924 as center of religious, cultural, and social life for Polish immigrant community.

CHURCH OF ST. JOSEPH (CATHOLIC) (9/6/2002)
7897 Elmer Rd., Elmer Twp.
Frame church built in 1913 for colony of Austro-Hungarian immigrants from Chicago, recruited by railroad company agent to settle logged-over land.

CHURCH OF THE HOLY FAMILY (CATHOLIC) (8/27/80)
307 Adams Ave., Eveleth
Gothic Revival brick-and-stone church designed by A. F. Wasielewski and built in 1909 as religious, cultural, and social center for Slovenian community.

CIVILIAN CONSERVATION CORPS CAMP S-52 (3/2/89)
off U.S. Hwy. 53, Leiding Twp.
Frame buildings erected in 1933 as shops for CCC logging and forest maintenance operation, 1933–ca. 1941.

CLYDE CREEK SITE (21SL35) (12/19/87)
unorganized territory (Voyageurs National Park)
Habitation site dating from Precontact Period.

COATES HOUSE (8/18/80)
817 S. 5th Ave., Virginia
Frame residence built ca. 1912 by a hotel owner and entrepreneur.

CHESTER AND CLARA CONGDON ESTATE (GLENSHEEN) (8/15/91)
3300 London Rd., Duluth
Jacobean Revival mansion/outbuildings designed by Clarence H. Johnston Sr. and built in 1905–09 for a prominent legal counsel and his wife; landscape design by Charles W. Leavitt Jr. of New York.

DELVIC BUILDING (7/17/80)
1st Ave. and Howard St. E., Hibbing (also in East Howard Street Commercial Historic District)
Brick commercial block built in 1922 by Oliver Iron Mining Company in town's relocated business district.

DEWITT-SEITZ BUILDING (9/5/85)
394 Lake Ave S., Duluth
Brick warehouse designed by John Wagenstein and built in 1909 in city's waterfront jobbing and manufacturing district.

DULUTH CENTRAL HIGH SCHOOL (11/9/72)
Lake Ave. and 2nd St., Duluth
Richardsonian Romanesque brownstone school with clock tower designed by Palmer, Hall, and Hunt and built in 1892.

DULUTH CIVIC CENTER HISTORIC DISTRICT (11/6/86)
5th Ave. W. and 1st St., Duluth
Classical Revival, government-building complex (including 1909 county courthouse) designed by Daniel H. Burnham, a proponent of the City Beautiful Movement.

DULUTH MISSABE AND IRON RANGE DEPOT (ENDION) (4/16/75)
100 Lake Place, Duluth
City's last remaining small passenger depot, a Richardsonian brick-and-sandstone depot designed by Tenbusch and Hill and built in 1899.

DULUTH PUBLIC LIBRARY (5/5/78)
101 W. 2nd St., Duluth
Classical Revival, sandstone-and-brick, Carnegie-funded
library designed by Adolph F. Rudolph and built in
1902 to replace rented quarters.

DULUTH SOUTH BREAKWATER INNER LIGHT (8/4/83)
South Breakwater, Duluth
Skeletal steel watchtower built in 1900–01 by the U.S.
Coast Guard to guide ships in and out of Duluth harbor.

DULUTH STATE NORMAL SCHOOL HISTORIC DISTRICT
(11/8/85)
E. 5th St. and 23rd Ave.,
Duluth
Campus established in
1898 as part of state school
system for teacher training;
includes two dormitories
and model school by
Clarence H. Johnston Sr.

Duluth Winnipeg and Pacific Depot

DULUTH UNION DEPOT (12/9/71)
5th Ave. W. and Michigan St., Duluth
Chateauesque stone passenger depot designed by
Peabody and Stearns of Boston and built in 1892 to
serve fast-growing commercial center.

DULUTH WINNIPEG AND PACIFIC DEPOT (8/18/80)
600 Chestnut St., Virginia
Brick-and-stone replacement depot built in 1913 for
major Iron Range supply and distribution center.

E. J. LONGYEAR FIRST DIAMOND DRILL SITE (7/20/77)
off Co. Hwy. 110, Hoyt Lakes
Site of 1890 drilling exploration for ore deposits on
Mesabi Iron Range.

EAST HOWARD STREET COMMERCIAL HISTORIC DISTRICT (4/1/93)
101-510 E. Howard Street, Hibbing
Business district established in 1920–21 by Oliver Iron Mining Company when town was relocated to expand mining operations.

ENDION SCHOOL (2/10/83)
1801 E. 1st St., Duluth
Richardsonian Romanesque brick-and-stone school designed by Adolph F. Rudolph and built in 1890.

EVELETH MANUAL TRAINING SCHOOL (8/18/80)
Roosevelt Ave. between Jones and Jackson Sts., Eveleth
State's first vocational school, built in 1914 to train skilled workers for iron mining industry; Moderne-style design by Bray and Nystrom.

EVELETH RECREATION BUILDING (11/25/80)
Garfield St. and Adams Ave., Eveleth
Public facility for physical development of workers, built by city in 1918 with tax revenues from mining operations.

FINNISH SAUNA (8/26/80)
105 S. 1st St., Virginia
Public bathhouse built ca. 1912 to serve Finnish immigrant miners and their families.

FIRE HOUSE NO. 1 (5/12/75)
1st Ave. E. and 3rd St., Duluth
City's first brick fire hall (1889), designed in Richardsonian style by Oliver G.Traphagen and Francis Fitzpatrick.

FITGER BREWING COMPANY (2/9/84)
600 E. Superior St., Duluth
Brewery complex (1886–1930) of largely Richardsonian Romanesque stone and brick buildings by Chicago's Louis Lehle and Duluth's Traphagen and Fitzpatrick.

FLINT CREEK FARM HISTORIC DISTRICT (3/2/89)
off Minn. Hwy. 1, Field Twp.
Summer farm operated ca. 1915–33 by lumbermen
Samuel J. Cusson and Chester H. Rogers to raise feed
and crops for winter logging operations.

JUN FUJITA CABIN (12/2/96)
*Wendt Island, Rainy Lake, unorganized territory
(Voyageurs National Park)*
Recreational frame cabin with log additions evoking
Japanese country house, used ca. 1928–41 by Japanese-
born Chicago photographer and poet.

GREGORIUS AND MARY HANKA FARMSTEAD (4/9/90)
off Twp. Rd. 6544, Embarrass Twp.
Subsistence farm with house, barn, and outbuildings of
traditional Finnish log construction built ca. 1910–15
by Finnish immigrant.

HARTLEY BUILDING (12/22/89)
740 E. Superior St., Duluth
Jacobean Revival brick-and-stone office building designed by Bertram G. Goodhue and built in 1914 for
business leader Guilford G. Hartley.

Hartley Building

HEIGHT OF LAND PORTAGE (7/23/92)
off Co. Rd. 138, Embarrass, White, and Pike Twps.
Overland transportation route along continental divide
used by Indians, fur traders, and other travelers ca.
1630s–1870s.

HIBBING CITY HALL (2/12/81)
21st St. E. and 4th Ave., Hibbing
Georgian Revival brick hall designed by Holstead
and Sullivan and built in 1922 as seat of municipal
government.

HIBBING DISPOSAL PLANT (8/9/91)
1300 E. 23rd St., Hibbing
Moderne-style concrete municipal sanitation complex
with innovative design by architect/engineer J. C. Taylor,
built in 1938–41 by PWA workers.

HIBBING HIGH SCHOOL (8/11/80)
21st St. at 8th Ave. E., Hibbing
Jacobean Revival brick-and-stone school designed by
W. T. Bray and built in 1919–24 with tax revenues from
mining operations.

Hibbing High School, 1929

EMMA AND MATT HILL FARMSTEAD (4/9/90)
off Twp. Rd. 303, Pike Twp.
Grouping of domestic and agricultural buildings of traditional Finnish log construction, erected ca. 1897–1920 by immigrant subsistence farmer.

HOTEL GLODE (11/25/80)
222 Adams Ave., Eveleth
Brick hotel built in 1904 as Mesabi Iron Range's leading hostelry; a major stop on Mesaba Railway's interurban trolley line.

Hotel Glode

HULL-RUST-MAHONING MINE (11/13/66)
(National Historic Landmark, 11/13/66)
off 3rd Ave. E., Hibbing
World's largest open pit mine complex (opened 1895), which revolutionized mining technology and transformed the U.S. steel industry.

IRVING SCHOOL (11/20/92)
101 N. 56th Ave. W., Duluth
Renaissance Revival brick-and-stone school where vocational training was introduced to Duluth system; designed by Palmer, Hall, and Hunt and built in 1894–95.

JOHN HARRIS HEARDING GRAMMAR AND HIGH SCHOOL AND JOHN A. JOHNSON GRAMMAR SCHOOL (1/16/97)
4th Ave. N. and 1st St. W., Aurora
Public schools (Tudor Revival Hearding school by Puck and Holstead) built in 1912 and 1914 to educate and assimilate immigrant miners and their children.

JUKOLA BOARDINGHOUSE (3/10/82)
201 N. 3rd Ave., Virginia
Frame residential dwelling constructed in 1912 to house unmarried miners.

KABETOGAMA RANGER STATION (6/18/93)
unorganized territory (Voyageurs National Park)
Rustic-style, board-and-batten and stone administrative/
residential/storage complex for forestry ranger, built by
CCC workers in 1933–41.

KETTLE FALLS HISTORIC DISTRICT (7/17/78)
Kettle Channel, unorganized territory
(Voyageurs National Park)
Portage used by Indians, fur traders, and explorers; dam
built ca. 1910–14 to facilitate commercial/recreational
use of boundary lakes.

KETTLE FALLS HOTEL (1/11/76)
*Kettle Channel, unorganized territory (Voyageurs National
Park) (also in Kettle Falls Historic District)*
Frame hotel built in 1913 on international waterway to
serve travelers, lumberjacks, and commercial and recre-
ational fishermen.

KITCHI GAMMI CLUB (4/16/75)
831 E. Superior St., Duluth
Jacobean Revival clubhouse designed by Cram, Goodhue, and Ferguson and built in 1912 for private businessmen's social club established in 1883.

LEMOINE BUILDING (3/2/89)
off Co. Hwy. 74, unorganized territory
False-front frame store/residence built in 1913 in townsite established to serve lumber industry.

CHARLES LENONT HOUSE (8/18/80)
202 N. 5th Ave., Virginia
Queen Anne brick residence (1900) owned by prominent physician.

LESTER RIVER BRIDGE (BRIDGE NO. 5772) (9/6/2002)
London Rd. (Minn. Hwy. 61) over Lester River, Duluth

Classical Revival, stone-faced concrete arch bridge designed by landscape architects Morell and Nichols and built in 1924–25 as part of city's parkway system.

LINCOLN SCHOOL (11/28/78)

3rd Ave. N. at 1st St. N., Virginia
Jacobean Revival brick-and-stone school designed by Kelly and Shefchik and built in 1922.

MIKE AND MARY MATSON FARMSTEAD (4/9/90)

off Co. Hwy. 21, Embarrass Twp.
Subsistence farm with barns, stable, and sauna of traditional Finnish log construction built ca. 1900 by Finnish homesteader.

MINNESOTA POINT LIGHTHOUSE (12/27/74)

Minnesota Point, Duluth
Ruins of brick lighthouse completed in 1858 at channel entrance to Superior Bay.

MITCHELL-TAPPAN HOUSE (12/2/80)

2125 4th Ave., Hibbing
Queen Anne frame residence built in 1897–98 by Oliver Iron Mining Company for use by superintendent of mining operations.

Kettle Falls Hotel

MOUNTAIN IRON MINE (11/24/68)
(National Historic Landmark, 11/24/68)
off 1st St. and Mountain Ave., Mountain Iron
First mine to ship ore (1892) from Mesabi Range, which encompassed world's largest iron ore deposit.

MUNGER TERRACE (12/12/76)
405 Mesabi Ave., Duluth
Massive Chateauesque stone-and-brick row house designed by Oliver G. Traphagen and Francis Fitzpatrick and built in 1891–92 (remodeled as apartments in 1915).

St. Mark's African Methodist Episcopal Church

ERICK AND KRISTINA NELIMARK SAUNA (4/9/90)
off Co. Rd. 615, Embarrass Twp.
Large log bathhouse built ca. 1930 using traditional Finnish construction techniques.

NORTHLAND (7/31/78)
off U.S. Hwy. 2, Proctor
All-steel private railroad car built by the Pullman Company in 1916 for business use by the president of Duluth Missabe and Northern Railway.

ORR ROADSIDE PARKING AREA (9/6/2002)

Minn. Hwy. 53 at 1st Ave., Orr

Rustic-style wayside rest and recreation area designed by landscape architect A. R. Nichols and built in 1935–38 for state highway department by CCC workers.

PIONEER MINE BUILDINGS AND "A" HEADFRAME (11/28/78)

off Pioneer Rd., Ely

Steel headframe, brick water tower, enginehouse, and dry houses supporting Ely area's first underground mining operation, opened in 1889.

SACRED HEART CATHEDRAL AND CATHEDRAL SCHOOL (6/26/86)

211 and 206 W. 4th St., Duluth

Gothic Revival brick cathedral (1894–96) designed by Gearhard A. Tenbusch and school (1904) by I. Vernon Hill and W. T. Bray.

ST. LOUIS COUNTY DISTRICT COURTHOUSE (6/18/92)

300 S. 5th Ave., Virginia

Beaux Arts brick government building designed by Bray and Nystrom and constructed in 1910 to serve Iron Range region.

ST. LOUIS COUNTY 4-H CLUB CAMP (3/4/85)

100 Pine Lane, Biwabik Twp.

Log lodge and stone amphitheater built by CCC and WPA workers in 1934 with prize money awarded by Sears Roebuck Company for county's 4-H achievements.

ST. MARK'S AFRICAN METHODIST EPISCOPAL CHURCH (4/16/91)

530 N. 5th Ave. E., Duluth

Gothic Revival brick church completed in 1913 by city's first black congregation as religious and social center for black community.

SS. PETER AND PAUL CHURCH
(UKRAINIAN CATHOLIC) (8/27/80)
530 Central Ave., Chisholm
Brick church with onion-dome tower built in 1916 as
religious and social center for the Iron Range's Ukrainian
immigrants.

ALEX SEITANIEMI BARN (4/9/90)
off Twp. Rd. 797, Waasa Twp.
Rare two-story log building combining dwelling, animal shelter, and crop storage, built ca. 1907–13 by
Finnish homesteader.

SONS OF ITALY HALL (11/25/80)
704 E. Howard St., Hibbing
Renaissance Revival brick building designed by J. C.
Taylor and constructed in 1930 as social center for
Italian immigrant fraternal organization.

SOUDAN MINE (11/13/66)
(National Historic Landmark, 11/13/66)
off Minn. Hwy. 1/169 (Tower Soudan State Park),
Breitung Twp.
State's oldest and deepest underground iron mine,
opened on Vermilion Range in 1884.

SWEETNOSE ISLAND SITE (21SL141) (12/31/87)
unorganized territory (Voyageurs National Park)
Habitation site spanning Precontact through Postcontact Periods (ca. A.D. 300–1900).

TANNER'S HOSPITAL (7/28/80)
204 E. Camp St., Ely
Queen Anne 20-bed hospital built in 1901 by enterprising local physician Dr. A. F. Tanner to serve booming
mining town.

WAINO TANTTARI FIELD HAY BARN (4/9/90)
off Twp. Rd. 585, Waasa Twp.

Special-purpose farm outbuilding of traditional Finnish log construction, built in 1935.

THOMAS WILSON SHIPWRECK (7/23/92)
vicinity of Duluth, Lake Superior
Steel-hulled whaleback steamer launched in 1892 to carry bulk cargoes of grain or iron ore; sinking in 1902 led to new harbor safety procedures.

Soudan Mine

TOWER FIRE HALL (7/17/80)
Main St., Tower
Commercial Queen Anne community fire station built of locally made brick ca. 1895, with on-site cistern for water storage.

OLIVER G. TRAPHAGEN HOUSE (REDSTONE) (4/4/75)
1509-1511 E. Superior St., Duluth
Imposing Richardsonian double house designed by prominent architect Oliver G. Traphagen and built of stone in 1892.

U.S. ARMY CORPS OF ENGINEERS DULUTH VESSEL YARD (10/23/95)
9th St. S. and Minnesota Ave., Duluth
Maintenance/storage/mooring facility (est. 1904) for floating plant supporting dredging and maintenance of Duluth shipping harbor.

U.S. FISHERIES STATION–DULUTH (11/28/78)
6008 London Rd., Duluth
Group of Shingle and Stick Style frame buildings constructed in 1880s as federal hatchery for Lake Superior fish propagation.

USS *ESSEX* SHIPWRECK (4/14/94)
Duluth, Lake Superior
Steam-powered, three-masted wooden sloop of war launched in 1876 as naval cruising vessel; transferred in 1904 to Great Lakes as training ship; scuttled in 1931.

VALON TUOTE RAITTIUSSEURA (FINNISH TEMPERANCE HALL) (8/24/79)
125 3rd St. N., Virginia
Brick meeting/performance hall built ca. 1906 by local chapter of national Finnish temperance society.

VIRGINIA BREWERY (8/27/80)
305 S. 7th Ave., Virginia
Richardsonian polychrome brick brewery complex designed by H. Eilenberger and Company of Chicago and built in 1905.

VIRGINIA COMMERCIAL HISTORIC DISTRICT (1/31/97)
Chestnut St. between 1st and 6th Aves., Virginia
Concentration of early-20th-century brick buildings constituting business district of leading commercial center for Mesabi and Vermilion Iron Ranges.

VIRGINIA–RAINY LAKE LUMBER COMPANY MANAGER'S RESIDENCE (8/18/80)
402-404 S. 5th Ave., Virginia
Jacobean/Tudor Revival frame house built by lumber company in 1910 for use by mill manager.

VIRGINIA–RAINY LAKE LUMBER COMPANY OFFICE (8/26/80)
731 3rd St. S., Virginia
Administrative headquarters (built ca. 1907) of region's largest processor of pine lumber.

VIRGINIA RECREATION BUILDING (2/4/82)
305 S. 1st St., Virginia
Georgian Revival brick community center housing ice rink, built in 1923 with tax revenues from mining operations.

WESTERN BOHEMIAN FRATERNAL UNION HALL (7/31/86)
Co. Hwy. 29, Meadowlands Twp.
Frame meeting hall for Czech fraternal lodges, community events, and Sokol gymnastics, built in 1925 to preserve Czech culture.

William A. Irvin and Aerial Lift Bridge

WILLIAM A. IRVIN (FREIGHTER) (7/13/89)
Minnesota Slip, Duluth Harbor, Duluth
Technologically advanced steel-hulled bulk freighter with passenger accommodations, launched in 1938 as flagship of U.S. Steel's Great Lakes fleet.

WIRTH BUILDING (7/25/91)
13 W. Superior St., Duluth
Richardsonian Romanesque brownstone commercial building (1886) designed by Oliver G. Traphagen of Duluth and St. Paul–based George Wirth.

SCOTT COUNTY

ABRAHAM BISSON HOUSE (4/17/80)
Co. Rd. 57, St. Lawrence Twp.
Rare surviving building associated with townsite of St. Lawrence, built in 1884 of sandstone quarried on site by Bisson.

BRIDGE NO. L-3040 (11/6/89)
Co. Rd. 51 north of Minn. Hwy. 19, Blakely Twp.
Early single-span stone arch highway bridge, built in 1878 with ornamental stonework.

CHURCH OF ST. WENCESLAUS (CATHOLIC) (2/19/82)
E. Main St., New Prague
Baroque Revival/ Georgian brick church (1907) designed by Hermann Kretz, 1908 rectory, and 1914 school built as focus for growing Czech community.

Church of St. Wenceslaus, 1939

JULIUS A. COLLER HOUSE (4/17/80)
434 S. Lewis St., Shakopee
Brick residence built in 1887 for statesman and civic leader.

EARLY SHAKOPEE RESIDENCES (4/17/80)
411 and 419 E. 2nd Ave., Shakopee
Two worker's houses facing rail line, built ca. 1864 of red Shakopee brick.

EPISCOPAL CHURCH OF THE TRANSFIGURATION (4/17/80)

Walnut and Church Sts.,
Belle Plaine
Small Stick Style clapboard
church with bell tower,
constructed in 1869.

Episcopal Church of the Transfiguration

FOSS AND WELLS HOUSE
(4/17/80)
613 Broadway St. S., Jordan
Italianate residence of locally
quarried sandstone, built in 1858 by two families oper-
ating nearby flour and grist mill.

HOOPER-BOWLER-HILLSTROM HOUSE (4/17/80)

Court and Cedar Sts., Belle Plaine
Frame residence built ca. 1871 by early settler and town
promoter S. A. Hooper; addition and two-story outhouse
built in late 1880s.

INYAN CEYAKA OTONWE (2/12/99)

Louisville Twp.
Site of Precontact mound group and Contact Period
Wahpeton Dakota village called "Village of the Rapids";
associated with Dakota leader Mazomani.

JORDAN BREWERY (4/17/80)

Broadway St. S., Jordan
Limestone brewery complex built ca. 1861–1900.

JORDAN HISTORIC DISTRICT (4/17/80)

vicinity of Water St. and Broadway St. S., Jordan
Group of brick commercial buildings (mid- to late-19th
century) constituting town's commercial and social center.

WENCL KAJER FARMSTEAD (4/17/80)

Co. Hwy. 2, New Market Twp.
Dairy farm with brick farmhouse (1920) and gambrel-
roofed, round frame barn (1918) built by Kajer.

Mudbaden Sulphur Springs Company, ca. 1925

MUDBADEN SULPHUR SPRINGS COMPANY (4/17/80)
Co. Hwy. 63, Sand Creek Twp.
Classical Revival brick health spa, a trackside hospital/
resort built in 1915 to treat a variety of ailments.

NEW MARKET HOTEL AND STORE (4/17/80)
Main St., New Market
Town's only surviving 19th-century commercial block,
an Italianate polychrome brick building constructed in
1897.

ROEHL-LENZMEIER HOUSE (4/17/80)
Minn. Hwy. 300, Jackson Twp.
Stone farmhouse built ca. 1860 by German immigrant
homesteader; brick addition built ca. 1895 by second-
generation family members.

ST. MARY'S CHURCH OF THE
PURIFICATION (CATHOLIC) (4/17/80)
Co. Hwy. 15, Louisville Twp.
Romanesque rubblestone church (1882), 1893 school,
1910 rectory, and 1921 convent built for county's oldest
parish, a German Catholic settlement.

SHAKOPEE HISTORIC DISTRICT (4/11/72)
Minn. Hwy. 101, Shakopee
Site of Precontact burial mounds; Dakota village spanning Contact and Postcontact Periods; and mill, inn, and ferry landing from white settlement period.

STRUNK-NYSSEN HOUSE (4/17/80)
off U.S. Hwy. 169, Jackson Twp.
Residence built by two successive brewery operators (brick portion ca. 1856; stone portion ca. 1880, with second-story boardinghouse).

SHERBURNE COUNTY

HERBERT M. FOX HOUSE (4/10/80)
1st St. and Bradley Blvd., Becker
Slab-construction farmhouse built of roughly sawn vertical planks in 1876.

OLIVER H. KELLEY FARMSTEAD (10/15/66)
(National Historic Landmark, 7/19/64)
U.S. Hwy. 10, Elk River
Italianate residence (1869) of founder of National Grange, a fraternal organization for farmers that led national agrarian reform movement.

Oliver H. Kelley Farmstead, 1979

STATE REFORMATORY FOR MEN HISTORIC DISTRICT
(7/17/86)
off Minn. Hwy. 301, St. Cloud
Reformatory complex (1887–1933) designed by J. Walter
Stevens and Clarence H. Johnston Sr., built largely of
granite from on-site quarry worked by inmates.

SIBLEY COUNTY

CHURCH OF ST. THOMAS (CATHOLIC) (9/16/91)
Co. Hwys. 6 and 19, Jessenland Twp.
Gothic Revival frame church built in 1870 as focal
point of state's oldest Irish farming settlement, established in 1850s.

GIBBON VILLAGE HALL (8/19/82)
1st Ave. and 12th St., Gibbon
Romanesque Revival brick municipal hall designed by
Charles Webster and built in 1895 to serve as government and community center.

HENDERSON COMMERCIAL HISTORIC DISTRICT (12/20/88)
Main St. between 4th and 6th Sts., Henderson
Group of Italianate and Queen Anne commercial buildings (1874–ca. 1905) of local red brick, constituting river
town's supply and trade center.

AUGUST F. POEHLER HOUSE (2/4/82)
700 Main St., Henderson
Queen Anne brick residence designed by George Pass
and built in 1884 for early settler and entrepreneurial
businessman.

SIBLEY COUNTY COURTHOUSE (1879) (7/2/79)
Main St., Henderson
County's first permanent courthouse, designed in Italianate style by Frank Barnard and built of local yellow
brick and stone in 1879.

Gibbon Village Hall

SIBLEY COUNTY COURTHOUSE AND SHERIFF'S RESIDENCE AND JAIL (12/29/88)

400 Court St. and 319 Park Ave., Gaylord
Classical Revival stone courthouse and Spanish Colonial Revival residence/jail designed by Burner and Macomber and built in 1916 after a county seat relocation.

STEARNS COUNTY

FRANCIS ARNOLD HOUSE (12/1/94)

32268 Co. Rd. 1, LeSauk Twp.
Italianate brick residence built in 1884 by owner of nearby waterpowered flour mill.

JOHN N. BENSEN HOUSE (2/11/82)

402 6th Ave. S., St. Cloud
Queen Anne brick residence and carriage house built in 1904 for civic leader Bensen.

BISHOP'S RESIDENCE/CHANCERY OFFICE (4/15/82)

214 3rd Ave. S., St. Cloud
Mansard-roofed, French Renaissance Revival stucco house with stone trim, designed by Louis Pinault and built in 1916.

CHRISTOPHER BORGERDING HOUSE (4/15/82)
Washburn Ave., Belgrade
Cross-gambrel-roofed, Colonial Revival brick-and-frame residence built in 1904–05 by town developer, banker, and lumberyard owner.

CARTER BLOCK (6/13/86)
501-511 1st St. N., St. Cloud
Brick commercial block combining retail, warehouse, and meeting space, built in 1902 by Wesley Carter, early settler and entrepreneur.

CHURCH OF ST. BONIFACE (CATHOLIC) (11/12/93)
203 S. 5th Ave. E., Melrose
Romanesque Revival church designed by George Bergmann and built in 1897–99 as center of religious, cultural, and social life of German-American community.

CHURCH OF THE SACRED HEART (CATHOLIC) (7/12/91)
110 3rd Ave. N.E., Freeport
Gothic/Romanesque Revival church built of St. Cloud brick in 1905–06 as spiritual, cultural, and social center of German community.

CLARK AND MCCORMACK QUARRY AND HOUSE (4/15/82)
Minn. Hwy. 23 at Pine St., Rockville
Georgian Revival home of quarry owner John Clark (1924), built of pink granite from adjacent quarry, a major producer of structural granite since 1907.

Clark and McCormack Quarry, 1990

NEHEMIAH P. CLARKE HOUSE
(4/15/82)
356 3rd Ave. S., St. Cloud
Queen Anne brick-and-granite residence designed by Charles S. Sedgwick and built in 1892–93 for business/civic leader and stock breeder.

COLD SPRING BREWERS' HOUSES:

Eugene Hermanutz House (4/15/82)
302 N. Red River Ave., Cold Spring
John Oster House (4/15/82)
201 N. Red River Ave., Cold Spring
Ferdinand Peters House (4/15/82)
214 N. Red River Ave., Cold Spring
Adjacent frame houses built in 1907–12 by co-owners of
Cold Spring Brewing Company, area's major industry.

FAIR HAVEN MILL (4/14/78)

off Co. Hwy. 7, Fair Haven Twp.
Frame, waterpowered flour mill built in 1867.

FIFTH AVENUE COMMERCIAL BUILDINGS (4/15/82)

14-30 5th Ave. S. (even numbers only), St. Cloud
(also in St. Cloud Commercial Historic District)
Group of six brick commercial buildings in various architectural styles, constructed in 1883–1914 in city's central
business district.

FIRST NATIONAL BANK (4/15/82)

501 St. Germain St. W., St. Cloud
(also in St. Cloud Commercial Historic District)
Romanesque Revival brick office building with cast-iron
ornament, designed by Charles S. Sedgwick and built in
1889 to house city's oldest bank.

FIRST STATE BANK (4/15/82)

23 Minnesota St. W., St. Joseph
Egyptian Revival brick bank with elaborate terra cotta
ornament; built in 1918.

FOLEY-BROWER-BOHMER HOUSE (5/5/78)

385 3rd Ave. S., St. Cloud
Richardsonian Romanesque brick residence designed
by A. E. Hussey and built in 1889–90 for lumberman/
industrialist Timothy Foley.

FREEPORT ROLLER MILL AND MILLER'S HOUSE (4/15/82)
Mary St., Freeport
Milling complex of steam-powered, frame flour mill
with attached brick powerhouse (1898, enlarged 1912)
and adjacent frame residence (1900).

ANTON GOGALA FARMSTEAD (4/15/82)
Co. Hwy. 39 and Minn. Hwy. 238, Krain Twp.
Small dairy farm homesteaded by Slovenian immigrant
family, with farmhouse, barns, and outbuildings, some
of log construction, built in 1875–1915.

KIMBALL PRAIRIE VILLAGE HALL (4/15/82)
Main St. and Hazel Ave., Kimball
False-front brick municipal hall built in 1908 to house
local government, library, theater, professional offices,
and telephone company.

SINCLAIR LEWIS CHILDHOOD HOME (5/23/68)
(National Historic Landmark, 5/23/68)
812 Sinclair Lewis Ave., Sauk Centre
Family home (1889–1903) of first American writer to
receive Nobel Prize for literature; author of *Main Street*,
satirizing small-town life.

Sinclair Lewis Childhood Home, 1975

MICHAEL MAJERUS HOUSE (5/5/78)

404 9th Ave. S., St. Cloud
French Second Empire brick residence designed by
Theodore Kevenhoerster and built in 1891.

MINNESOTA HOME SCHOOL FOR GIRLS HISTORIC DISTRICT (1/19/89)

off Minn. Hwy. 302, Sauk Centre
First state residential treatment
facility for delinquent girls, established in 1911; complex designed
on cottage plan by State Architect Clarence H. Johnston Sr.

MODEL SCHOOL, ST. CLOUD STATE NORMAL SCHOOL (12/29/88)

826 1st Ave. S., St. Cloud
Georgian Revival laboratory
school designed by Clarence H.

Michael Majerus House

Johnston Sr. and built in 1913 at teacher-training
school opened in 1869.

ORIGINAL MAIN STREET HISTORIC DISTRICT (8/5/94)

Main St. between S. 8th and N. 3rd Sts., Sauk Centre
Residential/commercial district along town's principal
thoroughfare; inspiration for Sinclair Lewis's 1920
novel *Main Street.*

PALMER HOUSE HOTEL (2/11/82)

500 Sinclair Lewis Ave., Sauk Centre
Commercial Queen Anne salesman's hotel built of brick
in 1901 (1916 addition designed by Roland C. Buckley).

PAN MOTOR COMPANY OFFICE AND SHEET METAL WORKS (1/31/84)

435-437 33rd Ave. N., St. Cloud
Part of automobile manufacturing complex established
by Samuel C. Pandolfo that produced roughly 750 Pan
cars between 1917 and 1922.

ST. BENEDICT'S CONVENT AND
COLLEGE HISTORIC DISTRICT (3/20/89)
College Ave. and Minnesota St., St. Joseph
Collection of architect-designed buildings, structures, and objects (1882–late 1920s) marking growth of Benedictine religious and educational community.

ST. CLOUD COMMERCIAL HISTORIC DISTRICT (2/26/98)
roughly along W. St. Germain St. between
5th and 10th Aves., St. Cloud
Concentration of commercial/civic buildings built in 1868–1938 largely of local brick and granite in city's central retail/service/banking/social district.

ST. JOHN'S ABBEY AND UNIVERSITY
HISTORIC DISTRICT (3/23/79)
Co. Hwy. 159, Collegeville Twp.
Complex of buildings (1868–1961) constituting core of Benedictine religious and educational community; modernistic concrete church by Marcel Breuer.

STEARNS COUNTY COURTHOUSE AND JAIL (4/15/82)
705 Courthouse Square, St. Cloud
Beaux Arts courthouse (1921) of brick, granite, and terra cotta by Toltz, King, and Day; Prairie School jail (1922) by Louis Pinault.

STEARNS COUNTY ETHNIC HAMLET CATHOLIC CHURCHES:
Church of St. Joseph (4/15/82)
Minnesota St. at College Ave., St. Joseph
Church of St. Mary Help of Christians (4/15/82)
Co. Hwy. 7, St. Augusta
Church of St. Stephen (4/15/82)
Co. Hwy. 7, St. Stephen
Church of the Immaculate Conception (4/15/82)
Co. Hwy. 9, Avon Twp.
Rural churches built as focus of Catholic colonies settled by German, Slovenian, and Polish immigrants beginning in 1850s.

STEELE COUNTY

EZRA ABBOTT HOUSE (6/10/75)
345 E. Broadway, Owatonna
Greek Revival brick residence built ca. 1860 for townsite surveyor, sawmill owner, and civic leader.

JOHN H. ADAIR HOUSE (7/3/86)
322 E. Vine St., Owatonna
Large Prairie School residence designed by Purcell, Feick, and Elmslie and constructed in 1913 for physician Adair.

ADMINISTRATION BUILDING, STATE SCHOOL FOR DEPENDENT AND NEGLECTED CHILDREN (5/12/75)
West Hills Circle, Owatonna
Richardsonian Romanesque main building designed by Warren B. Dunnell and built in 1887 for public school established in 1886 to house and educate wards of state.

BLOOMING PRAIRIE COMMERCIAL HISTORIC DISTRICT (8/5/94)
Main St. E. between Highway Ave.
and 2nd Ave. N.E., Blooming Prairie
Business district of trackside agricultural trade center, containing late-19th- and early-20th-century brick commercial buildings in various styles.

Administration Building, State School for Dependent and Neglected Children, ca. 1895

BRIDGE NO. L-5573 (1/25/97)
Twp. Rd. 95 over Straight River, Clinton Falls Twp.
Single-span metal Pratt through truss built in 1894 by
George E. King Bridge Company of Iowa.

CLINTON FALLS MILL AND DAM (7/3/86)
off Co. Hwy. 9, Medford-Clinton Falls Twp.
Fieldstone dam and three-story frame, waterpowered
flour and custom-grinding mill built in 1856–59.

KAPLAN APARTMENTS (7/3/86)
115 W. Rose St., Owatonna
Polychrome brick apartment house built in 1912 for
Godfrey J. Kaplan, founder of Owatonna Tool Company.

NATIONAL FARMERS' BANK OF OWATONNA (8/26/71)
(National Historic Landmark, 1/7/76)
101 N. Cedar St., Owatonna
Brick bank with terra cotta trim designed by Louis Sulli-
van and built in 1907–08 with lavish ornamentation by
George G. Elmslie.

OWATONNA CITY AND FIREMAN'S HALL (1/31/97)
107 W. Main St., Owatonna
Romanesque Revival brick municipal building housing
city offices and fire department, designed by William F.
Keefe and built in 1906–07.

OWATONNA PUBLIC LIBRARY (6/7/76)
105 N. Elm St., Owatonna
Classical Revival brick-and-stone library with second-
floor art gallery and meeting room, designed by Frank
A. Gutterson of Iowa and built in 1899.

PILLSBURY ACADEMY CAMPUS HISTORIC DISTRICT (1/22/87)
vicinity of Academy, Grove, and Main Sts., Owatonna
Richardsonian Romanesque/Classical Revival brick campus complex built in 1889–1914 for private Baptist college endowed by philanthropist George A. Pillsbury.

DANIEL S. PIPER HOUSE (2/24/75)
Co. Hwy. 45, Medford-Clinton Falls Twp.
Greek Revival frame farmstead complex built in 1877, featuring New England–style connected house, summer kitchen, shed, granary, and barn.

STEELE COUNTY COURTHOUSE (6/3/76)
111 E. Main St., Owatonna
Richardsonian Romanesque, brick-and-stone, second-generation courthouse designed by T. D. Allen and built in 1891.

STEVENS COUNTY

ALBERTA TEACHERS HOUSE (2/11/83)
Main St., Alberta
Living quarters for superintendent and teachers of consolidated school district, built in 1917 adjacent to school as experiment in rural teachers' housing.

MORRIS CARNEGIE LIBRARY (1/27/83)
Nevada Ave. and 6th St., Morris
Classical Revival brick-and-stone library with prominent portico, designed by Sedgwick and Saxton and constructed in 1905.

Morris Carnegie Library

**MORRIS INDUSTRIAL SCHOOL FOR
INDIANS DORMITORY** (5/10/84)
off 4th St., Morris
Brick dormitory built in 1899 after the U.S. government
took over mission schools to educate Indian students;
transferred to state control in 1909.

LEWIS H. STANTON HOUSE (THE CHIMNEYS) (8/19/82)
907 Park, Morris
Stick Style polychrome frame residence built in 1881
for stock farm owner.

SWIFT COUNTY

Sabin S. Murdock House

APPLETON CITY HALL (6/17/77)
23 S. Miles St., Appleton
Romanesque Revival brick municipal building and
community center built in 1895 to house city offices,
jail, fire department, and performance hall.

CHRIST CHURCH (EPISCOPAL) (8/15/85)
310 13th St. N., Benson

Gothic Revival board-and-batten church built in 1879 by congregation organized under leadership of Bishop Henry Whipple.

CHURCH OF ST. BRIDGET (CATHOLIC) (8/15/85)
3rd St. and Ireland Ave., DeGraff
Gothic Revival brick-and-stone church designed by Edward J. Donahue and built in 1901 in Irish Catholic community founded by Bishop John Ireland.

CHURCH OF ST. FRANCIS XAVIER (CATHOLIC) (8/15/85)
13th St. N. and Montana Ave., Benson
Large, Renaissance-inspired, brick-and-limestone parish church designed by Emmanuel L. Masqueray and constructed in 1917.

MONSON LAKE STATE PARK CCC/WPA/RUSTIC STYLE HISTORIC RESOURCES (10/25/89)
off Co. Rd. 95 (Monson Lake State Park), Hayes Twp.
Two buildings of split-fieldstone and timber construction, built in 1938 by CCC workers in park established to commemorate events of the Dakota War of 1862.

SABIN S. MURDOCK HOUSE (8/15/85)
Clara Ave., Murdock
Italianate frame residence built in 1878 by entrepreneurial town founder and developer.

SWIFT COUNTY COURTHOUSE (9/19/77)
301 14th St. N., Benson
Richardsonian Romanesque, brick-and-stone, second-generation courthouse with corner tower, designed by Buechner and Jacobson and built in 1897–98.

CHRISTIAN F. UYTENDALE FARMSTEAD (9/5/85)
Co. Hwy. 25, Benson Twp.
Frame farmhouse of Danish form built in 1887 for prosperous Danish farmer.

TODD COUNTY

BANK OF LONG PRAIRIE (9/5/85)
262 Central Ave., Long Prairie
Richardsonian Romanesque brick-and-stone bank/retail/office building designed by Omeyer and Thori and built in 1903.

CHURCH OF ST. JOSEPH (CATHOLIC) (9/5/85)
Main and 7th Sts., Browerville
Baroque Revival brick church with onion-domed tower designed by Boehme and Cordella and built in 1908–09 for growing Polish parish.

GERMANIA HALL (11/29/95)
Co. Hwy. 11, Germania Twp.
Small frame practice/performance hall built in 1917 for rural community brass band; also served as township meeting hall and social/political center.

GREY EAGLE VILLAGE HALL (9/5/85)
Spruce and Woodman Sts., Grey Eagle
Fieldstone municipal building constructed in 1934 under the CWA to house village offices, fire department, and auditorium.

Hotel Reichert

HOTEL REICHERT (9/5/85)
20 3rd St. N., Long Prairie
Classical Revival, first-class brick hotel built in 1902–03
by Reichert family of hostelers.

KAHLERT MERCANTILE STORE (9/5/85)
Main and 6th Sts., Browerville
Two-story, false-front frame store and social hall built
by Kahlert brothers in 1883 after branch rail line was
completed to new townsite.

ST. CLOUD AND RED RIVER VALLEY
STAGE ROAD: KANDOTA SECTION (8/30/91)
off Co. Hwy. 92, Kandota Twp.
Portion of road developed in 1859 by Minnesota Stage
Company during period when stage companies laid
major routes of travel through state.

TODD COUNTY COURTHOUSE AND JAIL (9/5/85)
215 1st Ave. S., Long Prairie
Romanesque Revival brick replacement courthouse
(1883) designed by P. J. Pauley and Brothers of St. Louis
and Charles H. Sparks; ca. 1900 brick jail.

TRAVERSE COUNTY

BROWNS VALLEY CARNEGIE PUBLIC LIBRARY (8/15/85)
Broadway Ave. and 2nd St., Browns Valley
Classical Revival library of patterned brick, built in
1915–16.

CHICAGO MILWAUKEE AND ST. PAUL DEPOT (8/23/85)
Front St. and Broadway Ave., Wheaton
Standardized frame passenger/freight depot built ca.
1906 to replace earlier depot lost in fire.

Fort Wadsworth Agency and Scout Headquarters

FORT WADSWORTH AGENCY AND
SCOUT HEADQUARTERS (7/17/86)
Broadway and Dakota Aves., Browns Valley
Log building constructed in 1864 by local Indians under command of military agent Major Joseph R. Brown; after 1871 served as Samuel J. Brown residence.

LARSON'S HUNTERS RESORT (8/15/85)
Co. Hwy. 76, Lake Valley Twp.
Large brick house/lodge (1901) and outbuildings of game-bird hunting resort run by farmers Andrew and Bertha Larson.

WABASHA COUNTY

BEAR VALLEY GRANGE HALL (1/5/89)
Co. Hwy. 3, Chester Twp.
Frame meeting hall for farmers' fraternal organization, built in 1874 as part of statewide expansion of agrarian reform movement.

BRIDGE NO. 5827 (6/29/98)
Minn. Hwy. 60, Zumbro Falls

Multi-plate arch bridge ornamented with stone facing, built in 1938 by WPA workers.

WILLIAM H. AND ALMA D. CAMPBELL HOUSE (5/15/89)
211 W. 2nd St., Wabasha
Greek Revival brick residence built in 1874 for the family of a prosperous farmer, merchant, and civic leader.

LORENZ AND LUGERDE GINTHNER HOUSE (5/15/88)
130 W. 3rd St., Wabasha
Elaborate Italianate brick residence built in 1882 for the family of a successful tailor and merchant.

GRACE MEMORIAL EPISCOPAL CHURCH (2/4/82)
205 E. 3rd St., Wabasha
English Gothic, random-course stone church (1900) designed by Clarence H. Johnston Sr., commissioned by lumberman Thomas Irvine.

HURD HOUSE/ANDERSON HOTEL (9/18/78)
333 W. Main St., Wabasha (also in
Wabasha Commercial Historic District)
Brick hotel built in 1856 by B. S. Hurd, enlarged in 1887 to serve booming steamboat port and railroad town.

KING COULEE SITE (4/8/94)
Pepin Twp.
Precontact habitation site occupied ca. 3500 B.C.–A.D. 1000.

LUCAS KUEHN HOUSE (7/29/94)
306 E. Main St., Wabasha
Italianate brick residence built in 1878 for Wabasha's leading merchant and downtown developer.

Archaeological fieldwork, King Coulee Site, 1987

LAKE CITY AND ROCHESTER STAGE ROAD:
MOUNT PLEASANT SECTION (8/30/91)
off U.S. Hwy. 63, Mount Pleasant Twp.
Portion of stage road built in 1858 by group of Lake
City property owners to increase trade.

LAKE CITY CITY HALL (6/16/81)
205 W. Center St., Lake City
Romanesque/Queen Anne brick-and-limestone municipal building constructed in 1899 to house city offices,
fire department, library, and opera hall.

LAKE ZUMBRO HYDROELECTRIC
GENERATING PLANT (3/14/91)
off Co. Hwy. 21, Mazeppa Twp.
Classical Revival concrete powerhouse and gravity dam
designed by engineer Hugh Lincoln Cooper and built
in 1917–19 by the city of Rochester.

PATRICK H. RAHILLY HOUSE (2/13/75)
Co. Hwy. 15, Mount Pleasant Twp.
Italian Villa–style brick residence and carriage house
built in 1880 by prosperous landowner, farmer, and
state legislator.

READS LANDING SCHOOL (1/19/89)
3rd St. and 1st Ave., Reads Landing
Italian Villa–style, two-story brick school built by Daniel
C. Hill in 1870 for fast-growing lumbering center.

CLARA AND JULIUS SCHMIDT HOUSE (5/15/89)
418 E. 2nd St., Wabasha
Italianate brick residence with tin ornamentation built
in 1888 for leading hardware dealer and his wife.

HENRY S. AND MAGDALENA SCHWEDES HOUSE (5/15/89)
230 E. Main St., Wabasha
Italianate brick residence built in 1882 for bookkeeper/

general manager of Kuehn Mercantile Company and his wife.

JAMES C. AND AGNES M. STOUT HOUSE (1/13/89)
310 S. Oak St., Lake City
Gothic Revival frame cottage built in 1872 for early town developer and his wife.

SWEDISH EVANGELICAL LUTHERAN CHURCH (1/19/89)
Bridge St., Millville
Small Gothic Revival church of locally quarried limestone, built in 1874 by Swedish immigrant farmers.

Reads Landing School

ALEXANDER THOIRS HOUSE (5/15/89)
329 W. 2nd St., Wabasha
Early Greek Revival brick residence, built in 1868 for shoemaker Thoirs.

WABASHA COMMERCIAL HISTORIC DISTRICT (4/15/82)
vicinity of Bridge and Bailey Aves. and Main St., Wabasha
River town's central business district, a concentration of largely 19th-century, Italianate commercial buildings constructed of local brick.

WABASHA COUNTY POOR HOUSE (8/26/82)
Hiawatha Dr., Wabasha
Complex of group residence (1883), hospital (1879), barn, and sheds, part of state-mandated system of county facilities to aid the destitute.

WEAVER MERCANTILE BUILDING (9/21/78)
U.S. Hwy. 61 and Minn. Hwy. 74, Minneiska Twp.
Italianate brick commercial building constructed in 1875 in once-thriving river town of Weaver.

WILLIAMSON-RUSSELL-RAHILLY HOUSE (3/8/84)
304 S. Oak St., Lake City
Large Greek Revival frame residence (ca. 1868) of postmaster Harvey Williamson; remodeled in Classical Revival style (1910) by Patrick H. Rahilly.

ZUMBRO PARKWAY BRIDGE (11/6/89)
Co. Rd. 68 over Zumbro River, Hyde Park Twp.
Multi-plate, double-arch bridge ornamented with stone facing and Gothic Revival detailing, built in 1937 by WPA workers

WADENA COUNTY

BLUEBERRY LAKE VILLAGE SITE (10/2/73)
Blueberry Twp.
Precontact seasonal habitation site near wild rice beds, yielding variety of ceramics.

COMMERCIAL HOTEL (12/22/88)
Jefferson St. S., Wadena
Commercial Queen Anne brick hotel built ca. 1885 as business-district boarding facility for growing railroad town.

NORTHERN PACIFIC PASSENGER DEPOT (1/3/89)
off 1st St. S.W., Wadena

County's only remaining passenger depot, a standard-ized brick replacement depot (1915) that spurred city's growth.

OLD WADENA HISTORIC DISTRICT (10/9/73)
Thomastown Twp.
Townsite established in 1856 to serve travelers on Red River Trail route; former site of trading post, ferry cross-ing, and area's first farming activity.

PETERSON-BIDDICK SEED AND FEED COMPANY (1/30/89)
102 S.E. Aldrich Ave., Wadena
Complex of warehouses and grain storage facilities built in 1916–36 for pioneering farm products wholesale company.

REAUME'S TRADING POST (12/24/74)
Wing River Twp.
Site of Leaf River post established in 1792 by trader Joseph Reaume in contested area between Dakota- and Ojibwe-controlled territories.

WADENA FIRE AND CITY HALL (1/19/89)
10 S.E. Bryant Ave., Wadena
Renaissance Revival, multipurpose brick municipal building with fire-bell tower, designed by Kirby T. Snyder and built in 1912.

Commercial Hotel

WASECA COUNTY

JOHN W. AUGHENBAUGH HOUSE (8/24/82)
831 3rd Ave. N.E., Waseca
Large Renaissance Revival brick residence with wrap-around porch, built in 1897 for innovative flour mill owner.

Philo C. Bailey House

PHILO C. BAILEY HOUSE (11/25/94)
401 2nd Ave. N.E., Waseca
Italianate brick residence built in 1872 by early civic leader active in business, public affairs, and local, county, and state politics.

JANESVILLE FREE PUBLIC LIBRARY (8/19/82)
102 W. 2nd St., Janesville
Classical Revival, brick-and-stone, Carnegie-funded library built in 1912.

SEHA SORGHUM MILL (6/4/79)
Co. Hwy. 5, Janesville Twp.
Complex of adjoining frame buildings constituting sorghum syrup mill, established ca. 1904–05 by farmer-miller Cornelius L. Seha.

VISTA LUTHERAN CHURCH (8/26/82)
15035 275th Ave., Otisco Twp.
Gothic Revival brick church with stone trim built in 1908 with labor and materials supplied by Swedish Lutheran congregation.

W. J. ARMSTRONG COMPANY
WHOLESALE GROCERS (8/19/82)
202 2nd St. S.W., Waseca
Brick warehouse built ca. 1900 on company's own side track of main line through railroading center.

ROSCOE P. WARD HOUSE (8/19/82)
804 Elm Ave. E., Waseca
Large Classical Revival clapboard residence designed by Edward S. Stebbins and built in 1897–98 for prominent banker and civic leader.

WASECA COUNTY COURTHOUSE (9/2/82)
307 State St. N., Waseca
Richardsonian Romanesque, brick-and-stone courthouse with clock tower, designed by Orff and Joralemon and built in 1897.

WILLIAM R. WOLF HOUSE (8/24/82)
522 2nd Ave. N.E., Waseca
Queen Anne frame residence built ca. 1895 for civic leader and head of family-owned mercantile business Wolf and Habein.

WASHINGTON COUNTY

CHICAGO MILWAUKEE AND ST. PAUL
DEPOT AND FREIGHT HOUSE (7/13/77)
233-335 Water St., Stillwater (also in Stillwater Commercial Historic District)
Brick combination depot (1883) on locally quarried limestone foundation; housed town's telegraph office.

JOHN COPAS HOUSE (7/21/80)
Minn. Hwy. 95, New Scandia Twp.
Frame residence (ca. 1880) built on site of 1857 homestead of early settler, merchant, and farmer.

CUSHING HOTEL (1/17/85)
3291 St. Croix Trail Ave. S., Afton
Modest frame hotel built in 1867 in small river town to lodge railroad workers, lumbermen, and travelers.

JOHN T. CYPHERS HOUSE (9/10/71)
661 Quinnell Ave N., Lakeland
Small cottage with thick exterior walls of grout, a form of early concrete construction, built by Cyphers in 1858.

JOHANNES ERICKSON HOUSE (6/17/76)
Co. Hwy. 3, New Scandia Twp.
Log dwelling with gambrel roof built in 1868 by Swedish immigrant Erickson.

JOHN P. FURBER HOUSE (4/20/82)
7310 Lamar Ave., Cottage Grove
Italianate frame residence constructed by Furber in 1871, the same year he platted Cottage Grove.

Grey Cloud Lime Kiln, 1967

GREY CLOUD LIME KILN (12/18/78)
Grey Cloud Island Trail, Cottage Grove
Kiln of loose-stone construction built ca. 1850 adjacent to limestone quarry to furnish building material to nearby cities and soil agent to local farmers.

HAY LAKE SCHOOL (7/1/70)
Co. Hwy. 3, New Scandia Twp.
Brick school with bell tower built in 1895 by Scandia residents.

ROSCOE HERSEY HOUSE (2/19/82)

416 S. 4th St., Stillwater
Eastlake/Queen Anne residence designed by George
Orff and built in 1879–80 for partner in land, lumber,
and mercantile company.

MITCHELL JACKSON FARMHOUSE (2/19/82)

16376 7th St. Lane S., Lakeland
Greek Revival frame house (ca. 1850) of farmer whose
diaries (1854–71) document mid-century agricultural
and civic pursuits.

AUSTIN JENKS HOUSE (4/20/82)

504 S. 5th St., Stillwater
Victorian brick residence with mansard-roofed tower
built in 1871 for Captain Jenks, a river pilot and ship
owner involved in log rafting.

ALBERT LAMMERS HOUSE (4/20/82)

1306 S. 3rd St., Stillwater
Elaborate Queen Anne frame residence built in 1893 for
partner in one of Stillwater's leading family lumber
businesses.

Albert Lammers House, ca. 1965

MARINE MILL SITE (1/27/70)
Maple St. at St. Croix River, Marine on St. Croix
(also in Marine on St. Croix Historic District)
Site of steamboat levee and state's first commercial saw-mill (opened in 1839), which set stage for Minnesota's white pine lumbering industry.

MARINE ON ST. CROIX HISTORIC DISTRICT (6/28/74)
vicinity of Spruce and Kennedy Sts., St. Croix River,
and Soo Line railroad tracks, Marine on St. Croix
Mid-19th-century lumbering town, encompassing civic/business district and residential areas populated by New England and Swedish settlers.

Marine on St. Croix Historic District

IVORY MCKUSICK HOUSE (4/20/82)
504 N. 2nd St., Stillwater
Small French Second Empire frame residence built in 1868 for lumberman and surveyor.

JOHN AND MARTIN MOWER HOUSE
AND ARCOLA MILL SITE (6/17/80)
12905 Arcola Trail N., May Twp.
Large Greek Revival residence (1847) of Mower brothers, who founded town of Arcola and built one of earliest St. Croix lumber mills.

NELSON SCHOOL (10/25/79)

1018 S. 1st St., Stillwater
Georgian/Classical Revival, two-story brick school designed by Orff and Guilbert and built in 1897.

JOHN OLIVER HOUSE (12/16/77)

1544 Rivercrest Rd., Lakeland
Greek Revival frame residence built in 1849 for Captain Oliver, a British naval officer, early Lakeland settler, and St. Croix River ferry operator.

PEST HOUSE (6/17/80)

Co. Hwy. 11, Stillwater Twp.
Frame building constructed ca. 1872 as community institution to house persons afflicted with contagious diseases.

Pest House, 1976

POINT DOUGLAS–ST. LOUIS RIVER ROAD BRIDGE (2/24/75)

off Co. Hwy 5, Stillwater Twp.
Stone arch bridge of locally quarried limestone built in 1863 on a U.S. government military road.

ST. CROIX BOOM COMPANY HOUSE AND BARN (6/3/80)

9666 N. St. Croix Trail, Stillwater Twp.
Queen Anne frame residence constructed ca. 1885 for superintendent W. F. McGray by company that built and managed St. Croix log boom.

ST. CROIX BOOMSITE (11/13/66)

(National Historic Landmark, 11/13/66)
off Minn. Hwy. 95, Stillwater Twp.
Terminus of state's great log drives, the earliest and longest-lived site (1856–1914) for storing, sorting, and rafting logs for mills downstream.

ST. CROIX LUMBER MILLS/
STILLWATER MANUFACTURING COMPANY (4/20/82)
318 N. Main St., Stillwater
Limestone powerhouse (1850) of Stillwater's second mill, purchased in 1869 by Isaac Staples, leading businessman and milling company founder.

ST. CROIX RIVER ACCESS SITE (8/23/84)
Stillwater Twp.
Habitation site with evidence of stone tool production dating from ca. A.D. 800 to 1700.

WILLIAM SAUNTRY HOUSE AND RECREATION HALL
(4/20/82)
626 N. 4th St. and 625 N. 5th St., Stillwater
Large Queen Anne frame residence (1891) and whimsical Exotic Revival recreation facility (1902) built by prosperous businessman for entertaining.

SCHILLING ARCHAEOLOGICAL DISTRICT (12/22/78)
Cottage Grove
Habitation site and mound group with several Precontact Period components.

CORDENIO SEVERANCE HOUSE (CEDARHURST) (6/3/76)
6940 Keats Ave. S., Cottage Grove
Country estate of prominent St. Paul attorney, an Italianate frame house transformed in 1917 through a Classical Revival addition by Cass Gilbert.

BENJAMIN B. SHEFFIELD HOUSE (CROIXSYDE) (6/3/80)
4 Croixside Rd., May Twp.

Soo Line
High Bridge

Early St. Croix summer residence, a large log house designed in 1922 by Chilson D. Aldrich for grain milling executive.

SOO LINE HIGH BRIDGE (8/22/77)
Stillwater Twp.
Multiple-span steel arch railroad bridge with technical innovations by engineer/designer C. A. P. Turner and built in 1910–11.

CHARLES SPANGENBERG FARMSTEAD (12/5/78)
9431 Dale Rd., Woodbury
Large farmhouse (1871) of locally quarried limestone, frame barn (ca. 1887), and granary (ca. 1875) built by German immigrant farm family.

STATE PRISON HISTORIC DISTRICT (7/10/86)
5500 Pickett Ave., Bayport
Brick prison complex (1910–14) built on French "telegraph pole" plan, and two wardens' residences, all designed by State Architect Clarence H. Johnston Sr.

STILLWATER BRIDGE (6/2/89)
Minn. Hwy. 36/Wis. Hwy. 64 over St. Croix
River, Stillwater (also in St. Croix County, Wis.)
Ten-span, concrete-and-metal vertical lift highway bridge of Waddell and Harrington type, built in 1931.

STILLWATER COMMERCIAL HISTORIC DISTRICT (3/26/92)
vicinity of Main, 2nd, and Chestnut Sts., Stillwater
Central business district of 19th-century river town, encompassing largely brick commercial buildings of various styles (1860s–1930s).

HENRY STUSSI HOUSE (4/20/82)
9097 Mendel Rd., Stillwater Twp.
Victorian Gothic brick residence built in late 1870s for miller Stussi from plan in Palliser and Palliser's *American Cottage Homes.*

Twine factory, Territorial/State Prison, ca. 1910

TERRITORIAL/STATE PRISON (4/20/82)
Main and Laurel Sts., Stillwater
Brick warehouse and manufacturing buildings (1884–98) of prison operated 1849–1914, with convict labor contracted to local manufacturers.*

TERRITORIAL/STATE PRISON WARDEN'S HOUSE (12/17/74)
602 N. Main St., Stillwater
Greek Revival dwelling of locally quarried limestone with frame additions; served as warden's residence 1853–1914.

VALLEY CREEK RESIDENCES:
Erastus Bolles House (4/20/82)
1741 Stagecoach Tr., Afton
Newington Gilbert House (4/20/82)
1678 Stagecoach Tr., Afton
Greek Revival dwellings remaining from Old-Stock American immigrant community: Bolles House built in 1856 by blacksmith; Gilbert House built in 1864 by mill owner.

---

* Destroyed by arson in September 2002

WASHINGTON COUNTY COURTHOUSE (8/26/71)
W. Pine and S. 3rd Sts., Stillwater
Italianate/Classical Revival, second-generation brick courthouse, jail, and sheriff's residence designed by Augustus F. Knight and built in 1867–70.

MORTIMER WEBSTER HOUSE (4/20/82)
435 S. Broadway, Stillwater
Italian Villa–style frame residence built in 1865–66 for New York immigrant and real estate developer.

WATONWAN COUNTY

FLANDERS' BLOCK (3/8/84)
30 W. Main St., Madelia
Italianate brick commercial build-ing constructed in 1872 in then-county seat, leased by owner Joseph Flanders to house county government, jail, and bank.

Flanders' Block

NELSON AND ALBIN COOPERATIVE MERCANTILE STORE (1/7/87)
Co. Hwy. 6, Nelson Twp. (Godahl)
False-front frame general store (1894) and warehouse (1895) built by members of local farmers' cooperative established in village of Godahl.

ALFRED R. VOSS FARMSTEAD (10/27/88)
Co. Hwy. 27, Rosendale Twp.
Farmstead complex (1893–1920) with distinctive barn developed by leading stock farmer for large-scale farm-ing operation.

WATONWAN COUNTY COURTHOUSE (1/7/87)
7th St. S. and 2nd Ave. S., St. James
Romanesque Revival brick-and-limestone courthouse designed by Henry C. Gerlach and built in 1895–96.

WILKIN COUNTY

FEMCO FARM NO. 2 (7/17/80)
Co. Rd. 153, Roberts Twp.
One of five farms established in 1920s by newspaper publisher Frederic E. Murphy to experiment with stock raising and crop rotation.

J. A. JOHNSON BLACKSMITH SHOP (2/23/96)
Main Ave. W. and 2nd St. W., Rothsay
False-front frame blacksmith shop built in 1903 to serve small agricultural trade center, equipped with tools forged by proprietor.

J. A. Johnson Blacksmith Shop

WALTER J. PEET FARMSTEAD (7/17/80)
Co. Hwy. 32, Deerhorn Twp.
Family farm with large Queen Anne frame house (1902), 1901 barn, 1912 wood-hoop silo, and 1920 metal-frame windmill.

STIKLESTAD UNITED LUTHERAN CHURCH (7/17/80)
Co. Rd. 17, Brandrup Twp.
Late Gothic Revival frame church with bell tower built

in 1897–98 by congregation as focal point of Norwegian Lutheran community.

TENNEY FIRE HALL (7/17/80)
Concord Ave., Tenney
Small frame hall with fire-bell tower built in 1904 to house town's hand-drawn pumpers.

WILKIN COUNTY COURTHOUSE (7/17/80)
316 S. 5th St., Breckenridge
Beaux Arts brick courthouse (1928–29), with interior mural-filled central dome, designed by Buechner and Orth.

WOLVERTON SCHOOL (7/17/80)
N. 1st St., Wolverton
Two-story brick school built in 1906, expanded in 1917 to serve growing community.

WINONA COUNTY

ANGER'S BLOCK (1/31/78)
116-120 Walnut St., Winona (also in Winona Commercial Historic District)
Early Italianate brick commercial building in central business district, designed in 1872 by Charles Maybury.

BRIDGE NO. L-1409 (7/5/90)
Twp. Rd. 62 over Garvin Brook, Hillsdale Twp.
Stone arch highway bridge (1895) of a scale and sophistication unusual among rural stone arch bridges of southeastern Minnesota.

WILLARD BUNNELL HOUSE (4/23/73)
Homer and Matilda Sts., Homer Twp.
First known permanent house in Minnesota below St. Paul, an 1850s Gothic-style residence built by frontier settler and town planner.

Benjamin Ellsworth House, 1983

CHOATE DEPARTMENT STORE (6/3/76)
*51 E. 3rd St., Winona (also in Winona
Commercial Historic District)*
Richardsonian brick commercial building built in 1881
for Hannibal Choate, one of Winona's leading and most
innovative merchants.

CHURCH OF ST. STANISLAUS (CATHOLIC) (11/8/84)
601 E. 4th St., Winona
Beaux Arts brick church constructed in 1895 by Winona's
Polish community, then the largest in Minnesota.

CHURCH OF THE HOLY TRINITY (CATHOLIC) (8/9/84)
off Rollingstone Rd., Rollingstone
Gothic Revival stone church built in 1869 by Luxembourg immigrants as centerpiece of community's religious, social, and academic life.

EAST SECOND STREET COMMERCIAL
HISTORIC DISTRICT (1/25/91)
*66-78 Center, 54-78 E. 2nd, and
67-71 Lafayette Sts., Winona*
Winona's main business district, a concentration of late-
19th-century, largely Italianate brick-and-stone buildings.

BENJAMIN ELLSWORTH HOUSE (8/9/84)
U.S. Hwy. 14, Utica
Italianate brick house built in 1873 by Utica founder.

J. W. S. GALLAGHER HOUSE (11/8/84)
451 W. Broadway St., Winona
Prairie School residence of stucco with cypress trim
(1913) designed by Purcell and Elmslie.

GRAIN AND LUMBER EXCHANGE (12/2/77)
51 E. 4th St., Winona
Renaissance Revival brick-and-stone office building
(1900) designed by Kees and Colburn.

WILLIAM HEMMELBERG HOUSE (10/23/86)
Co. Hwys. 26 and 37 (Whitewater
Recreation Area), Elba Twp.
Farmhouse of native limestone built in 1858 by one of
Elba Township's first settlers.

ABNER F. HODGINS HOUSE (11/8/84)
275 Harriet St., Winona
Outstanding frame example of Queen Anne residential
architecture (1890), designed by Charles Maybury for a
prominent Winona lumberman.

HUFF-LAMBERTON HOUSE (12/12/76)
207 Huff St., Winona
One of Minnesota's earliest
and best-preserved residences
in Italian Villa style, built in
1857 of brick with stone trim;
Exotic Revival porch added
1876; home successively of
land speculator/newspaper
owner Henry Huff and
lawyer/businessman Henry
W. Lamberton.

Huff-Lamberton House, 1975

KIRCH-LATCH BUILDING (5/21/75)
114-122 E. 2nd St., Winona
Transitional Italianate/Gothic commercial architecture
with first-floor colonnade of cast-iron columns.

NICHOLAS MARNACH HOUSE (1/31/78)
off Co. Hwy. 26 (Whitewater Wildlife
Management Area), Whitewater Twp.
Early example (ca. 1857) of stucco-covered stone building type transposed from Luxembourg to rural Midwestern residential architecture.

MERCHANTS NATIONAL BANK (10/16/74)
102 E. 3rd St., Winona (also in Winona
Commercial Historic District)
Prairie School bank of
brick with elaborate
terra cotta and stained
glass ornament, de-
signed in 1912 by Pur-
cell, Feick, and Elmslie.

PICKWICK MILL (9/22/70)
Co. Hwy. 7, Homer Twp.
One of Minnesota's
oldest surviving water-
power gristmills, built
of limestone in 1854.

Nicholas Marnach House

ST. CHARLES CITY BAKERY (8/9/84)
501 Whitewater Ave., St. Charles
Italianate brick commercial building constructed in
1876 in town's original business district.

SCHLITZ HOTEL (8/26/82)
129 W. 3rd St., Winona (also in Winona
Commercial Historic District)
Hotel and cafe (1892) built and operated by Joseph
Schlitz Brewing Company.

SUGAR LOAF (8/3/90)
southwest of U.S. Hwy. 61 and Minn. Hwy. 43, Winona
Mississippi River bluff associated with Dakota legend; a
visual landmark known to travelers and tourists since
mid-19th century.

SUGAR LOAF BREWERY (3/31/78)
Lake Blvd. and Sugar Loaf Rd., Winona
Stone-and-brick brewery built in 1872 at base of Sugar
Loaf.

TRINITY EPISCOPAL CHURCH (8/9/84)
807 St. Charles Ave., St. Charles
Carpenter Gothic–style church with bell tower, built in
1874.

TRINITY EPISCOPAL CHURCH (8/9/84)
E. Main St. and Broadway, Stockton
Sophisticated example of Carpenter Gothic church with
spire, built in 1859.

PAUL WATKINS HOUSE (11/8/84)
175 E. Wabasha St., Winona
Jacobean Revival brick house designed in 1927 by Cram
and Ferguson for owner of J. R. Watkins Company, one
of Winona's most prominent businesses.

**WHITEWATER AVENUE COMMERCIAL
HISTORIC DISTRICT** (8/9/84)
900-1012 Whitewater Ave. (even numbers only), St. Charles
Cohesive group of two-story brick commercial buildings
constructed after 1891 fire.

**WHITEWATER STATE PARK CCC/WPA/RUSTIC STYLE
HISTORIC RESOURCES** (10/25/89)
*off Minn. Hwy. 74 (Whitewater State Park),
southwest of Elba, Elba Twp.*
Diverse collection of buildings/structures of native
limestone in state park developed 1934–41 by CCC and
WPA workers.

WINONA AND ST. PETER ENGINE HOUSE (1/12/84)
75 Gould St., Winona
Brick repair shop constructed ca. 1890 to service engines
for rail line that made Winona a major shipping hub.

WINONA AND ST. PETER FREIGHT HOUSE (1/26/84)
58 Center St., Winona
Brick freight warehouse built in 1883 for rail line that
spurred Winona's growth and development.

WINONA CITY HALL (7/8/99)
207 Lafayette St., Winona
PWA-financed, Moderne-style, brick-and-stone civic
building (1939) designed by Boyum, Schubert, and
Sorenson.

WINONA COMMERCIAL HISTORIC DISTRICT (10/1/98)
3rd St. between Franklin and Johnson Sts., Winona
Mix of 19th- and 20th-century commercial buildings,
many designed by Maybury and Son, that supported
river town's economy.

WINONA COUNTY COURTHOUSE (12/2/70)
171 W. 3rd St., Winona
Richardsonian courthouse of local stone, designed by
Winona firm of Maybury and Son and built in 1889 by
local artisans.

WINONA FREE PUBLIC LIBRARY (7/29/77)
151 W. 5th St., Winona
Classical Revival domed library with interior frescoes
and stained glass, built in 1899 and presented to city
by philanthropist William Laird.

WINONA HOTEL (3/31/83)
*157 W. 3rd St., Winona (also in Winona
Commercial Historic District)*
City's first full-service hotel, a Victorian Gothic brick

building funded by local business owners to house out-of-town theater guests.

WINONA MASONIC TEMPLE (2/26/98)
255 Main St., Winona
Regional headquarters for Masonic organizations, a 1909 Classical Revival brick building with hand-painted scenic stage backdrops.

WINONA SAVINGS BANK (9/15/77)
204 Main St., Winona
Egyptian Revival stone building designed by George W. Maher and built in 1914–16, with interiors and art glass by the architect and Tiffany Studios.

Winona Savings Bank, 1957

WRIGHT COUNTY

AKERLUND PHOTOGRAPHIC STUDIO (4/11/77)
390 Broadway Ave., Cokato
Frame residence/studio with dressing room, skylit posing room, and darkroom, built in 1903 for portrait photographer August B. Akerlund.

ALBERTVILLE MILL (12/11/79)
5790 Main Ave. N.E., Albertville
Steam-powered brick roller mill constructed ca. 1909 in railroad town for commercial production of flour.

CHURCH OF ST. MICHAEL (CATHOLIC) (12/11/79)
Central Ave. and Main St., St. Michael
Late Gothic Revival brick church with clock tower, erected in 1890 as religious and social center of German Catholic community.

CLEARWATER MASONIC LODGE–GRAND ARMY OF THE REPUBLIC HALL (12/11/79)
205-215 Oak St., Clearwater
Italianate brick meeting hall with ground-floor retail space, built in 1888 to house Masons fraternal order and Civil War veterans group.

COKATO TEMPERANCE HALL (12/12/76)
Co. Hwy. 3 and Co. Rd. 100, Cokato Twp.
Small frame assembly hall built in 1896 by Finnish temperance organization that served as community's civic, cultural, and social center.

First Congregational Church

DELANO VILLAGE HALL (12/11/79)
127 River St., Delano
Romanesque Revival municipal building (1888) with fire-bell tower (1896), built of local brick to house city offices, jail, fire department, and civic events.

DISTRICT NO. 48 SCHOOL (12/11/79)
U.S. Hwy. 12, Franklin Twp.
Small frame school built in 1871 to serve rural district.

EAGLE NEWSPAPER OFFICE (12/11/79)
300 Railroad Ave. E., Delano
Italianate brick commercial block built in 1883–85 for proprietor I. Gulzwiller to house newspaper offices, commercial printing shop, and book bindery.

FIRST CONGREGATIONAL CHURCH (12/11/79)
Bluff and Elm Sts., Clearwater
Greek Revival frame church built in 1861 by community's New England settlers; fortified against possible attack during the Dakota War of 1862.

DAVID HANAFORD FARMSTEAD (12/11/79)
off Co. Hwy. 106, Monticello Twp.
Farm homesteaded by New England settlers in 1855, with Federal-style brick farmhouse (1870) and frame barn and outbuildings (ca. 1870s–1900).

HANOVER BRIDGE (BRIDGE NO. 92366) (12/11/79)
off Co. Hwy. 19 over Crow River, Hanover
(also in Hennepin County)
Pratt through truss metal bridge built in 1885 by Morse Bridge Company of Youngstown, Ohio.

HAWKINS CLINIC, HOSPITAL, AND HOUSE (12/11/79)
Buffalo St., Montrose
Brick residence/clinic (ca. 1885) and frame hospital (1903) built by Dr. E. P. Hawkins; adjacent building acquired in 1913 for nurse training.

HOWARD LAKE CITY HALL (12/11/79)
737-741 6th St., Howard Lake
Queen Anne brick municipal building constructed in
1904 to house city offices, fire department, post office,
public library, and meeting hall.

MARYSVILLE SWEDESBURG LUTHERAN CHURCH (12/11/79)
Co. Hwy. 9, Marysville Twp.
Late Gothic Revival church of local brick, built in 1891
for Swedish immigrant congregation.

TOBIAS G. MEALEY HOUSE (12/12/76)
Territorial Rd., Monticello
Greek Revival frame residence (1855) of early
Monticello settler, businessman, and state legislator.

NICHERSON-TARBOX HOUSE AND BARN (12/11/79)
514 E. Broadway, Monticello
Queen Anne/Shingle Style residence built in 1889 for
lumberman E. A. Nicherson; earlier board-and-batten
barn moved to site by Judge James C. Tarbox.

RUFUS RAND SUMMER HOUSE
AND CARRIAGE BARN (12/11/79)
Washington St., Monticello
Country estate of prominent Minneapolis businessman,
with large Queen Anne house built in 1884 as wedding
present to his bride, Susan Mealey.

ST. MARK'S EPISCOPAL CHURCH (12/11/79)
off Minn. Hwy. 24, Corinna Twp.
Gothic Revival board-and-batten rural church constructed in 1871 under direction of parish founding
member Octavius Longworth.

SIMPSON METHODIST EPISCOPAL CHURCH (12/11/79)
4th and Linn Sts., Monticello
Early Methodist church, a Greek Revival/Italianate

frame edifice built in 1857 for congregation founded by town father the Rev. Samuel T. Creighton.

THAYER HOTEL (8/24/78)
60 Elm St. W., Annandale
False-front, frame, trackside hotel with three-tiered front verandah, built in 1895 by Albert A. Thayer for growing tourist and agricultural trade center.

Waverly Village Hall

WAVERLY VILLAGE HALL (6/6/2002)
4th St. N., Waverly
Moderne-style, reinforced-concrete municipal building constructed by WPA workers in 1939–40 for social and recreational community activities.

WILLIAM W. WEBSTER HOUSE (12/11/79)
Spring and Linn Sts., Clearwater
Greek Revival frame residence built ca. 1863 by early Clearwater merchant, civic leader, and Civil War veteran.

SIMON WELDELE HOUSE (12/11/79)
309 River St. N., Delano
Queen Anne frame residence built in 1893 for prominent businessman.

YELLOW MEDICINE COUNTY

CANBY COMMERCIAL HISTORIC DISTRICT (11/25/80)
vicinity of 1st and 2nd Sts. and St. Olaf Ave., Canby
Second-generation central business district of one-
and two-story, largely brick commercial buildings constructed after 1893 fire.

JOHN G. LUND HOUSE (10/2/78)
101 4th St. W., Canby
Frame residence (1891) of early land speculator, banker,
and politician; transformed by 1900 remodeling into
Queen Anne showplace.

LUNDRING SERVICE STATION (6/20/86)
201 1st St. E., Canby
English Cottage–style station (1926) with low-pitched,
shingled roof to simulate thatching, likely designed by
Sinclair Oil Company architect.

SWEDE PRAIRIE PROGRESSIVE FARMERS CLUB (6/13/86)
Co. Hwy. 9, Swede Prairie Twp.
Small frame meeting hall built in 1915 for grassroots-
level, local farmers' organization arising from national
agricultural reform movement.

John G. Lund House

UPPER SIOUX AGENCY (10/15/70)

Minn. Hwy. 67 (Upper Sioux Agency State Park), Sioux Agency Twp.
Site of U.S. government administrative center (1854–62) for Dakota Indian reservation, where failed policies contributed to causes of the Dakota War of 1862.

ANDREW J. VOLSTEAD HOUSE (12/30/74)
(National Historic Landmark, 12/8/76)

163 9th Ave., Granite Falls
Residence (1894–1930) of U.S. Congressman who drafted 1919 National Prohibition Enforcement Act (Volstead Act) interpreting newly ratified 18th amendment to the Constitution.

Lundring Service Station

F. Scott Fitzgerald House (right)

NATIONAL HISTORIC LANDMARKS

National Historic Landmark status is conferred on properties of transcendent value to the nation as a whole. As of December 31, 2002, a total of 21 Minnesota properties have been designated National Historic Landmarks.

F. SCOTT FITZGERALD HOUSE (11/11/71)
St. Paul, Ramsey County

FORT SNELLING HISTORIC DISTRICT (12/19/60)
Ft. Snelling Military Reservation, Hennepin County

JAMES J. HILL HOUSE (11/5/61)
St. Paul, Ramsey County

HULL-RUST-MAHONING MINE (11/13/66)
Hibbing, St. Louis County

KATHIO HISTORIC DISTRICT (7/19/64)
Kathio Twp., Mille Lacs County

OLIVER H. KELLEY FARMSTEAD (7/19/64)
Elk River, Sherburne County

FRANK B. KELLOGG HOUSE (12/8/76)
St. Paul, Ramsey County

SINCLAIR LEWIS CHILDHOOD HOME (5/23/68)
Sauk Centre, Stearns County

CHARLES A. LINDBERGH HOUSE (12/8/76)
Pike Creek Twp., Morrison County

MOUNTAIN IRON MINE (11/24/68)
Mountain Iron, St. Louis County

NATIONAL FARMERS' BANK OF OWATONNA (1/7/76)
Owatonna, Steele County

**1914 BUILDING AND PLUMMER BUILDING,
MAYO CLINIC** (8/11/69)
Rochester, Olmsted County

**PEAVEY-HAGLIN EXPERIMENTAL CONCRETE
GRAIN ELEVATOR** (12/21/81)
St. Louis Park, Hennepin County

PILLSBURY A MILL (11/13/66)
Minneapolis, Hennepin County

O. E. ROLVAAG HOUSE (8/4/69)
Northfield, Rice County

ST. CROIX BOOMSITE (11/13/66)
Stillwater Twp., Washington County

**ST. CROIX RECREATIONAL
DEMONSTRATION AREA** (9/25/97)
*Crosby, Clover, Ogema, Munch, and
Chengwatana Twps., Pine County*

SOUDAN MINE (11/13/66)
Breitung Twp., St. Louis County

THOMAS VEBLEN FARMSTEAD (12/21/81)
Wheeling Twp., Rice County

ANDREW J. VOLSTEAD HOUSE (12/8/76)
Granite Falls, Yellow Medicine County

WASHBURN A MILL COMPLEX (5/4/83)
Minneapolis, Hennepin County

THEMATICALLY RELATED PROPERTIES

When thematically related properties are nominated for listing on the National Register of Historic Places, they are submitted under the umbrella of a Multiple Property Documentation Form. This cover document serves as an evaluation tool for determining the significance of each related property in a given category. The form defines an historical framework for the nomination, identifying the themes, geographical area, and time period represented by the property.

As of December 31, 2002, Multiple Property Documentation Forms have been submitted for the following categories of historic properties in Minnesota.

A range of years after a category name covers a period of historic activity; the year in parentheses indicates the date that the form was accepted by the Keeper of the National Register.

American Indian Rock Art (1996)
Architecture of Olof Hanson, 1895–1901 (1990)
Commercial Logging in Minnesota, 1837–1940s (1999)
Federal Relief Construction in Minnesota, 1933–41
     (1991)
Grain Elevators in Minnesota (1990)
Hydroelectric Power in Minnesota, 1880–1940 (1991)
Iron and Steel Bridges in Minnesota, 1873–1945 (1989)
Minnesota Masonry-Arch Highway Bridges, 1870–1945
     (1989)

Minnesota Military Roads, 1850–75 (1991)

Minnesota State Park CCC/WPA/Rustic Style Historic Resources (1989)

Minnesota's Lake Superior Shipwrecks, 1650–1945 (1992)

Overland Staging Industry in Minnesota, 1849–80 (1991)

Portage Trails in Minnesota, 1630s–1870s (1992)

Precontact American Indian Earthworks, 500 B.C.– A.D. 1650 (1996)

Red Brick Houses in Wabasha Associated with Merchant-Tradesmen (1989)

Red River Trails in Minnesota, 1835–71 (1991)

Reinforced-Concrete Highway Bridges in Minnesota, 1900–45 (1989)

Rural Finnish Log Buildings in St. Louis County, Minnesota (1990)

Shipwrecks of Minnesota's Inland Lakes and Rivers, 9500 B.C.–A.D. 1945 (1999)

PROPERTIES REMOVED FROM THE NATIONAL REGISTER

Properties may be removed from the National Register if the qualities for which they were listed have been lost. The following properties have been officially removed because they were destroyed by fire or storm, demolished, moved, or severely altered.

Additional properties in this guide may have lost their eligibility for listing but have not yet gone through the formal process for removal from the National Register.

BECKER COUNTY

St. Benedict's Mission School (demolished, 1995)
Co. Hwy. 133, White Earth Twp.

BIG STONE COUNTY

Shannon Hotel (demolished, 1999)
Studdart Ave. and 2nd St., Graceville

BLUE EARTH COUNTY

Adam Jefferson House (dismantled and moved, 1985)
west end of Cleveland St., Mankato

Oscar Schmidt House (demolished, 1988)
111 Park Lane, Mankato

Winnebago Agency House (practice burn by fire department, 1986)
Co. Hwy. 173, McPherson Twp.

BROWN COUNTY

Chicago North Western Section House (moved, 1988)
Railroad and Brown Sts., Comfrey

Cobden Jail (severely altered, 1989)
2nd St., Cobden

New Ulm Roller Mill (burned, 1981 and 1982)
222 1st St. S., New Ulm

Ruemke Mercantile Store (demolished, 1981)
226 N. Minnesota, New Ulm

Tivoli Gardens (demolished, 1985)
313 1st St. N., New Ulm

Twente Farm Elevator and Granary (demolished, 1986)
off Co. Rd. 16, Albin Twp.

CARVER COUNTY

Chanhassen Township Hall (moved, 1988)
Great Plains Blvd., Chanhassen

Iltis Brewery and Ice House (demolished, 1989)
597 Stoughton Ave., Chaska

Kusske and Hahn Saloon (severely altered, 1980s)
Co. Hwy. 23, Watertown Twp. (Helvetia)

CASS COUNTY

Sixth Street Commercial Building (demolished, 1985)
525 6th St., Walker

CHISAGO COUNTY

Chisago County Courthouse (moved, 1990)
Main St., Center City

Aaron Diffenbacher Farmhouse (burned, 1985)
Rushseba Twp.

Johnson Block (burned, 1981)
4th St. and Ave. D., Rush City

DAKOTA COUNTY

Chicago Milwaukee St. Paul
and Pacific Depot (demolished, 1984)
400 2nd St., Farmington

Horticulture Building, Dakota
County Fairgrounds (demolished, 1988)
Co. Hwy. 74, Castle Rock Twp.

Jacob Marthaler House (demolished, 1993)
1746 Oakdale Ave., West St. Paul

Kusske and Hahn Saloon, Carver County, before and after

DODGE COUNTY

Andrew Holtermann House (moved, 1990s)
Minn. Hwy. 30, Vernon Twp.

DOUGLAS COUNTY

Osakis Milling Company (demolished, 1990)
Lake St. and Central Ave., Osakis

FARIBAULT COUNTY

Constans Hotel (demolished, 1988)
121-127 N. Main St., Blue Earth

FREEBORN COUNTY

John Niebuhr Farmhouse (burned, 1997)
Mansfield Twp.

GOODHUE COUNTY

Just C. Gronvold House (moved, 1991)
Co. Hwy. 8, Wanamingo Twp.

Orrin I. Hall House (moved, 2000)
206 W. 3rd St., Zumbrota

Kenyon Opera House (demolished, 1994)
Main St., Kenyon

Roscoe Store (demolished, ca. 1997–99)
Co. Hwy. 11 Roscoe Twp. (Roscoe)

Wanamingo Township Hall (moved, 1990)
Co. Hwy. 1, Wanamingo Twp. (Aspenlund)

HENNEPIN COUNTY

Century Mill (burned, 1990)
545 Oak St. S.E., Minneapolis

Dania Hall (burned, 2000)
427 Cedar Ave., Minneapolis

Excelsior Fruit Growers Association (demolished, 2001)
450 3rd St., Excelsior

Dania Hall, Hennepin County, before and after

Forum Cafeteria (demolished and interior dismantled, 1979)
36-38 7th St. S., Minneapolis

Nicollet Hotel (demolished, 1991)
235 Hennepin Ave., Minneapolis

Philander Prescott House (demolished, 1980)
4458-4460 Snelling Ave. S., Minneapolis

HOUSTON COUNTY

Houston County Poor Farm (demolished, 1988)
Co. Hwy. 12, Caledonia Twp.

HUBBARD COUNTY

Hubbard Lodge No. 130 (arson, 1991)
off Co. Hwy. 6, Hubbard Twp. (Hubbard)

JACKSON COUNTY

Heron Lake Public School (demolished, 1986)
6th Ave. and 10th St., Heron Lake

Winter Hotel (demolished, 1990)
111 Main St., Lakefield

KANABEC COUNTY

Coin School (moved, 1995)
Co. Hwys. 4 and 16, Brunswick Twp.

KANDIYOHI COUNTY

Mount Tom Lookout Shelter, Sibley State Park
(severely altered, 1992)
off U.S. Hwy. 71 (Sibley State Park), Lake Andrew Twp.

Mount Tom Lookout Shelter, Kandiyohi County, before and after

KOOCHICHING COUNTY

Scenic Hotel (demolished, 1996)
Main and 3rd Sts., Northome

LAC QUI PARLE COUNTY

Hotel Lac qui Parle (demolished, 1999)
202 6th Ave., Madison

Andreas Thoreson Farmhouse (burned, 1989)
off Co. Rd. 64, Lac qui Parle Twp.

Yellow Bank Church Campground Bridge (moved, 1994)
Twp. Rd. 76 over Yellow Bank River,
Agassiz and Yellow Bank Twps.

LAKE OF THE WOODS COUNTY

Spooner School (demolished, 2001)
1st St. N. and 8th Ave. E., Baudette

LE SUEUR COUNTY

Elysian Water Tower (demolished, 1989)
Frank St., Elysian

MCLEOD COUNTY

American House Hotel (demolished, 1988)
12th and Ford Sts., Glencoe

Ansgar College (demolished, 1980)
700 N. Main St., Hutchinson

MEEKER COUNTY

West End Elevator (burned, 1987)
4th St. and Atlantic Ave., Dassel

MILLE LACS COUNTY

***Ellen Ruth* Launch** (moved, 1989)
Main and 5th Sts., Wahkon

MORRISON COUNTY

O. A. Churchill Store (demolished, 1988)
55 Bay St., Little Falls

MURRAY COUNTY

Murray County Courthouse (1891–92) (demolished, 1981)
Main and 7th Sts., Slayton

Murray County Courthouse, before (built 1891–92) and after (built 1981)

NICOLLET COUNTY

St. Peter Central School (destroyed by tornado, 1998)
300 S. 5th St., St. Peter

NORMAN COUNTY

Faith Milling Company (burned, 1989)
Co. Rd. 40, Fossum Twp.

OLMSTED COUNTY

Chicago Great Western Depot (moved, 1987)
19 2nd St. S.E., Rochester

Cutting Barn (burned, 1982)
3210 19th St. N.W., Rochester

Hotel Zumbro (demolished, 1987)
101 1st Ave. S.W., Rochester

Charles H. Mayo House (demolished, 1987)
419 4th St. S.W., Rochester

OTTER TAIL COUNTY

Henry G. Page House (moved, 1977)
219 N. Whitford St., Fergus Falls

Edward J. Webber House (moved, 1991)
506 W. Lincoln Ave., Fergus Falls

PINE COUNTY

Pine City Naval Militia Armory (demolished, 2000)
1st Ave., Pine City

PIPESTONE COUNTY

Christianson House and Store (moved, 1981)
208 E. 2nd St., Jasper

POPE COUNTY

Lowry School (demolished, 1992)
Florence Ave. and Maple St., Lowry

RAMSEY COUNTY

William Dahl House (moved, 1997)
136 13th St., St. Paul

Selby Avenue Bridge (demolished, 1993)
Selby Ave. over Soo Line railroad tracks. St. Paul

Smith Avenue High Bridge (demolished, 1985)
Smith Ave. over Mississippi River, St. Paul

Wabasha Street Bridge (demolished, 1996)
Wabasha Street over Mississippi River, St. Paul

REDWOOD COUNTY

Lamberton Farmers Elevator (demolished, 19879)
1st Ave. at Douglas St., Lamberton

Milroy Block (demolished, 1998)
Euclid Ave. and Cherry St., Milroy

Milroy Block, Redwood County, before and after

RICE COUNTY

Dump Road Bridge (demolished, 2001)
Twp. Rd. 45 over Straight River, Walcott Twp.

ROCK COUNTY

**Close Brothers Land Company
Tenant House** (demolished, 1989)
Co. Hwy. 5, Beaver Creek Twp.

**Worthington and Sioux Falls
Freight Depot** (demolished, 1992)
E. Fletcher St. at Freeman Ave., Luverne

ST. LOUIS COUNTY

Otto Johnson House (demolished, 1997)
202 3rd Ave., Mountain Iron

SCOTT COUNTY

Merchants Hotel (demolished, 1987)
221 E. 2nd St., Shakopee

Reis Block (demolished, 1986)
1st Ave. and Holmes St., Shakopee

SHERBURNE COUNTY

Sherburne County Courthouse (demolished, 1995)
326 Lowell Ave., Elk River

STEARNS COUNTY

Church of the Sacred Heart (Catholic) (moved, 1989)
off Co. Hwy. 9, Holding Twp. (Arban)

St. Cloud Post Office (demolished, 1986)
314 St. Germain St., St. Cloud

St. Cloud Public Library (demolished, 1981)
124 5th Ave. S., St. Cloud

Church of the Sacred Heart (Catholic), Stearns County, before and after

STEELE COUNTY

Owatonna High School (severely altered, 1998)
333 E. School St., Owatonna

**Owatonna Water Works
Pumping Station** (demolished, 1992)
W. School St. and Mosher Ave., Owatonna

Steele County Courthouse (1874) (demolished, 1987)
139 E. Main St., Owatonna

WABASHA COUNTY

First Congregational Parsonage (moved, 1987)
305 W. 2nd St., Wabasha

WASECA COUNTY

Seth S. Phelps Farmhouse (moved, 1992)
Co. Hwy. 2, St. Mary's Twp.

WASHINGTON COUNTY

Heath Summer Residence (arson, 1986)
Arcola Trail, Stillwater Twp.

WILKIN COUNTY

IOOF Hall (demolished, 1988)
1st Ave. S.W. and 1st St., Rothsay

WINONA COUNTY

E. L. King House (Rockledge) (demolished, 1988)
U.S. Hwy. 61, Homer Twp.

***James P. Pearson* Steamboat/
Julius C. Wilkie Steamboat** (arson, 1981)
foot of Main St. at Mississippi River (Levee Park), Winona

Stockton Mill (arson, 1988)
8th St., Stockton

WRIGHT COUNTY

Henry C. Bull House (demolished, 1988)
195 E. 3rd St., Cokato

Marsh Octagon Barn (burned, 1992)
off Co. Hwy. 14, Rockford Twp.

Middleville Township Hall (practice burn by fire department, 1994)
off Co. Hwy. 6, Middleville Twp.

Titrud Barn (destroyed by tornado, 1992)
Co. Hwy. 30, Stockholm Twp.

NATIONAL REGISTER CRITERIA FOR EVALUATION

The quality of significance in American history, architecture, archaeology, engineering, and culture is present in districts, sites, buildings, structures, and objects that possess integrity of location, design, setting, materials, workmanship, feeling, and association and:

(A) that are associated with events that have made a significant contribution to the broad patterns of our history; or

(B) that are associated with the lives of persons significant in our past; or

(C) that embody the distinctive characteristics of a type, period, or method of construction, or that represent the work of a master, or that possess high artistic values, or that represent a significant and distinguishable entity whose components may lack individual distinction; or

(D) that have yielded, or may be likely to yield, information important in prehistory or history.

CRITERIA CONSIDERATIONS

Ordinarily, cemeteries, birthplaces, or graves of historical figures, properties owned by religious institutions or used for religious purposes, structures that have been moved from their original locations, reconstructed historic buildings, properties primarily commemorative in nature, and properties that have achieved significance within the past 50 years shall not be considered eligible for the National Register. However, such properties will qualify if they are integral parts of districts that meet the criteria or if they fall within the following categories:

(A) a religious property deriving primary significance from architectural or artistic distinction or historical importance; or

(B) a building or structure removed from its original location but that is significant primarily for architectural value, or that is the surviving structure most importantly associated with a historic person or event; or

(C) a birthplace or grave of a historical figure of outstanding importance if there is no other appropriate site or building directly associated with their productive life; or

(D) a cemetery that derives its primary significance from graves of persons of transcendent importance, from age, from distinctive design features, or from association with historic events; or

(E) a reconstructed building when accurately executed in a suitable environment and presented in a dignified manner as part of a restoration master plan, and when no other building or structure with the same association has survived; or

(F) a property primarily commemorative in intent if design, age, tradition or symbolic value has invested it with its own historical significance; or

(G) a property achieving significance within the past 50 years if it is of exceptional importance.

Rock County Courthouse and Jail

INDEX

Zumbrota Covered Bridge, Goodhue County

PICTURE CREDITS

The name of the photographer, when known, appears in parentheses along with any other additional information.

Unless otherwise noted below, images reproduced in this book are from the files of the State Historic Preservation Office, Minnesota Historical Society. Many of the photographs from the files were taken by Michael Koop; exceptions include photographs on pages 6, 22, 95, 104, 112, 205, 220, 227, 230, & 250 (all by Joseph M. Van Ryn), 90 (Holly Wahlberg), 120 *top* (Geoffrey Gyrisco), 120 *bottom* (Rolf Anderson), 137 (Michael Larson), 145 (Tim Rummelhoff), 229 (National Park Service).

From the Sound and Visual Collections, MHS—Pages i (Niels Larson Hakkerup), xiv (Charles P. Gibson), 9, 19 (Olson Photograph Company), 25, 34, 38, 47 (National Park Service), 48, 57, 77, 78, 81 (William H. Illingworth), 85, 93 (Charles J. Hibbard), 96 & 99 (both Minneapolis *Star Tribune*), 100, 108, 118, 125, 127 (Norton & Peel), 133, 134, 138, 144, 148 (Eugene D. Becker), 160, 163, 172, 174 (Harry W. Bradow), 176, 179 (Gibson), 180 (Riehle Studios), 183 (Donaldson Photo Company), 184 (Stan Waldhauser), 187 (Kenneth M. Wright), 188, 191 (Gibson), 196 (Edward A. Bromley), 202, 211, 226 (Harry Buetow), 233, 236, 238, 239, 242 (Jet Lowe), 244 (Henry Harren), 247, 262 (Alan Ominsky), 263, 265 (Liza Nagle), 268, 272, 273, 277, 284 (Becker), 293 *top* (Charles W. Nelson), 337

Courtesy of Public Relations, MHS—Page 169

Courtesy of Douglas A. Birk, Institute for Minnesota Archaeology—Page 147

Mickey's Diner, St. Paul, 1982

ALSO AVAILABLE FROM THE MINNESOTA
HISTORICAL SOCIETY PRESS

**The Minnesota Book of Days:
An Almanac of State History**
by Tony Greiner

A fun and fascinating day-by-day account
of Minnesota history, chronicling important events, famous firsts, notable individuals, and interesting incidents. A perfect gift
for any fan of Minnesota history and trivia.

$13.95, paper, ISBN 0-87351-416-5

**Minnesota History along the Highways:
A Guide to Historic Markers and Sites**
Compiled by Sarah P. Rubinstein

A handy travel guide to more than 254
historic markers, 60 geologic markers,
and 29 state historic monuments
throughout the state.

$13.95, paper, ISBN 0-87351-456-4

**The Pocket Guide to Minnesota
Place Names**
by Michael Fedo

The pocket version of the authoritative
Minnesota Place Names, 3rd Edition. This
handy guide is the perfect companion for
anyone who travels the highways and
waterways of the North Star state.

$11.95, paper, ISBN 0-87351-424-6

JOIN THE MINNESOTA HISTORICAL SOCIETY TODAY! IT'S THE BEST DEAL IN HISTORY!

The Minnesota Historical Society is the nation's premier state historical society. Founded in 1849, the Society collects, preserves, and tells the story of Minnesota's past through innovative museum exhibits, extensive collections and libraries, educational programs, historic sites, and book and magazine publishing. Membership support is vital to the Society's ability to serve its ever-broadening and increasingly diverse public with programs and services that are educational, engaging, and entertaining.

What are the benefits of membership?

Members enjoy:

- A subscription to the quarterly magazine *Minnesota History;*
- *Member News* newsletter and events calendar;
- Unlimited free admission to the Society's 25 historic sites;
- Discounts on purchases from the Minnesota Historical Society Press and on other purchases and services in our museum stores, library, Café Minnesota, and much more;
- Reciprocal benefits at more than 70 historical organizations and museums in over 40 states through Time Travelers; and
- Satisfaction of knowing your membership helps support the Society's programs.

Membership fees/categories:

- $55 Household (2 adults and children under 18 in same household)
- $50 Senior Household (age 65+ for 2 adults)
- $45 Individual (1 adult)
- $40 Senior Individual (age 65+ for 1 adult)
- $100 Associate
- $250 Contributing
- $500 Sustaining
- $1,000 North Star Circle

Join by phone or e-mail. To order by phone, call 651-296-0332 (TTY 651-282-6073) or e-mail membership@mnhs.org. Benefits extend one year from date of joining.

The National Register of Historic Places in Minnesota was designed and set in type by Percolator, Minneapolis, who used Stone Serif, designed by Sumner Stone in 1987, for the text type. This book was printed by Transcontinental Printing, Peterborough, Ontario.

9 780873 514484